Care-full Creativity in Theatre and Dance Education

Care-full Creativity in Theatre and Dance Education: Consent-Forward, Trauma-Informed, Psychologically Safe Movement Pedagogy is an interactive text that provides theory and tools for practice on creating a movement pedagogy of care.

This book brings together theories and tools of consent-forward, trauma-informed, and psychologically safe pedagogies and pedagogies of care, specifically for dance and movement teachers. It begins with power assessments for educators, then offers insights on the ripple effects of those powers in the classroom on students' consent, agency, and psychological well-being. Each chapter includes reflective prompts for educators to examine their current classroom practices, as well as imagine new possibilities. Specifically in the second half of the book, chapters include multiple tools and/or templates for movement educators to use in incorporating new pedagogic practices into their classroom, including their syllabus, class design, and assessment. Reminders of the big ideas or highlight concepts conclude each chapter.

Care-full Creativity in Theatre and Dance Education is written for dance and movement educators as they develop consent-forward, trauma-informed, psychologically safe classrooms, rehearsals, and studio spaces.

Additional tools and templates are available for download from https://resourcecentre.routledge.com/books/9781032979502.

Nicole Perry, MFA, CLMA, CIC/D, is a movement artist and educator. Nicole has taught movement and dance for the past twenty years in private and public educational institutions, from middle school to university levels. Her intimacy choreography can be seen on many regional theatre stages in South Florida, as well as Netflix, Showtime, Hulu, and Peacock. Nicole regularly teaches on movement and consent topics for university faculties through Momentum Stage and a professional development course for the National Dance Education Organization. She is the Director of Praxis at Intimacy Professionals Education Collective. www.nicoleperry.org

Care-full Creativity in Theatre and Dance Education

Consent-Forward, Trauma-Informed, Psychologically Safe Movement Pedagogy

Nicole Perry

NEW YORK AND LONDON

Designed cover image: Dancers: Kalin Basford, Abbie Fricke, Mélanie Martel, and Sarah Romeo in *Prove It*, choreographed by Nicole Perry. Part of the *Totentanz* Project at Momentum Stage, funded by the Doris Duke Foundation. Photo by Morgan Sophia Photography.

First published 2026
by Routledge
605 Third Avenue, New York, NY 10158

and by Routledge
4 Park Square, Milton Park, Abingdon, Oxon, OX14 4RN

Routledge is an imprint of the Taylor & Francis Group, an informa business

© 2026 Nicole Perry

The right of Nicole Perry to be identified as author of this work has been asserted in accordance with sections 77 and 78 of the Copyright, Designs and Patents Act 1988.

All rights reserved. No part of this book may be reprinted or reproduced or utilised in any form or by any electronic, mechanical, or other means, now known or hereafter invented, including photocopying and recording, or in any information storage or retrieval system, without permission in writing from the publishers.

For Product Safety Concerns and Information please contact our EU representative GPSR@taylorandfrancis.com. Taylor & Francis Verlag GmbH, Kaufingerstraße 24, 80331 München, Germany.

Trademark notice: Product or corporate names may be trademarks or registered trademarks, and are used only for identification and explanation without intent to infringe.

ISBN: 978-1-032-97951-9 (hbk)
ISBN: 978-1-032-97950-2 (pbk)
ISBN: 978-1-003-59630-1 (ebk)

DOI: 10.4324/9781003596301

Typeset in Goudy
by KnowledgeWorks Global Ltd.

Access the Support Material: https://resourcecentre.routledge.com/books/9781032979502

Contents

Acknowledgments — vii

Introduction — 1

PART 1
Theory — 15

1 Assessing power dynamics in the movement classroom: Understanding power and power dynamics — 17

2 Moving to power-with — 40

3 The connections of power, consent, and trauma — 63

4 Psychological safety: Creating spaces for learning and art-making — 78

PART 2
Praxis — 95

5 Practices for ensemble building: Creating inclusion safety — 97

6 Practices in the syllabus: Setting the stage for learner safety — 131

7 Practices in class: Structure, language, and experiences for learner safety and beyond — 163

8 Practices in class: Touch and contact — 187

9 Practices in assessment: Personal reflection and (un)grading — 208

10 Practices in assessment: Feedback — 253

11 Conclusion — 272

PART 3
Resource Section   **277**

    References   279

    Resources to support material in the text: Tools and
templates referenced from Momentum Stage
and Nicole Perry   286

    Resources to support material in the text: Other links
and offerings   288

    Index   292

Acknowledgments

A book, like a theatre or dance production, or a collaborative classroom, is a team effort.

I am so grateful for the editing work of Jessica Bennett, Caryl Fantel, and Cassie Kris. Stacey and Lucia, my editors at Routledge, thank you for answering every question and being so supportive!

My movement and dance teacher colleagues, who were so gracious to give me feedback on content: Suzanne Ankrum-Harris, Ian Bond, D Granke, and Kristin Mellian. Thank you for your excitement about this book—it kept me going. Double thanks to Ian who also read my thesis, which was my first articulation of many of these thoughts.

I give my deepest gratitude to the excellent teachers I have had along the way. They helped me think deeply, and often differently, about moving, teaching, and learning: Karen Clemente, Dr. Joselli Deans, Lisa Troutman Welsh, Joy Friedlander, William "Bill" Evans, Debbie Knapp, Colleen Wahl, Erin C. Law, Peggy Hackney, JuPong Lin, and Michael Love.

I must also acknowledge my colleagues in theatre, dance, intimacy, and academia, who never seem to tire of having conversations with me about how to create more care in the arts and arts training programs: Alex Alvarez, Halie Bahr, Meredith Bartmon, Geri Brown, Dr. Jimmy Chrismon, Joseph Cloud, Crystal U. Davis, Elaine DiFalco Daugherty, Bill Fennelly, Hannah Fisher, Niki Fridh, Colleen Hughes, Carol Kaminsky, Cat Kamrath, Margaret Ledford, Susannah LeMarquand, Sarah Lozoff, Daimien Matherson, Ricky Morisseau, Cara Rawlings, Renee Redding-Jones, Dr. Danielle Rosvalley, Kunya Rowley, Molly W. Schenck, Matt Stabile, Dr. Nicole Stodard, Ed Talavera, Jason Paul Tate, Heather Trommer-Beardslee, Rebecca Jane Vickers, and Dr. Jessica Zeller. So much of who I am, as an artist, teacher, and human, is due to being in relationship with you.

The team at Intimacy Professionals Education Collective: Rachel, Charlie, Jess, Matt, Chels, and Jon, without your support and cheerleading I would have struggled to balance it all and get it all done. Thank you for your grace and your wisdom.

Thanks to Brooke M. Haney for facilitating the introduction that made this book a reality.

The folks who have attended sessions at Momentum Stage or that I have led for conferences or festivals provided wonderful feedback, questions, and engagement that helped build this book.

A big acknowledgment for the dancers who participated in the *Totentanz* Project, some of whom are pictured on the cover: Kalin Basford, Abbie Fricke, Mélanie Martel, and Sarah Romeo in *Prove It*, captured beautifully by Morgan Sophia Photography.

My partner, Pedram Nimreezi, believes and supports every wild idea I come up with. This book has been no different, and I would not have been able to index it without his expertise and generosity.

And finally, I must acknowledge and honor the students I have taught over the past nearly twenty years, who have entered with curiosity, vulnerability, and creativity. I am humbled by the teachings you gave me.

In memory of Cadence Whittier. Your joy in teaching, moving, creating, performing, writing, and living fully present remain an inspiration.

Introduction

Setting our expectations

I wrote this book for all movement educators working to incorporate and cultivate a culture of care in their movement classes. Since 2020, I have worked with hundreds, if not thousands, of artists and educators in:

- Power and consent workshops for creators of dance, theatre, opera, and film in college programs and professional companies, as well as at international and national arts conferences.
- Pedagogy courses specifically for movement teachers, examining touch as an instructional method.
- Trainings for performers and students on knowing, communicating, and holding their boundaries.
- Sessions for students and teachers on giving and receiving actionable feedback.
- Workshops for performing artists and students on creating personal grounding and/or closure practices.

In the teacher training sessions, I witness "Aha!" moments as educators become attuned to previously unrecognized power dynamics in classrooms and how these impact the psyches and performances of their students. After every session I facilitate, I am energized by the commitment of these educators to creating processes for art-making that are safer, braver, and more compassionate.

This book is to support teaching artists as they do just that. *Care-full Creativity in Theatre and Dance Education: Consent-Forward, Trauma-Informed, Psychologically Safe Movement Pedagogy* is meant to be an interactive text that provides theory and tools for practice in creating a movement pedagogy of care. It is a combination textbook (with theoretical underpinnings from scholars like Amy Edmonson, Paulo Freire, Mary Parker Follett, and Alfie Kohn[1]), guidebook (with tools and templates that can be immediately implemented), and workbook (with reflective prompts for self-assessment and to imagine potential solutions to classroom challenges) for movement educators as they establish or continue consent-forward,[2] trauma-informed, psychologically safe[3] classrooms, rehearsals, and studio spaces. Developing such spaces also creates more equitable systems for everyone in those movement classrooms or creative processes.

Creating not only systems, but relationships, is at the heart of this book. Our learning experiences in the movement classroom are defined by teacher-student and student-student interactions. Real people, with their feelings, decisions, and actions, are key to teaching and learning. We experience power, and its impact(s), in relationship. Trauma occurs, or is avoided, in relationship. Likewise, care is relational—we experience consent, or a lack thereof, in relationship. In fact, in her introduction to *Performing Care*, editor Amanda Stuart Fisher (2020) says, "care can only be experienced as a live, embodied encounter …" (12).

Why "care-full" pedagogy?

This book offers practices for care-full creativity. When I refer to "care-full" pedagogies, I do not mean that we tread lightly, for fear of hurting someone's feelings or "triggering[4]" them, or teach in ways that do not require engagement from students. Quite the contrary! I propose pedagogies full of care so we can move boldly into the processes of creating and learning with confidence in our abilities to support the students in the room while they honor their bodies, take risks, and explore sensitive or difficult material.

In his essay, "Towards an Aesthetics of Care," included in a 2015 issue of *Research in Drama Education*, James Thompson offers:

> An "aesthetics of care" is then about a set of values realized in a relational process that emphasise engagements between individuals or groups over time. … it is always one that notices inter-human relations in both the creation and the display of art projects. It is an aesthetics that is unafraid to lay bare what Shannon Jackson calls the "supporting infrastructures of […] living beings" (2011, 39), but importantly this is an aesthetics that could both present those mutually beneficial structures and foster them. (437)

This definition deeply informs my idea of care-full creativity. As I use it in this book, care-full creativity is experienced in relationship, uses both consent-forward and trauma-informed structures to build psychological safety, and leads to confidently embodied creative processes and performances.

Care-full approaches to teaching are responses to practices that harm (directly or indirectly), like punitive grading structures that foster fear, syllabus policies that reinforce power dynamics or competition, and classroom practices that do not prioritize bodily autonomy, psychological safety, or equity. Care-full pedagogic practices stand in opposition to many of the teaching methods and traditions of European and European-derived dance and theatre performance found in many classrooms. These ways of doing and learning are steeped in hierarchy, capitalism, colonialism, and binary thinking over collaboration, consent, or a multiplicity of solutions.

Many movement educators do incorporate care-full approaches in their work. For some this looks like requesting consent in touch, providing options for physical participation, creating an accessible syllabus, exploring different ways of assessing that account for individuality, or another practice intended to cultivate a culture of care. Throughout this book, I offer my collection of tools and resources to support care-full experiences and relationships between students and teachers and between students in movement classrooms, in all these categories and more. These examples are not meant to be prescriptive (although you can certainly use them "as is"), but rather to spark your imagination for possibilities to demonstrate care in your own classes.

When I speak of demonstrating "care" in the classroom, I mean engaging in practices that prioritize bodily autonomy, psychological safety, and equitable relationships. However, it is important to note that care exists only when the one "cared-for" experiences it as such. Nel Noddings, who wrote the definitive book on care in education, *Caring*, in 1984, reminds her readers, in the preface to the second edition, "A primary message of *Caring* is that we cannot justify ourselves as carers by claiming 'we care' if the recipients of our care insist that 'nobody cares,' caring relations do not exist" (2003, xiv).

The movement classroom

When I speak of "movement" in these pages, I mean story-telling movement: dance, movement for actors and modalities that may be taught in such a class, such as Laban, Viewpoints, Suzuki, etc., and staged combat and intimacy. However, I suspect many of these pedagogic practices could apply to teaching movement for function (such as Dance or Movement Therapy) and/or fitness as well!

When I speak of "classroom," I am mainly envisioning a studio space for the practice of movement in higher and graduate level education. I developed the tools found in this volume while teaching multiple levels of Ballet, Modern Dance, and Movement for Actors classes, as well as courses like Stretching and Bodywork, Movement for Musicians, Jazz Dance, and Choreography and Composition. In these spaces, learning and creativity are the goals, more than the final product. I've also included the syllabus and grading tools for lecture classes like Dance History and Dance Appreciation.

Care is especially important in the movement classroom because the work relies on bodies. Bodies are inextricably tied to our identity, and when in the movement classroom, our potential for academic and professional success as well. The idea that there is a lack of bodily autonomy in dance and theatre may seem counterintuitive, as these fields rely on the body for expression. However, they also typically attempt to mold every body into certain ideals of "body," and/or perceive the body as other than a human, as an instrument or tool. Bodies, particularly bodies of students, remain objects throughout much of Eurocentric dance and theatre training, regardless of age, ability, expertise, needs, boundaries, or interests.

I would suggest that this "body as outside object" way of thinking is part of why students may not experience care in the movement classroom. Carol Lynne Moore, whose work is documented in Judith Gray's *Dance Instruction*, writes of four categories of body metaphor: a beast, a machine, an object d'arte, and a child (1989, 146–148). These categories could apply to bodies in theatre movement classes as well.

When it is a beast or animal, the body is learning physical skills, but it is also susceptible to overwork and injury and being seen as without thought or emotion. As a machine, the body is incredibly skillful and efficient, yet it is only so in one area. It cannot change or adapt; it cannot be creative.

An art object is aesthetically valued on stage and in performance. With the focus on outer appearance, it is meant to be looked at and appreciated. However, the inner life of the performer is ignored. There is no reflection on sensation or meaning-making. Additionally, anatomical and biological reality may become warped as flexibility is forced, or certain body sizes are mandated.

Paulo Freire ([1973] 2006), an influential educator, community activist, and author, shares in his book, *Pedagogy of the Oppressed*, "The capability of banking education to minimize or annul the students' creative power and to stimulate their credulity serves the interests of the oppressors, who care neither to have the world revealed nor see it transformed" (73). As objects, bodies remain in a state of oppression, as objects cannot be in equal relationship to subjects, and objects cannot transform their worlds. Conversely, when students are validated, as subjects, then they can be truly creative and develop their own "voice" (which is what we as teachers often have as a goal in our dance and theatre classes), even to the point of transforming their world.

A child is open to creativity and play. But children do not have a professional level of skill. Seeing the body as a child may also make the student and/or their teacher risk-averse in explorations, feeling the need to protect, patronize, or condescend. The body as child does not allow for full expression of personal autonomy, as children do not always understand the consequence of their actions, nor are ready for accountability. A view of the body as child may cause a teacher to not offer opportunities for consent or to express boundaries.

All these (rather dismissive) categories of the body appear in the Eurocentric dance and movement education available in academic institutions and keep the body and the student-performer as less-than-fully-human. But educator Felicia Rose Chavez, author of *The Anti-racist Writing Workshop* reminds us, "The body is where liberation lives" (2021, 99). Providing space and time for students to experience freedom and actualization are what I strive for in dance and movement classes.

When I describe my classes, I refer to my experiences teaching in undergraduate dance minor programs in both public and private universities and Movement for Actors classes inside BFA acting programs in private universities, as well as a graduate-level movement course. Many of these tools and resources are useful for middle school and high school academic settings, and I include when I have used them in those ways. The tools in Chapters 7 and 8 are likely applicable in recreational arts settings, like dance studios and children's and youth theatre programs as well.

My applications speak specifically to my experiences as a human and educator. My introduction to consent-forward work in intimacy training at Intimacy Directors International in 2018 inspired an examination of the power dynamics, traditions, and "status quo" underpinning my creative processes and ways of teaching and assessing. I continued exploring power dynamics and their effects on consent, as well as trauma-informed practices in my certification work first at Intimacy Directors and Coordinators and now with Intimacy Professionals Education Collective, as well as my MFA in Interdisciplinary Arts at Goddard College. While learning, I was engaged in both teaching and professional creative practice. As I applied consent-forward adjustments, I found new areas for growth in my pedagogy and praxis. You will find citations of the books and articles that formed my thoughts throughout the book, but especially in Chapters 1 through 4 that share the theories behind the applications in Chapters 5 through 10.

How to use this book

In her article "The Messages behind the Methods: The Authoritarian Pedagogical Legacy in Western Concert Dance Technique Training and Rehearsals" in *Arts Education Policy Review*, Robin Lakes (2005) cautions educators that the subject is not all we teach in the classroom:

> There are actually two subject matters in the classroom. Unconsciously or not, ideas about many other aspects of life, including power, gender, and equity—and about how the teacher believes learning takes place—are being conveyed in the room. …Teaching behaviors and methods of the teacher teach a set of rules, beliefs, and ideologies as powerfully as does the curriculum, the syllabus, or the lesson plan. (4)

In the first half of the book, you will have occasions to clarify and articulate your beliefs and ideologies regarding power, agency, and safety in the classroom. These reflection exercises will help you make connections to how your beliefs may become part of the curriculum and impact students. Some of these questions also ask you to connect to your own embodied experiences.

Then, as later chapters offer tools and examples for the syllabus, class experiences, and assessments, the reflection space is for you to examine your current practices and imagine new possibilities. You will develop methods to support and promote those life and learning lessons through movement technique and training.

All educational spaces are influenced by power dynamics, so I know at least some of these tools will be useful in your space, whatever it is! While my examples may not speak specifically to your situation, they are meant to serve as inspiration and a spark for your imagination of what is possible in your movement classroom. Tools in this book are for every educator wishing to create more care in their teaching practices. You can document these possibilities in the reflection[5] spaces.

Chapters in this book

The first step in addressing harm[6] is understanding the conditions that allow it. In movement classrooms, the power dynamics of both European and European-derived academic and performance traditions create conditions that can enable harm. The first part of the book lays out theories of power in practice, along with reflective prompts that create a power assessment for movement classrooms.

Chapter 1 is an examination of both power and power dynamics. The Social Power theories of French and Raven (1959) are accompanied by reflective assessments of how power appears in, and affects, the spaces you lead. This chapter also details the relationship of power and competition, and how they inhibit trust and collaboration.

In Chapter 2, the integrative power theories of Mary Parker Follett (1929) illustrate how educators can use their power to create more opportunities for, rather than limit, the agency and personal power of students. This chapter lays the groundwork for facilitating collaborative processes, by understanding Follett's "law of the situation" and "power-with." The collaborative processes and tools are explored in depth in the next section of the book.

The next chapter, Chapter 3, draws on the work of Paulo Freire (1972) and mental health policies, as well as Follett, and my own work to demonstrate the necessity of addressing power dynamics, if educators are to create movement classrooms that are truly trauma-informed and based on consent and agency. A new theory of consent, Working Consent, created specifically for performance and education spaces, is offered.

The final chapter in this, the theory section of the book, takes the business concept of psychological safety, as articulated by Amy C. Edmonson in *The Fearless Organization: Creating Psychological Safety in the Workplace for Learning, Innovation, and Growing* (2019), and applies it to the classroom. This idea is furthered by Timothy R. Clark's *The Four Stages of Psychological Safety* (2020) to creates a scaffold for classroom experiences that build psychological safety. This chapter connects consent, trauma, and psychological safety, with the influences of power.

I situate all the theories around power, consent, and trauma with primary sources that date back nearly 100 years, up through current scholarship in education and movement. In doing so, I demonstrate that these conversations are not new; yet we are still not applying the insights and offerings from these researchers as fully as we could. These early thinkers on how power influences people still have much to offer us, as hierarchies, kyriarchies,[7] and interpersonal dynamics still play out in movement studios and classrooms every day.

We cannot build practices that center consent or are trauma-informed without an understanding of power. Honest assessment of where we are is required to make change. Similarly, to create collaboration, trust and safety are required, demanding an understanding of power dynamics. Chapters 1 through 4 provide the theoretical underpinnings for developing consent and psychological safety, resulting in a trauma-informed movement classroom. So please, read and do these first! But, after that, feel free to jump to the chapter that is most applicable or tools that are most exciting to you.

Following the chapters of theoretical frameworks are those offering deep-dives into the practices of care-full creativity and pedagogy in the movement classroom. These chapters feature case studies of syllabus language, classroom experiences and exercises, and assessment. These are accompanied again by reflective prompts, meant to let you explore how you may bring more care to your classroom.

In Chapter 5, the first tools, those for building and maintaining inclusion safety (Clark, 2020), a requirement for psychological safety and belonging, are offered. This chapter includes templates, handouts, and illustrations for classroom community agreements, boundary conversations, and more.

Chapter 6 looks specifically at the syllabus. While traditionally a document of rules and the penalties for breaking them, in care-full pedagogy, the syllabus is a tool for communication and connection. This type of syllabus details not only what the educator expects of students, but what the students can expect from their instructor, and what they all should expect from each other. As many institutions have requirements for their syllabi, this chapter offers ways educators might incorporate language around participation, community, conflict resolution, and more to support consent-forward, trauma-informed, psychologically safe classroom experiences. This language provides the baseline for the practices of Chapters 7 and 8.

Using the psychological safety scaffold, Chapter 7 offers distinct practices for incorporating care-full pedagogy into the movement classroom, from start to finish of each class period. The care theories of Thompson, the pedagogic theories of Freire, and the consent-forward principle of staged intimacy work provide the foundation. The tool of grounding strategies draws on the work of Molly W. Schenck in *Trauma-Informed Creative Practices*

(2021). With each tool, examples of actual classroom use are offered, as well as templates and/or handouts as possible.

In Chapter 8, I examine the use of touch in the classroom. I offer reasons and alternatives for no-touch and low-touch teaching in movement spaces, as consent-forward and trauma-informed methods of teaching. This chapter was developed from not only my own classroom work, but from teaching a course on touch in dance instruction for the National Dance Education Organization every summer since 2021.

Chapter 9 was perhaps my favorite chapter to write. This chapter views traditional assessments and grades as tools of power dynamics, while offering ungrading options to support consent and mitigate trauma. The work of Alfie Kohn (2006), and other "ungrading" experts support the case for care-full assessments. Policies and rubrics for both lecture and studio courses are offered. This chapter also includes example assignments and student feedback about ungrading. Offerings from several other movement educators, including Dr. Jessica Zeller (author of *Humanizing Ballet Pedagogies*, 2024) are included.

To conclude this section, we will view feedback in class, from both the instructor and students, through the lens of care. Feedback is, like touch, an often taken for granted part of movement classes, which means the power dynamics and issues around consent and trauma are often unexamined, too. In this chapter, I share a care-full method for giving feedback. The scripts for feedback and notes are supported by the work of Larry Lavender (1996), Liz Lerman (2003), and Felicia Rose Chavez (2021), as well as principles of nonviolent communication.

The conclusion of this book is my letter to you, as you go forward, developing and sustaining a consent-forward, trauma-informed, psychologically safe, care-full pedagogy in your academic movement classroom. Resources for each chapter can be found in the Resource Section. Included here is a collection of links to and citations of supportive resources, as well as the bibliography. Part of ethical academic and creative work is citing one's sources, and this book has many.

This book will give you language to name what you are already doing, and how it fits in a care-full pedagogy. Tools and resources will help you grow and find new ways of teaching and creating with care. Reflections are there for you to review your current practice and/or understandings, as well as to imagine next steps. Each chapter concludes with a list of the main points of each chapter.

Conclusion

Through the course of this book, you may be challenged or inspired. You may get mad or excited. You may feel overwhelmed at times with the amount of change there is to make. If you are here, it is because you desire to teach with care; to honor consent and autonomy, to deal with students equitably, and to create excellent works of art. Nel Noddings wrote in *Caring*, "The student is infinitely more important than the subject" (20). In teacher training workshops I often say, "I don't teach movement; I teach humans." I suspect you are here because you feel the same way.

I want to recognize that teaching in consent-forward, trauma-informed ways takes time. You may read some of the policies and practices I offer and think, "I do not get paid enough to do that." And, I believe you! In fact, you are probably reading this book that you bought with your personal funds on your unpaid break. I have had full-time positions with a salary, adjunct positions that paid a flat fee per class, and adjunct positions that paid hourly. In each, I have included policies and practices for consent-forward, trauma-informed work, while also recognizing that they had to be sustainable, equitable and demonstrate care for me, as well as students. There is no singular or "right" way for you to implement this work. Please experiment, adapt, and get creative!

Please give yourself time to:

1. *Reflect:* Professional development is an opportunity to learn not just more about your field, but about yourself. This takes time and honesty. While you may feel some urgency around getting this knowledge now, resist that. Please don't skip the reflections!
2. *Return often:* This is not a "one and done" kind of book. Use it often! It may be worth revisiting every school year, or at least every time you teach a new class. Or when something you have done "a million times" suddenly doesn't connect with a group of students. You don't have to use every tool or tip now (see the above on urgency). You have time to make changes.
3. *Strategize:* The need for systemic change often feels urgent, but it takes time. Make changes with intention, and in ways that are sustainable. Moving too fast may result in unintended consequences that you could have foreseen and/or prepared for if you had discussed your choices with others or implemented in steps. Making changes with intention, and with support, will also provide care for you in resisting burnout.
4. *Share:* The work we are talking about here starts with you, but likely also requires institutional shifts. This will necessitate transparent conversations with your co-workers, your boss, and maybe even your boss's boss.

As you read and reflect, bring these discussions forward. Change can start with one person, but it is only sustainable with support.
5. *Resource yourself:* Part of developing care-full creativity includes you being equitable with your own time and resources and bringing yourself the same care you bring to students. We are both supportive and supported. The Resources section contains not only a bibliography for sources cited in this text, but a section of additional reading and tools that can support a care-full pedagogy.
6. *Resource those around you:* Please share the resources freely and widely!

My goal in writing *Care-full Creativity in Theatre and Dance Education: Consent-Forward, Trauma-Informed, Psychologically Safe Movement Pedagogy* was to share my learning and application in ways that might lead you to know yourself and your classroom methods more deeply and feel confident in your ability to create movement spaces that are collaborative and full of care.

We have all made mistakes, me, included. I continue to work on creating a more care-full pedagogy every time I teach, and sometimes it doesn't work as well as I had hoped. When that happens, I look for what I can learn from it, engage in some closure practices, and try to do better in the next class. Nel Noddings wrote in *Caring*, "the test of my caring is not wholly in how things turn out; the primary test lies in an examination of what I considered, how fully I received the other, and whether the free pursuit of his projects is partly a result of the completion of my caring in him" (81). As you proceed into the text, I hope you will give yourself grace for past mistakes, and those that will occur as you make changes (change is hard!).

REFLECTION SECTION: Designing a care-full pedagogy

What drew me to this book? Why do I want to bring more care into my teaching?

_____
_____
_____
_____
_____

What chapter, described above, is most interesting to me? Why? What do I do with this information?

_____
_____
_____
_____
_____

Which sound the most challenging? Why? What do I do with this information?

_____
_____
_____
_____
_____

Chapter reminders

- Care-full creativity is experienced in relationship, uses both consent-forward and trauma-informed structures to build psychological safety, and leads to confidently embodied creative processes and performances.
- We don't teach dance or movement; we teach humans.
- There is no single way to create a care-full pedagogy.
- As you create a care-full pedagogy of movement, give yourself time to: reflect, return to the material, strategize, share your discoveries with others, and resource yourself and others.

Notes

1. You will see my references run from the early 1900s to 2024. The ages of some of these ideas may surprise you! I try to use primary sources whenever possible, as giving credit is part of ethical and care-taking work. See the Resources Section for not only the sources cited in the text, but supplemental texts and tools, as well.
2. "Consent-forward" is the phrase used by the training organization Intimacy Directors and Coordinators to describe their approach to staged intimacy work and education. For Colleen Hughes, their former Director of Core Training who helped define this term, the language helps position consent with a positive, "you can do it," mindset because often the changes the work requires us to do in creation and teaching can feel overwhelming. I choose to use this idea of consent-forward in my own discussions of the work because I believe it supports the idea of ongoing consent, as described in my definition of Working Consent in Chapter 3.
3. While there are occasions of the term "psychological safety" being used in clinical settings in the mid1900s, for the purposes of this book, we will be using the definition that arises in organizations, like businesses and schools, as developed by Edmonson. At no point is this phrase meant to convey a medical status or condition.
4. A word I try not to use, choosing to go with "activated" for two reasons: (1) the word itself can be activating because of the connotation of violence and (2) a "trigger" is either pulled or not, allowing not room for a spectrum of responses. An activation, like a dimmer switch, encompasses an entire range of reactions. You will see "activate" and "activation" frequently from Chapter 3 onward.
5. For more on the pedagogy of reflection, see p. 213–214 in Chapter 9
6. "Harm" is used in this book as "an action or behavior by a person or system(s) that leads to unmet needs." This definition comes from Chels Morgan in their video lecture *Accountability, Apology, and Healing* available at Intimacy Professionals Education Collective. In this way, harm may be physical but could be emotional or psychological. In this lecture Chels is also very clear that (1) harm is defined by the person experiencing it and (2) academia and performance spaces are systems that can cause harm.
7. See p. 18 in Chapter 1 for a definition of "kyriarchy."

Part 1
Theory

1
Assessing power dynamics in the movement classroom: Understanding power and power dynamics

It is impossible to talk about demonstrating care (engaging in practices that prioritize bodily autonomy, psychological safety, and equitable relationships) in the classroom without first assessing the conditions which create a need for care. In academic movement spaces, abuse(s) of power, a lack of consent or ability to access bodily autonomy, trauma, and/or a lack of psychological safety all contribute to a need for a care-full pedagogy.

This chapter and the next one look at power in the classroom. In the "Introduction," I said care is relational. So is power—which makes care the perfect antidote for abuse of power and for mitigating power dynamics.

Defining power dynamics

I define power dynamics as conditions that influence how I choose, speak, or behave in the moment, because I feel I must do so, in proximity to a certain person or group of people, so that my relationship with them functions in the way I would like it to. Another way to think about power dynamics is to consider the ways we as educators may hold power over the students we work with and how that power impacts students.

Power dynamics are my favorite things to talk about. Understanding how they affect working relationships is key to transforming hierarchical spaces into collaborative ones. But power dynamics are often taken for granted. We accept them as "just the way it is."

Power dynamics:

- Occur in relationship. That is, they happen between people or groups of people. And, they happen in a particular context.

DOI: 10.4324/9781003596301-3

- Are anything that affect a person's ability to act (including making choices or speaking) fully autonomously in the moment.

Power dynamics might be summed up as "the politics of the situation." In the next section, we will use French and Raven's Social Powers to name the power dynamics that may be affecting students in your classes and/or rehearsals.

This is not to neglect the existence and truth of power experienced because of the bodies we are in, or embodied power. In European and European-derived societies, certain bodies, most often white, cis-male, thin, abled, neurotypical, and young, and those in closest proximity to those traits, carry more power in organizational spaces than bodies that do not have these characteristics. For example, I am an intimacy director[1] and dance choreographer for theatre, a modern concert dance choreographer, an intimacy coordinator for TV and film, a dance and movement educator in higher education, who also does teacher training, and a trainer of intimacy professionals. I show up to each of these jobs in a white, cis-female, heterosexual, thin, middle-aged body that has survived a period of disability and chronic illness, and continues to exist, move, and work with an (often debilitating) injury. The body I carry into my workspaces holds power, simply because I fit the typical ideas of how a "dance teacher" or "choreographer" (of both dance and intimacy) presents in the world. As you read and reflect, keep in mind that the Social Powers or power dynamics we are discussing can be compounded or negated by the body someone is in.

Elizabeth Schüssler Fiorenza called this collection of embodied powers a "kyriarchy," defined in the glossary of her 2001 book, *Wisdom Ways: Introducing Feminist Biblical Interpretation*, as "a complex pyramidal system of intersecting multiplicative social structures of superordination and subordination, of ruling and oppression" (211). Throughout the rest of this book, I will use both hierarchy and kyriarchy and will use hierarchy specifically when referring to arrangement and/or rank, and kyriarchy when referring to embodiment. Coupled with the idea of "intersectionality," kyriarchy provides a view of oppression and privilege as the interplay of both systems and bodies.

Powers over

History and theory

In 1958, two social psychologists, French and Raven, wrote a paper called "The Bases of Social Power." In it, they named five different ways that power was experienced in hierarchical structures, like companies, which could include companies that perform dance, theatre, and opera, and institutions that train students in the arts. French and Raven described power as presenting as Expert, Legitimate, Reward, Coercive, and Referent. A few years later, they added a sixth power, Informational, to their theory. While their theory is not new, it is still relevant. When I was introduced to this framework in my training for intimacy work, I recognized that in the intervening 60-plus years, the powers French and Raven analyzed and described haven't really changed in business or in education.

These are called Social Powers because they exist within the context of a certain relationship or institution. Most people in European and European-derived societies experience these powers similarly, regardless of the institution we work or participate in, because our institutions and societies are structured similarly. We could also call Social Powers "power dynamics."

Defining French and Raven's powers over

French and Raven define Social Power as influence that creates change (1959, 151). This supports our premise that power dynamics are the conditions of a relationship that cause someone to change how they think, speak, and/or behave in the presence of someone who they feel holds power. In these ways, the Social Powers French and Raven describe are "powers over," that is, they are exerted on someone or a group to cause a thought or behavior that is in accordance with the thoughts and/or behaviors of those doing the influencing. The idea of "power over" is often how we define[2] the broad concept of power.

Expert Power

French and Raven consider a person to hold this type of power when they are considered an "expert," whether because of their knowledge or experience. People will often act in deference to an expert because of this status. Students assume their teachers have more expertise in the subject matter than they do. An instructor is assumed to be an expert. When I show up to facilitate a workshop, my visual presentations, tone of voice, and location at the front of the room add to my Expert Power. Other examples of "experts" are choreographers in a room of dancers, a junior or senior in a class of first- or second-year students, someone who has worked with this director before, students in advanced levels when in the room with beginners, etc.

Legitimate Power

Legitimate Power, also called Title Power, is power conferred by an official position. Usually, this power is given from someone *outside* the relationship impacted by it—think of the hiring committee choosing a professor, or the studio owner who hires a teacher. The Legitimate Power vested in these titles is experienced between the instructors and their students, but not necessarily with the person who gave them the title. Other examples of Legitimate Power are anyone with a title, such as director, choreographer, etc. In movement classrooms. Professors often hold both Expert and Legitimate Powers.[3]

Reward and Coercive Powers

These are two sides to the same coin; one cannot exist without the other. These forms of power exist when the power holder can give a perk (Reward Power) for behavior they approve of, or a penalty (Coercive Power) for behavior they don't approve. It's a carrot-and-stick arrangement for behavior modification.

Reward and Coercive Powers are possibly the first power dynamics we encounter as children, as we interact with parents or other caregivers. According to Alfred J. Deikman, M.D., who studied and wrote about cult behavior[4] in America, "Biological survival requires that we become adept at pleasing these powerful people …" (1990, 70). Life is the ultimate reward and fear of death is very coercive! So, we quickly learn to please those in power, and tend to keep this conditioning with every other person in an authority role we encounter, even in our adult lives.

Alfie Kohn, pedagogue and author, writes extensively on the flaws of Reward Power as both a management theory and pedagogic method in his book *Punished by Rewards: The Trouble With Gold Stars, Incentive Plans, As, Praise and Other Bribes*. He reminds us that rewards are just as much a control method as coercive tactics, by quoting a 1987 study by Deci and Ryan, "In the final analysis, they are not one bit less controlling since, like punishments, they are 'typically used to induce or pressure people to do things they would not freely do'—or rather, things that the controller believes they would not freely do" (26). In fact, he says, rewards are "dehumanizing," because they negate the possibility of a "natural love of learning, and the desire to do good work …" (26).

Another pitfall of rewards is that a reward is only a reward once. After that it is a coercion. Most of us don't think of ourselves as manipulative people. And yet, this is exactly what a system of rewards allows us to do.

Obvious examples of Reward and Coercive Powers in the movement classroom are grades and assigning students to appropriate placement/levels. Less obvious cases may be casting, dressing room or costume assignments, even assigning material or partners for classroom exercises.

There is an important fact about power that Reward and Coercive Powers highlight for us: power is perceived as well as actual. Power, like beauty, is in the eye of the beholder. It does not matter if you, as the teacher, know that a certain participation grade was given for reasons that you feel are legitimate. If a student feels it is a punishment for a question they asked in class or a skill they are working on, but have not mastered, it will be perceived as a punishment, and that will affect their behavior in your presence. If a student feels that you placed them in the back of a dance formation or scene, not because they are tall, but because you "don't like them," they will behave as if they are being punished, and that will impact your relationship with them.

Kohn writes later in the book:

> If your parent or teacher or manager is sitting in judgment of what you do, and if that judgment will determine whether good things or bad things happen to you, this cannot help but warp your relationship with that person. You will not be working collaboratively in order to learn or grow; you will be trying to get him or her to approve of what you are doing so you can get the goodies. (57)

Since one of the skills we hope to build in the movement classroom is collaboration, Reward and Coercive Powers present a distinct challenge, as fear often negatively affect students' abilities to work together and take creative risks.

Punishment discourages creativity. Deikman writes, "Although innovation and creativity may be given lip service, even insignificant mistakes are usually punished despite their being the inevitable price of developing ..." (82). There will be a lot more on how to mitigate these types of power in the chapter on assessment.

Informational Power

Informational Power comes from the information, or knowledge, a person has. This is very similar to Expert Power but has the qualifier that this information must be knowledge others need or want. In fact, that information is crucial to others experiencing success.

Gatekeeping is a way to keep people in a certain order of importance or value. Deikman wrote of cult behavior, "hierarchy was maintained through limiting access to information" (145). He continues, "By promoting the idea that the leader ... [has] special information and expertise, they remove themselves from criticism and justify the exclusion of others from the decision-making process" (145). An example of this in the arts is often coupled with Legitimate and Expert Powers: "Because I'm the director/choreographer/teacher, and it's my vision." Another example is grading an artistic performance, particularly if there is no rubric provided to make the values on which art is assessed transparent. In both situations, the leader is the only one who holds this information in its fullness, and it is a reliance on a power dynamic to have this be the end of the conversation.

Some other examples of those who hold Informational Power are teachers (especially right before an exam), a jury panel, or a casting panel. All these folks hold information that will help those in front of them be more successful, and they may or may not be willing to share it.

Referent Power

Interestingly, Referent Power occurs both inside and outside the group we are in together. A student may assume their behavior or performance in my class will influence what I say about them when I see them outside the academic environment in the professional world, like at an audition. The student is thinking, "What group do I want to belong to," or "what do I want a particular group to think about me?" So, their behavior in front of me changes in anticipation of my use of Referent Power in my sphere of influence. Similarly, think of a letter of reference—a student assumes my standing in the university will persuade another university or organization of what I say about them.

Deikman asserts, "Reference groups influence our behavior greatly, although we may not be conscious of how and when this occurs" (50). Because Referent Power has results outside our immediate situation, it can be a bit tricky to recognize. Other examples of Referent Power, beyond letters of reference, include the possibility of being extended professional recommendations, audition invitations, etc.

Like Reward and Coercive Powers, Referent Power is often more perceived than actual. But students' perceptions of me influence our shared reality.

Also, like Reward and Coercive Powers, Referent Power developed from a biological need. Deikman writes in *The Wrong Way Home*, "Imitation of our peers is basic to learning and development and the reference group is an important influence throughout life" (51). It is safe to fit in. Deikman reminds, "Compliance with a group increases with one's psychological and economic dependence on it" (61). In this way, the Reward is being seen as part of the group, and so Referent Power compounds with Reward and becomes a doubly influential dynamic.

Recognizing power dynamics in the movement classroom: Power is experienced in relationship

French and Raven's Social Powers are power dynamics, because they occur in relationship and influence a member of that relationship to behave in a certain way.

There are a few things to keep in mind about power dynamics:

- Power dynamics are the ways leaders exert influence, whether they are aware of this or not. Many educators think they don't have power because they don't abuse power or use power negatively. But that is an entirely different thing than having power.
- In fact, power dynamics can influence behavior whether they are perceived or actual, because power dynamics affect someone's ability to choose, speak, and/or act; people will be influenced when they *think* someone has the power, whether they really do or not. This is a crucial perspective, as often educators are aware of the power they *don't* have in a space—but to the students they lead, they still have power and influence.
- Power dynamics are neither linear, nor singular. You don't have to have one to have another. And usually you don't have just one, rather several are enmeshed.

In his essay "On Authoritarianism in the Dance Classroom" in the book *Dance, Power, and Difference* (1998), Clyde Smith writes, "The dance class situation offers so much power to the teacher, however, that this power is readily abused, as I myself later discovered..." (128). This is a teacher deeply desiring to be collaborative and compassionate, and realizing that the structures of dance and movement classes, particularly the power dynamics that exist in them, make that extremely challenging, and require constant monitoring and redress.

REFLECTION SECTION: Defining and identifying powers over

French and Raven open their article by stating, "The processes of power are pervasive, complex, and often disguised in our society" (1959, 151). I couldn't agree more! The following pages offer definitions and examples of each Social Power or power dynamic.

Use the space below the definitions to write about:

- A time you experienced someone as having this power, especially in an educational setting.
- How students do or may perceive you as holding this type of power.

By reflecting on your experience of these, you will remove the masks of power and start to expose how power affects your creative processes and classroom.

Expert Power

Held by a person because of their expertise, knowledge, or experience.

_____

_____

_____

_____

_____

Legitimate Power

Held by a person because of the title they hold or position they were hired for. Usually, this power is given by someone else.

_____

_____

_____

_____

_____

Reward Power

Held by a person because of their ability to grant perk(s) for behavior(s) that they approve of.

_____
_____
_____
_____
_____

Coercive Power

Held by a person because of their ability to penalize behavior(s) they don't approve of.

_____
_____
_____
_____
_____

Informational Power

Held by a person because of the knowledge they have AND their information is crucial to the success of others.

_____
_____
_____
_____
_____

Referent Power

Held by a person because of their sphere of influence.

Intersecting Powers

How have I seen these compound each other?

How have I seen these powers compound because of the body someone is in?

Which of French and Raven's Social Powers do I feel/guess most affect the students I work with?

Remember: These powers apply even if you don't want them or you don't think you have them! Power is perceived as well as actual.

___

Which of these powers, as defined by French and Raven, do I feel I most hold?

These do change, depending on context.

___

What are my feelings about recognizing myself as someone who holds, and uses, power?

___

How are these power dynamics different in a movement classroom than a traditional classroom? *There may be both positive and negative differences.*

_____

_____

_____

_____

_____

What do I wish students knew about my power, or lack thereof?

_____

_____

_____

_____

_____

When and/or why have I used power dynamics to shape my pedagogy?

"I don't know" and "that's what was modeled for me" are perfectly valid answers, but you may also have some anecdotes about how leaning on power dynamics was beneficial.

_____

_____

_____

_____

_____

What are ways I am/could address Social Powers in my classroom experiences and conversations?

"I don't know" is again a valid answer. The second section of this book provides tools to help you do exactly this.

Recognizing power dynamics in the movement classroom: Effects of hierarchies and kyriarchies

I included in "Power Dynamics in Dance" for the *Dance Geist*[5] ezine in early 2021 a quote from dance historian Deborah Jowitt,

> When Marius Petipa worried about pleasing "the public," he was speaking of a power elite. Dancers on the stage of the Maryinsky could look out into an orderly assemblage, seated according to rank and prestige .... The spectators looked back at a stage world that flatteringly mirrored theirs in protocol, decorum, and elegance .... The parades, grand entrances, and large ensemble dances in the ballets affirmed the power of ceremony. The surviving works from this period—*The Nutcracker, Swan Lake, The Sleeping Beauty,* and *La Bayadère*—contain courts of their own. (243–4)

Hierarchies and kyriarchies are traditional parts of professional work with the director and/or choreographer over performers, so it is no wonder that these ideas of rank and prestige are duplicated in movement classrooms with the teacher over the students.

Alfred J. Deikman wrote, "The evidence is strong that all of us show the effects of having been raised in a hierarchical world in which there were those above us and those below" (172). Hierarchies and kyriarchies are supported in movement classes not only with official ranking systems like grades and juries, but also unofficial ones like favoritism, body prejudices, people-pleasing, and competition.

These unofficial systems of power maintenance carry the possibility of abuse of power beyond the relationship between teacher and student. Through them, every student is affected. When these systems are in place, students exist in the space not to learn, but to please or impress the person in power. I call this desire to achieve favor or rewards from someone outside myself a "competition mindset."

Competition mindset

Competition mindset is prevalent in movement training programs and performance spaces. It reinforces kyriarchies, hierarchies, and power dynamics. In doing so, it also creates fear and distrust, as students view each other as obstacles to achievement, rather than co-creators. Competition mindset often leads students and performers to violate or give up their own boundaries, to ensure that they get a job or a good grade or stay in favor with a power holder. There will be more on the toxicity of this mindset when it comes to formal assessments in the Chapter 9 but, for now, let's look at how competition supports power dynamics.

Competition mindset holds the values and expectations of the one with power over as more important than my own, and unquestionably correct.

The person who places well or wins at competition, whether in an event or a classroom experience, is the person who has pleased the power holder, be it a judge or a teacher. They have been able to achieve seemingly objective benchmarks of what it means to be "good." I say "seemingly" because art is subjective, and to make objective benchmarks[6] out of it goes against what it is. In addition, the benchmarks are not always made clear to the participants. In competition, Expert, Legitimate, and Reward Powers are reinforced: the preferences and ideals of the expert become the unquestioned standard, as reaching them results in a reward.

What's more, those setting and enforcing these standards may or may not have done any work to examine their unconscious biases or how their expectations of technical execution may be coupled with the reality of genetic benefits or bodily limitations, access determined by class or wealth, or Eurocentric assumptions.

Competition mindset asserts that I am only as valuable as I am better than the person next to me.

Deikman wrote, "Adult human beings stand together in a horizontal plane, but they all too often try to organize it vertically" (171). Competition automatically creates ranking systems, even if that is not the goal of the competition. Existing power dynamics can go unaddressed or unmitigated because while these exist everyone at least feels clear on their rank and value.

Alfie Kohn devotes a whole chapter to competition's effect on relationships in his book, *No Contest: The Case Against Competition*. In it, he writes, "When we compete, then, we objectify others, lose our ability to empathize, become less inclined to help. A chasm opens up between us leaving us distrustful, envious, and contemptuous" (266). Competition alters our view of the people we are learning and working with. Kohn quotes Karen Horney: "Competitiveness creates easily aroused envy toward the stronger ones, contempt for the weaker, and distrust toward everyone…" (262).

While a competitive event may provide a student with tangible proof of progress, feedback for improvement, or an opportunity to celebrate their skills, competition mindset is a barrier to equitable, collaborative relationships. It encourages students to see peers not as persons but as threats to their success. Others are ignorable at best, and in worst-case scenarios, students may view them with fear, treat them with disrespect, or consider them exploitable.

We cannot collaborate with those we don't trust. Or, as Kohn concludes, "Competition is the worst possible arrangement as far as relationship is concerned" (277). This is because competition is a relationship of power, not a relationship of care.

For those of you saying, "well, that is just in auditions or solos, not for competition teams, ensembles, or class levels," I would remind you that those group settings often started as competitive ones—auditions, juries, etc. Kohn cites several studies showing that cooperation within a group does not increase when the group engages in competition outside of the group (283–5). It would be silly to expect that competitive behavior that was previously rewarded would not continue, even after someone has "made it." Competition requires hierarchies and kyriarchies and, therefore, creates a possibility of the abuse of power, particularly Expert, Reward and Coercive, and Referent Powers.

Competition mindset doesn't just make it difficult for me to trust others; it makes it difficult to trust myself.

In competition, self-worth is dependent on meeting the expectations of an outside power holder and knowing one's place in a rank of others. A student's sense of personal power or agency may become invisibilized.[7] They may no longer see themself as a powerful being with the ability to change their world; their identity is that of a group member. In this case, listening to themself, their needs and boundaries, is too dangerous, because following through on those requests may cause them to be dismissed from the group.

To quote Deikman again, "The security of a cult is bound up with the idea of being special, better than those outside the group" (101). That measure of "specialness" is policed by the group, and everyone must live up to the standards, usually set by the leader. But, if one has no power, one will not advocate for themself; it's too risky, as they may be cast out of the group. Therefore, a student may accept touch they do not want or tones of address that do not help them learn. They will work to move up the ranks of favor with the power holder or, at the very least, not go lower. The standards of the power holder and the group will, for better or worse, become their own. Other people will be rivals. In these instances, one is not making these choices freely—they are making them out of fear.

Referent Power carries its full force when competition mindset exists. Students will be constantly seeking to stay in a group, to belong, even if, particularly in the case of movement classes, they are putting themselves at risk of injury or exploiting their own trauma to meet performance benchmarks.

In environments that foster competition mindset, students are not using self-reflection and critical thinking to make choices about what they need or want, instead they accept imposed frameworks. Students become divorced from their own needs and boundaries more and more with every choice to ignore them. One becomes an unreliable narrator of one's own experience, so much so that they can only trust those in power to create it for them.

Recognizing power dynamics in the movement classroom: Institutional influence

Ideology and institutionalism are partners to power. Deikman writes in *The Wrong Way Home*, "We will surrender a great deal to institutions that give us a sense of meaning and, through it, a sense of security" (67). The organizations that we are a part of tell us:

- What power is.
- Who gets to have power.
- What power looks like when it's used well.
- If there are any consequences if power is used poorly.

You are likely also feeling some Referent Power regarding your institution that may be causing you to think that implementing more care-full practices in your classes may hinder your ability to fit in. These thoughts may take the form of:

- Dance and/or theatre are already so undervalued at my institution. If I challenge the traditional power dynamics of academia, enable practices of consent, talk about being trauma-informed, etc., I will play into their bias that my work is not valuable because I am going against the status quo.
- As a woman, gender nonconforming person, person of color, or other marginalized identity, I must always surpass expectations to succeed in

my institution. If I challenge the traditional power dynamics of academia, enable practices of consent, talk about being trauma-informed, etc., I will play into their bias that I am "too soft" and/or "not good enough" for this work.

If you are feeling these things, your experiences are valid. This goes back to the introduction and giving yourself the care you bring to your classes. Not all the changes or tools in this book are right for every person, class, or institution. This is why the reflective work is so important. Please make the changes that feel right and sustainable for you in your setting.

The power dynamics described in this chapter exist in most hierarchical structures, aka most educational institutions. But these do not need to be used in abusive ways or ways that make collaboration impossible. The next chapter explores power as a tool for collaboration and to support everyone's power.

REFLECTION SECTION: Recognizing unofficial systems of power

How do I see "competition mindset" at work in my classes?

_____
_____
_____
_____
_____

Are there other unofficial power systems at work in my classes?

These may be "majors or BFAs are more important than minors or BAs," certain body types are valued, etc.

_____
_____
_____
_____
_____

What are ways I am/could address competition or other unofficial power systems in my classroom experiences and conversations?

_____
_____
_____
_____
_____

Institutional influence

What does my organization say about power in public ways?

What is said in things like vision statements, syllabi, and/or accountability policies regarding power use and/or abuse?

_____
_____
_____
_____
_____

What does my organization imply about power?

What is said through actions like hiring, promoting, firing, etc.?

_____
_____
_____
_____
_____

What Social Powers does my institution value? What values around power are communicated through this?

For example, some programs constantly talk about grades and evaluations, some about professional preparation.

_____
_____
_____
_____
_____

Assessing power dynamics in the movement classroom

What conversations need to be had around power, and with who?

While the goal of this book is to give you language and tools for creating a care-full pedagogy, you are probably not doing it in a vacuum. Do you need to speak with your chair about how your department uses or values power? A co-teacher? Be more transparent with students?

_____
_____
_____
_____
_____

Conclusion

This chapter may have been a bit of a bummer. It can be illuminating, but also challenging, to come to terms with the powers that we hold, or are perceived to hold, in the creative processes we facilitate, as well as the influences of our institution and society, and systems like hierarchy and kyriarchy. Regarding hierarchy and freedom, dance educator and researcher Naomi M. Jackson wrote in *Dance and Ethics* (2022), "In other words, this is not just a case of a few bad actors but of a system and culture that allow teachers and choreographers to assume extensive control and dominance of the dancers (and staff) in their charge" (72). Similarly, Robin Lakes writes, "A contradiction exists between the liberating power that an arts education can provide and the continuing history of authoritarian teaching modes in this field" (2005, 3).

And yet, you are reading this book because you do not want to rely on power dynamics to get things done.[8] You want to work in collaboration. You want students to bring their full, creative, authentic selves to your classroom! You want to teach and create with care. But power over methods of teaching create fear, an emotion that limits expression and risk-taking, crucial elements of the creative process.

Concerted efforts must be taken to mitigate these power dynamics so that we can create in consent-forward, trauma-informed, equitable ways. The next chapter will offer a different approach to power that centers the humanity of everyone in the creative process. As you work on making changes in your own teaching methods and classes, remember that change for the better is indeed better, even if you are only able to change *your* system, and not *the* system.

Chapter reminders

- Power dynamics are conditions that influence how I choose, speak, or behave in the moment, because I feel I must do so in proximity to a certain person or group of people, so that my relationship with them functions in the way I would like it to.
- Power dynamics:
    - Occur in relationship.
    - Affect a person's ability to act fully autonomously in the moment.
    - Are "the politics of the situation."

- Social Power is influence that creates change.
- Power is perceived as well as actual.
- Social Powers are compounded (or negated) by the bodies we show up in.
- Competition mindset elevates power holders, pits students against each other, and discourages students from trusting their own bodies and choices when those are different than the power holder's.
- Having power (and all of us as educators do) isn't a bad thing. Unfortunately, abuse of power is common in our institutions.
- Not abusing power is not the same thing as not having power.
- Ideology and institutionalism are partners to power.
- Naming and acknowledging power dynamics, and how they can impact others, are the first steps in mitigating them.

Notes

1. An intimacy professional, in whatever medium, creates both protocols and choreography for scenes of simulated sex, nudity or hyperexposure, and/or complex physical intimacy.
2. You will get a chance to define power at the start of next chapter, but you can start thinking about it now!
3. Legitimate and Expert Powers are very similar, but they are not quite the same. Think of a job you had in which your manager or supervisor certainly held that title, but they had very little expertise to offer.
4. If you don't think teaching and learning can become cult-like behaviors, keep track of how many times I quote Deikman in this section.
5. Sadly, this ezine no longer exists, even in archives. You can find this article, however, on my website.
6. In Chapters 9 and 10, we will talk about how biases can impact assessing and giving feedback.
7. See more on Invisible Power in the next chapter.
8. For those of you keeping track at home, I quoted Alfred J. Deikman's work on cult mentality and behavior 11 times in this chapter (and it will show up other places in this book). The cultures of both performance and academia can lead to this mentality and behavior if we, as the leaders, are not careful.

2
Moving to power-with

REFLECTION SECTION: Defining power

This chapter begins with a reflection to help you know your baseline idea of "power."

What is power? The word is used a lot. What is my definition of it?

_____
_____
_____
_____
_____

During workshops I've led on power and power dynamics, high school and college students have most often defined "power" as "control" or "influence."

How do these words fit my definition of power? What is my reaction to these words?

_____
_____
_____
_____
_____

Defining power as it relates to collaboration

The definition of power we will use going forward comes from Mary Parker Follett, a community activist and management theorist living and working in New England in the 1910s and 1920s. Follett is one of the unsung heroes of community work, which we now would call social work, a field which, to her, included politics, education, labor, economics, and, importantly, community. Her work was not really taken seriously by her contemporaries, as she was a woman, writing about "men's" spheres like industry and politics. Her theories were also dismissed because her emphasis on collective action allowed some to paint her as a "Communist," and her long-term living arrangement with another woman had others judging her morality (Tonn 2003, 309). As so often happens, capitalism, patriarchy, and heteronormativity stifled brilliance and new ways forward.

However, many of her writings and speech notes, both of which she engaged in prolifically, still exist. For this chapter, we will find much of our support in *Creative Experience*, a book first published in 1924, and *Dynamic Administration*, a collection of notes and speeches from the 1930s, published in posthumously in 1940 as well as another collection of her papers and speeches, *Mary Parker Follett: Prophet of Management*. Well before French and Raven wrote the paper "The Bases of Social Power," Mary Parker Follett was considering how power affected relationships in industry, civil life, and education. As she looked at factories, politics, and community centers, she realized a lot of interpersonal and bottom-line problems were caused by power dynamics. She was fascinated with how people could create change, and examined how groups could work well together.

Mary Parker Follett defined power as, "the power to do something" (1924, 191). She also uses another definition, "simply the ability to make things happen, to be a causal agent, to initiate change" ([1933] 1973, 98). In order to do something, one must have the opportunity to do it and the ability to do it. Therefore, my definition of power, based on Follett's is "the ability and opportunity to do."

Most movement teachers want their classrooms to be a space where people *do*, which, according to Follett, is power. And yet, most Western classrooms and performance traditions are not set up for students to experience their power. Sometimes, they know they have the ability, but there is no opportunity to put it to work. Sometimes, they have an opportunity they are unprepared for. People are fully in their power when they can take confident action. Her analysis of power,[1] as practiced in groups, is discussed in following section.

Mary Parker Follett's types of power

Power-over

Power-over is how Follett found industry, education, politics, and community life in America and England to be structured in the 1920s and 1930s. In this experience, someone has power, and someone doesn't. Someone gets it, and keeps it, and no one else can have it. She found this to be so much the case that her biographer, Joan C. Tonn, wrote of her, "Follett not only repeatedly acknowledged the presence of 'domination' and 'power-over' in social life; she also wrote her book specifically to propose a method that might effectively replace it" (2003, 387). The book was *Creative Experience*, published in 1924, and it serves as a foundational text for my personal practice and this chapter.

Unfortunately, not much has changed in the intervening 100 years. Only certain people are seen as having the ability to do, so only certain people are given the opportunity to do. All the forms of Social Power defined by French and Raven included in Chapter 1 could go in this category of power-over. And way back in 1924, Follett made the case that "Power-over, nevertheless, is resorted to time without number, because people will not wait for the slower process of education" (190).

However, we are in the business of educating. So, we should take the time to examine Follett's counter to power-over, power-with. This sees power not as a singular trait, but as action, as collaboration. In this premise, every person, by nature of being a person, has power. Yet, we know that power dynamics compromise or challenge our ability to take action. Follett's definition of power-with demonstrates how every person can experience and grow their power and use their power to truly collaborate with others.

Power-with also known as coactive control or collaboration

Follett writes, "Power is not a pre-existing thing which can be handed out to someone, or wrenched from someone …. You cannot confer power because power is the blossoming of experience" (1933, 110). As such, everyone has power. She also wrote, "I do not think that power can be delegated, because genuine power is capacity" (1933, 108). In this way, we see power as "an attribute, or even a verb, not as a possession" (Beard 2018, 87).

If I am a powerful being who wants to impact my world, and I start doing that, I am eventually going to realize that I can create more change with others than alone. Mary Parker Follett stated clearly, "for genuine power is not coercive control, but coactive control" (1924, vii). Valerie Miller and Just Associates (JASS) in the 1980s developed a tool called *The Power Matrix*, in which they called this "Power With." I'd call it collaboration—I'm going to seek out others who want to change their world in ways like how I want to change mine, and work with them.

I suspect power-with,[2] or collaboration, is what we, as educators, desire to experience or create in classrooms. And yet, the hierarchies of academia, coupled with the hierarchies of European, or European-derived movement traditions, often do not lend themselves to this. Most of our classrooms operate in power-over. Students get to experience achievement, but only within the structures and approval systems the people in power have created. But in true power-with or coactive control, everyone would be using their power not only to do something, but to decide what that something is, and how best they can contribute to it. When we work together, we are not only creating the thing we are working on, but we are also creating more power, and experiences of power, for everyone involved.

Collaboration as power-with

Just like "power," the word "collaboration" gets tossed around a lot in performing spaces. But I don't think we use it well. Often when someone in power over someone else tells that person, "You are such a good collaborator," what they really mean is "thanks for always doing what I say." This is not collaboration. To be collaboration, an activity has some requirements that must be met:

- *Collaboration requires power*
  Collaboration involves the creative power of everyone. Collaboration is everyone using their power to do their role, and therefore developing power with each other. Follett called this type of working together "integration," instead of compromise (1924, 46). We don't each have to give up something to agree. Rather, we start with what we agree are the needs and priorities of the work and the workers, and find a way to support all these things. Being collaborative requires a lot of creativity, and it often means not doing the thing that was the first idea, because it incorporates ideas from all.
- *Collaboration requires consent*
  I can only be a collaborator if I have all the information about a process and am able to make choices that affect its outcome. This means

collaboration requires consent.[3] To truly be in collaboration, I must be working to expose and mitigate power dynamics so that others can enter the creative process as equals.

- *Collaboration is humanizing*
  To be collaborators, we must recognize the full and equal humanity of our co-artists. Yet dehumanizing tactics are often used in the creative and/or pedagogic process. In the opening chapter of *Pedagogy of the Oppressed*, Freire ([1973] 2006) writes, "[humanization] is thwarted by injustice, exploitation, oppression and the violence of the oppressors .... Dehumanization...is a *distortion of the vocation of becoming more fully human*" (emphasis original) (44). Injustices and exploitation cause harm not only among the collaborators, but through the larger world, as humanity is destroyed rather than validated, restored, or created. Art-making and teaching should be ways of guiding others in explorations of what it means to be human.

Roles, responsibilities and relationships in power-with

Power is not a noun, simply existing. Rather power exists in action and reaches its fullest expression, according to Follett, in "co-action." We are most powerful when we pool our resources, without abandoning our roles. So, power exists both in action and in relationship. She wrote in *Creative Experience*:

> There is an idea prevalent, which I think very harmful, that we give up individual power in order to get joint activity. But first, by pooling power we are not giving it up; and secondly, the power produced by relationship is a qualitative, not a quantitative thing. If we follow our rule throughout of translating everything into activity, if we look at power as the power to do something, we shall understand this. (1924, 191)

As a movement educator and creator, I know relationships are crucial to our work. In academic settings, we have teachers, students, and administrators. Much of performance requires a director or choreographer, actors or dancers, designers, and audience. While these may be seen as hierarchies, they are really relationships of equal humans with differing responsibilities. Shawn Wilson, an Indigenous scholar and researcher wrote the book *Research is Ceremony* to codify an Indigenous research paradigm, which particularly values relationality as a way of developing and sharing knowledge. In it, he offers, "everything needs to be seen within the context of the relationships it represents" (2008, 64). Mary Parker Follett said, "We, persons, have relations with each other, but we should find them in and through the whole situation. We cannot have any sound relations with each other as long as we take them out of that setting which gives them their meaning and value" ([1933] 1995, 128).

All our roles are part of the structures we are in, and no amount of wishing it were otherwise or pretending these roles do not exist will make it so (of course, if you have developed a beautifully egalitarian devising, improvising or other type of creating group, you may not have these roles, but in academia, we certainly do). As a matter of fact, to create our work, we actually *need* all of these roles and responsibilities to exist.

Being responsible is not the same as relying on power dynamics. As a teacher, I have a responsibility to both the students and the subject I am teaching to create a curriculum that meets certain learning outcomes to prepare students for the next steps in their academic and professional lives. I also have a responsibility to the students to create and hold a learning space where they can safely engage in the subject. I have a responsibility to my institution to turn in grades at the end of the semester. None of these are powers. They are part of my role (i.e., granted, imbued with Expert and Legitimate Powers) as teacher.

Students also have responsibilities. They are responsible for their bodies, caring for them, and preparing them for learning. They have a responsibility to our learning community to be present and engaged. They have a responsibility to themselves and their futures to do their best work. When all of us take responsibility for the functions of our roles, we can show up in our power.

"The law of the situation"

All these roles, responsibilities, and rules contribute to what Mary Parker Follett termed "the law of the situation" and described it as:

> One *person* should not give orders to another *person*, but both should agree to take their orders from the situation. If orders are simply part of the situation, the question of someone giving and someone receiving does not come up. Both accept the orders given by the situation. ... Our job is not how to get people to obey orders, but how to devise methods by which we can best *discover* the order integral to a particular situation. (emphasis original) (1933, 58)

"The law of the situation" defines the working parameters of our class. Or, in a rehearsal, we might call it "Given Circumstances."[4] Given Circumstances is a familiar concept for theatre folks: the things we take as true when entering the world of the play, such as the setting, time, relationships, etc.

"The law of the situation" doesn't change and is accepted as the context in which we develop power-with. That may include class start date, class time, there is a teacher and there are students, we are in ballet class, final grades must be given, etc. When we enter any situation, we accept these as conditions of being in the work.

In other words, the work we've come together to do tells us what we need to do! Nel Noddings recognized this as a factor of caring, writing that in caring for "those for whom we have personal regard" we must consider "what the situational relationship requires of us" (46). When it comes to clarifying "the law of the situation" and the unequal power dynamics within our Given Circumstances, the syllabus and the class contract are all tools of care-full pedagogy. These are addressed in Chapters 6 and 5, respectively.

Accommodations to "the law of the situation"

Just because the situation is defined does not mean it cannot be modified, or that accommodations cannot be made so that everyone can thrive and succeed in that situation. When I led workshops for the Dance Education Equity Association (DEEA) on power and consent in dance spaces, Geri Brown, their founder, would say that "the law of the situation" helps us "meet students where they are, in service of the work."

We're there to do the work, with real and powerful humans! Sometimes that means that, as a teacher or leader, I must make "reasonable accommodations" to support the work getting done. These might look like:

- Asking dancers to choose a single, double, or triple turn, and reassuring them that those are all acceptable options.[5]
- Ensuring we take a break after eighty minutes of work or making it clear anyone can take a break when they need.
- Offering the option for students to consent to corrective touch or be cued verbally.
- Hiring a specialized professional, like an intimacy or fight director, or lift or tumbling coach, for extreme physical work.
- Supporting academic accommodations as necessary.

In each of these examples, I do not let go of the work to be done nor has "the law of the situation" changed. I simply found ways to support the needs of the people doing the work, so that they can engage fully, and hopefully successfully. When we do this, we treat people equitably and acknowledge their full humanity and agency, and experience power-with.

Just because we all have different roles in the making of art does not mean that one role is over the others. We all contribute to the process; we all have work to do. Focusing on the work frees us to be in relationships of equality, rather than hierarchy. Follett said of power-with, "*With* is a pretty good preposition ... because it connotes functional unity" (1933, 61). That is how I imagine our different roles in a power-with setting—functional unity, all working toward the same goal. Power-with only occurs when we pool our respective powers and humanities. As sometimes the fulfillment of responsibilities can be achieved through the abuse of power, there will be more on how to facilitate collaboration and power-with in the next section of this book.

REFLECTION SECTION: Power-with: Creating collaboration

What does collaboration look like?

_____
_____
_____
_____
_____

When was a time I experienced true power-with or collaboration?

This would be a time that everyone was functioning in the role, bringing their expertise to the room, and creating space for others to do the same.

What factors allowed that to be true?

_____
_____
_____
_____
_____

How can I (re)create those factors that allow for power-with or collaboration in my class?

_____
_____
_____
_____
_____

REFLECTION SECTION: Law of the situation: With accommodations

What are some givens, or "laws of the situation," I do/could articulate in my class(es)?

_____
_____
_____
_____
_____

What are ways I can/could make clear that collaboration and humanity are prioritized, as is getting the work done, in the above situation?

_____
_____
_____
_____
_____

In a class I lead,

- Have there been requests for accommodations to support the work?
- Were those able to be met, or not?
- How did that meeting of needs (or not meeting) affect the work? Affect the working relationship?

_____
_____
_____
_____
_____

What are other accommodations I could foresee being asked for, or that I could offer to support my class or creative process?

___

How can I communicate the availability (or lack thereof) of accommodations in my class or creative process?

"I don't know" is a valid answer. The second section of this book provides tools to help you do exactly this.

___

Creating power-with

Power-with doesn't happen accidentally or by chance. *The Power Matrix* of Valerie Miller and JASS offers key insights for building "Power With", or power-with as described by Follett.

Power Within

This is the first step to collaboration, knowing that I, and everyone around me, is a powerful being. Every human being has inherent dignity and worth. Every person, because they are a person, wants to affect their world in ways that benefit them.

It is our Power Within that makes us want to speak up about our boundaries or needs, or when we feel we have been treated unfairly. It is our Power Within that fuels our desires to grow and learn. Power Within causes us to want to improve, both ourselves and the world around us.

Invisible Power

If I don't recognize my Power Within, or I lose the truth of it, I experience Invisible Power. When I am experiencing this dynamic, my own power, my ability and opportunity to change my world, have become invisibilized to me.

This can happen in a few ways:

- I look at folks who hold power over me, and I see no one who is like me. The kyriarchy has molded who is "powerful." So, I start to think I have no ability to do anything to change my world.
  - Western society has preferences for who is represented as powerful. As mentioned in the previous chapter, this has a lot to do with the body we are in.
- I never get an opportunity to put my power into action to affect my world. I think I have the ability, but because I never get the opportunity, I never experience power. And then, I start to doubt my ability as well.

In these scenarios, I either believe I have no ability to do or have no opportunity to do, so my own power simply becomes invisible to me. In academia, this might look like faculty who are a majority white or white-passing teaching mainly students of color, or a majority male faculty teaching a student body that is a majority female or other marginalized genders.

Similarly, students who do not get an opportunity to apply their knowledge, or make decisions, can dismiss their own power, as they never experience it. This can occur when an acting teacher gives a line read or a movement teacher instructs by demonstration. Insistence on the teacher's way being the only right way can invisibilize the power of students.

This is very apparent in the professional dance industry where women are consistently displayed onstage, but rarely in leadership. According to the Dance Data Project's 2025 report on Performing Arts Centers' Programming and Leadership, "The median percentage of women-choreographed works was 26.2%." And,

> Among the 116 centers examined, DDP identified 3,162 individuals occupying the highest leadership position within executive staff, artistic staff, and members of the center's governing board. Of these 3,162 individuals, 1,379 are women (43.6%). Women comprised 43.5% of centers' governing boards and 44.7% of staff at the highest decision-making level.[6]

Despite a visible presence, the power of women can, and likely is, invisibilized in dance. While not from academia, it is a clear example that representation does not equal power.

Gaslighting makes one's power invisible

Another way people experience an invisibilizing of their power is through gaslighting. The term "gaslight" comes from Patrick Hamilton's 1938 play by the same name. In it, a woman notices that every night the gas lamps flicker and dim. Her devious husband tells her she is simply imagining things. Of course, she is not; he is turning on a lamp in the attic, affecting the gas supply to all the other lamps in the house, while he searches for treasure he believes is there. He also moves and removes objects in the house purposefully so that she begins to doubt her memory and reality.

The nefarious husband's goal is the goal of all gaslighters—to convince you that your own mind cannot be trusted. If you are disconnected from reality in this way, then you cannot be trusted to make your own decisions. Your Power Within becomes invisible to you.

If you cannot make your own decisions, well, then you need someone to make them for you. The only one you can trust, of course, is the person who has put you in this position to start with—the person doing the gaslighting.

In movement classes we don't usually turn off the lights and insist that they are still on. But teachers can gaslight students in subtle ways that may remove their self-trust.

- A student tells us they are injured/ill, and we insist it's "not that bad."
- A student feels bullied or excluded, and we dismiss their hurt.
- A student expresses that the way a note was delivered was not respectful, and we tell them it wasn't what we meant, they are "too sensitive," or tell them to "toughen up."
- A student in a marginalized group experiences a microaggression from us or another student, and we tell them that harm wasn't the intention, or not to "make a big deal out of nothing."
- We tell students to "leave their baggage at the door."

I've heard that last one a lot. I've even said it myself. I am now convinced it is a form of gaslighting, because it tells students that their reality is "too much." With this, we also tell them that class has a different reality than the rest of their lives.

Students' experiences are their reality. Gaslighting reinforces that only one experience is valid, and it isn't theirs. This reinforcement of Expert and Legitimate Powers can result in invisibilizing students' own Power Within. As movement teachers, we should be giving them the tools to listen to and honor their bodies. We need to be resourcing them so that they can be present and take care of themselves in appropriate ways.

Devin Hill, a dancer, dance educator, and convention adjudicator, as well as an advocate for disability access in dance, has another take on "leave your baggage at the door." They believe that the phrase is meant to turn dancers into empty vessels, to be filled by the art, or lumps of clay, to be molded by the choreographer or teacher. In asking students to "leave their baggage at the door," we are setting them up for grooming or abuse as they exchange their experiences for the idea of what their teacher or choreographer expects them to be (Hill, 2024).

This idea is backed up by Clyde Smith's learning and teaching experiences, reflected in his essay "Authoritarianism in the Dance Classroom" in *Dance, Power, and Difference* (1998). He writes:

> I understood the dance classroom to be an ideal climate for authoritarian behavior. The student has already consented to being in a situation in which he or she is usually attempting to replicate as perfectly as possible the example and the demands of the teacher. ... most choreography

involved a process in which dancers became the material for the choreographer's work .... (128)

Robin Lakes echoes the sentiment, "When dancers are being utilized for an artistic vision, their feelings do not matter. They are a distraction to the artistic process of the teacher" (2005, 5). The same thing can happen in a theatre process in which the director's way is the only way, or in a classroom where only "perfect" or an "A" is an acceptable demonstration of learning.

When students are required to accept the teacher, director, or choreographer's version of reality as the only possible or true version, we are creating an atmosphere of acquiescence. This attitude will carry over into other classrooms and rehearsal rooms students enter. Even if we do not abuse or manipulate students, we have trained them to develop behaviors that make them more likely to be abused or manipulated.

REFLECTION SECTION: Invisible power

When was a time my own power was invisible?

Did I lose sight of my ability? Or was I never given opportunities?

_____
_____
_____
_____
_____

What are ways students may have their power invisibilized in my classroom? In my institution?

What factors may obscure their abilities? What factors limit their opportunities?

_____
_____
_____
_____
_____

What are ways I can mitigate the invisibilize-ing of students' power?

"I don't know" is again a valid answer. The second section of this book provides tools to help you do exactly this.

_____
_____
_____
_____
_____

Are there inadvertent episodes of gaslighting that students experience in my classroom? How can I change these?

_____

_____

_____

_____

_____

Power To

Recognizing and owning Power Within is necessary to build Power To. As our definition of power reminds us, it is "the ability and opportunity to do." Power Within recognizes our innate ability to create change. But, for power to be fully realized, we also need the opportunity, which takes us to Power To, and ultimately, power-with. If I recognize that I want to, and have the ability to, change my world, I'm going to take (or make) opportunities to do so. This is where, as educators, our power over others can come in handy—we can use our power in the rooms we are in to create opportunities for students to step into their Power Within and develop their power to do.

Power To is not empowerment

This is not the same thing as "empowerment." This is a word and concept I deeply dislike, especially when it comes to our work as educators.

- "Empowerment" ignores Power Within.
  "Empowering" students is the opposite of working with care and equity. It is not liberating, it is limiting. As teachers or leaders, we do not "empower" others. They are already powerful!

  Stating that we want to "empower" others would mean that power is something we can grant. It is not. Alex Shevrin Venet writes in *Equity-Centered Trauma-Informed Education*, "Rather, true empowerment is claiming and using one's own power" (2021, 69).

  We also had that Mary Parker Follett quote back a few pages, "Power is not a pre-existing thing which can be handed out to someone or wrenched from someone …. You cannot confer power because power is the blossoming of experience" (1933, 110). She continues, "We can confer authority; but power or capacity, no man can give or take. The manager cannot share his power with division superintendent or foreman or workmen, but he can give them opportunities for developing *their* power" (emphasis original) (111–2). As educators, we can use our power to create opportunities for students to step into their power, practice their power, or realize their power more fully. By doing so, we give students the opportunity to be their full selves. Not only that, but the work we are doing is benefited by everyone's full power.

- "Empowerment" is based on the maintenance of power-over.
  To "empower" someone would inherently mean that they are not in a position of power. The very idea of "empowerment" assumes that someone has no power, and that power must be given, granted, or permitted from someone who holds power-over, rather than something to be lived into or claimed by any and all. Hierarchies and kyriarchies are required with the idea of "empowerment." Instead, we should be working with a desire for everyone to be operating in their full power.

Tonn quotes Follett as telling the community centers she advised, "the attitude of the manager and leaders is that all are there to help the young people get what they want, not to 'uplift' them" (241). This is a powerful reminder for educators as well. We are not there to uplift students but help them achieve their goals. The assessment chapter, Chapter 9, will have more on helping students set, measure, and achieve their goals, as again, it should be about them, not us.

REFLECTION SECTION: Power Within, To, and With: Creating collaboration

What sensations/feelings/thoughts do I have when I think about sharing power with students?

_____
_____
_____
_____
_____

How would I describe the sense of power in my classroom?

Are students confident in their power within and their abilities to do, or learn to do what is asked of them? Do they get to step into Power To and take opportunities to do? Are we all creating Power With?

_____
_____
_____
_____
_____

How am I creating opportunities for students to practice Power To and Power With?

What exercises or experiences in my class have students stepping into their power to do? What exercises or experiences in my class require the pooling of power and experience between students?

If there are not these opportunities currently in your classroom, do you have any ideas of what these could be? "I don't know" is again a valid answer. The second section of this book provides tools to help you do exactly this.

_____
_____
_____
_____
_____

What do I hope students will learn about themselves from being in their own power?

_____
_____
_____
_____
_____

Conclusion: Power-over versus power-with

Follett was clear that in coactive control, roles and experiences of the invested parties don't go away. That is, there are still teachers and students, choreographers and dancers. Plus, administrators, bus drivers, marketing folks, board members, colleagues, audiences, etc.!

A key feature of coactive control, or collaboration, is that we recognize all these folks and their roles as crucial to getting the work done. Follett's biographer Joan C. Tonn points out:

> Follett insists that expertise must be understood and accepted 'as expressing an attitude of mind which we can all acquire,' This change in attitude, she admits, will not make us professional experts, but 'it will enable us to work with professional experts and to find our place in a society which needs the experience of all, to build up a society which shall embody the experience of all.' (363)

This is what Follett was seeing in group dynamics as she worked in her community—people came together from their disparate backgrounds, pooled their power and ideas to support an outcome they believed in, and were able to create change. But these ways of working were not being replicated in industry or education. In those fields, a "top down" model was how decisions were made, often resulting in inefficient methods, poor relationships, and changes that were unsustainable.

I like to remind students that we are all experts in the room. My expertise is in the certain subject matter, theirs is in their bodies and experiences. All of us need everyone else's expertise if we are going to fully learn, because of our different perspectives. We need everyone to be in their power, in their role, so that we can make the best art we can or learn to the fullest extent that we can!

Power-with is how many of us in arts and movement education want to be working and creating. We often say we are in collaboration. Yet, the power structures we are a part of keep reinforcing power-over! In the next chapter, we will examine the interlocking relationships of power, consent, and trauma, and how those influence our classrooms and studios, and our ability to collaborate.

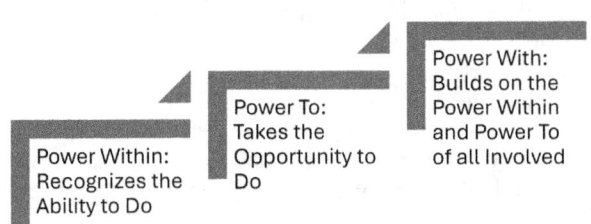

Figure 2.1 Building Power Within to Power To to Power With. Created by the author, 2024.

Chapter reminders

- All of French and Raven's Social Powers could be defined as power-over.
- Every person has Power Within, simply because they are human.
- Therefore, every person wants to use their power to do something, to change their world.
- Power Within is required to build Power To, which is required to build to Power With.
- Collaboration is everyone using their power to do their role, and therefore developing power with each other.
- Power-with requires us to all bring our power to our roles, which are all required to do the work of making art.
- Teachers simply create opportunities for students to practice their power, or they deny students' inherent power.
- Empowering someone is the opposite of working toward liberation for everyone.

Notes

1. We see Follett's categories of power-over and power-with often in activist and justice spaces, so you may be surprised to know she wrote and spoke these words in her work from 1929 to 1933. Bringing her name and writings back into the discourse on power dynamics is edifying, as a feminist perspective on power is not often cited in research.
2. Jessica Zeller writes in *Humanizing Ballet Pedagogies*, "While teacher affiliated with dominant identity groups might readily consider sharing power with students, teachers in historically marginalized groups might feel they need to retain some of their given pedagogical power to offset the biases they may encounter in an educational space" (2024, 45). In my privilege as a white cis-woman, I do not want to discount this reality that may make power-with feel unsafe for some educators. While it is important to note that power-with is a sharing of power, not a giving up of power, for those who may not experience much power because of the social context in which they must work, this sharing may feel like losing.
3. See more on consent in the next chapter.
4. This was first described as part of Stanislavski's System for Actor Training in his book *An Actor's Work: A Student's Diary*, translated by Jean Benedetti (2008).
5. See more on choice as contributor safety in Chapter 7.
6. The numbers only slightly improve within dance companies. According to another Dance Data Project (DDP) report on dance companies, "In the 2023/2024 season, women choreographed 30.6% of works presented by the Largest 150 companies." They continue, "Despite their considerable financial capacity (combined expenditures of $380,115,421 in FY 2022, representing 52.9% of the Largest 150's aggregate budget by expenditure), the Largest 10 continue to severely limit opportunities for female choreographers."

3
The connections of power, consent, and trauma

Consent in education

When I speak of "consent," I am speaking of more than conversations around the contact that occur in instructional touch given by a teacher in a movement class, or even partnering exercises between students in class. I am referencing the ability of students to be authentically engaged in their bodies and fully committed to the content we are working on, and the context in which we are working.

Consent matters in educational spaces and movement classes because young people are training their bodies and psyches to be available to take on a variety of work in their performance lives. Learning to listen to and honor the requests of those bodies and psyches should be part of the training. However, we cannot ask students to "listen to" their bodies or psyches if they don't have the opportunity to honor those requests or statements.[1] Consent in movement education spaces also matters because students are human and have personal sovereignty and autonomy—the right to boundaries[2] and to say "no" to anything, at any time.

I don't think we'd find many educators who would disagree with the idea of consent mattering in class. And yet, spaces that operate on the assumption of power over make consent not only difficult, but impossible.

Consent-forward pedagogy

The FRIES of Planned Parenthood[3] is an acrostic frequently associated with consent. This imagistic reminder tells us that consent in our intimate relationships should be:

DOI: 10.4324/9781003596301-5

- Freely given
- Reversible
- Informed
- Enthusiastic
- Specific

While I do want to emphasize healthy relationships in the movement classroom, if this were to be our definition for consent with students, we would find it unsustainable and incomplete in the following ways:

- Freely given (it cannot exist if someone has been/is being coerced, manipulated, or influenced).
  - This means consent cannot exist when power dynamics are in play, because power dynamics have the potential to alter how we choose, speak, and act in the presence of another! So, basically, that includes all of theatre, dance, opera, film, academia, as we said in previous chapters. We feel the pressure to please the power holder, so we say "yes," even when we want to say "no."
  - It is important for movement instructors to realize; we are never truly getting consent from our students. See the section on "Working Consent" on the next page for more on this.
- Reversible (I could change my mind).
  - While a student may be able to change their mind about certain activities in a class, they may not be able to remove themselves from an academic setting that feels unsafe or a teacher they find activating or harmful.
    - Add/drop deadlines create academic and/or financial consequence(s) to a student changing their mind.
    - Requirements of a specific major can hold a student in a class in to accrue course credits deemed necessary for successful matriculation or graduation.
- Enthusiastic (I am happy about it).
  - This one is simply too hard to assess.
    - Every student has a different way of showing enthusiasm and commitment.
    - Alternatively, a student could be enthusiastic about being in the class and not be enthusiastic about every single exercise or assignment. But that moment doesn't discount the fact that they are here, ready to work. That's real life. We don't love every second of our job, either.

So, on the best of days, in a Eurocentric, academic movement classroom, we're getting Informed and Specific (and I bet even those could be improved upon), which doesn't make for comprehensive consent.

Working Consent

My definition of consent in movement classrooms is what I call "Working Consent." Working Consent is the ongoing process of:

- Centering the focus on the overarching work we all have agreed to accomplish, and need to fulfill our roles in, to accomplish it.
- Opening dialogue between all parties involved to mitigate the power dynamics as much as possible.
- Acknowledging the power dynamics in performance and learning spaces.

- The **"Work ..."** reminds us that the focus is on the work we are there to do or the art we are there to create, rather than the titles of people in the creative roles. By focusing on the work, we disrupt the power dynamics of roles, of teacher and students, and instead center on a shared goal we are achieving through particular relationships. It is power-with, as we, in our individual roles, pool our power to get the work done.

And, as mentioned in the point regarding "Enthusiastic," while participants may not be thrilled about every action they engage in on stage or in the classroom, they are often enthusiastic about the overall work and the final outcome of that work, whether it be a performance or credits toward graduation. When we, as educators, responsibly frame directions, corrections, and dialogue in the context of the work we are all here to do—learn, create art, etc.—we use our role to address power dynamics and open the space for collaboration around the many ways we might get to that creation.

- The **"...ing"** in "Working Consent" reminds us that consent is a process. Consent is not a destination to reach and then it is done. Rather, consent requires consistent and frequent check-ins, reiterations, and adaptations. All of this requires dialogue.

Dialogue

Dialogue is inherently disruptive to power. Paulo Freire writes in *Pedagogy of the Oppressed*, the paradigm-shifting idea that most of current Western education has a "banking model." He declares this model is flawed and does not value humanity, because "dialogue cannot be reduced to the act of one person's 'depositing' ideas in another .... Because dialogue is an encounter among women and men who name the world, it must not be a situation where some name on behalf of others" (1972, 89). He continues "Without dialogue there is no communication, and without communication, there can be no true education" (92–3).

Referencing Freire, Felicia Rose Chavez, who uses dialogue as a tool in her writing classroom, cautions in *The Anti-racist Writing Workshop* (2021), "Shut down dialogue, and you shut down authentic thinking, liberation, and freedom" (50). In fact, she calls dialogue "an act of love and humility that subverts the teacher's authority and elevates students to critical co-investigators," highlighting dialogue's disruptive properties (50). Nel Noddings describes it as, "when I spend time in dialogue with my students, I am rewarded not only with appreciation but also with all sorts of information and insights" (1983, 52).

If we are going to engage in dialogue, I must believe that your point of view is valid for you, and equal to mine. This does not mean that I must adopt your point of view, but I must be able to see how and why you would hold this opinion and accept it as an alternative. As Freire writes later in the same book, "Dialogue does not impose, does not manipulate, does not domesticate, does not 'sloganize'" (168).

True dialogue, like collaboration, happens between equals, between humans operating in their power. Dialogue reminds us, in the words of Alfred J. Deikman, M.D., "when we face each other we find companions" (1990, 173). It's not about one person waiting for their turn to talk. Dialogue is both parties seeking to understand each other, and, where they can, support the points of view of the other.

For example, if I invited you to my house for breakfast and said I was making scrambled eggs, and you said, "Oh, I love ketchup on my scrambled eggs!" I would reply with something along the lines of, "Wow, that's good to know. I love hot sauce, but I will make sure we have ketchup for you." I listened to you and recognized that your point of view was valid. Then, I was able to make an accommodation[4] to meet your request. Similarly in movement classes, I can make modifications or accommodations to support injured students, offer corrections without touch, and/or provide multiple forms of assessment.[5]

In *A Pedagogy of Kindness*, Cate Denial writes, "An experiential form of learning, Dialogue asks participants to think critically about their own and others' socialization into systems of power by talking frankly about personal experience" (2024, 6). In this agreement to hold multiple perspectives, those with power acknowledge that their way is not the only way, or even the right way.

Remember Mary Parker Follett's "power-with," or "coactive control? (1924, vii)" This "jointly developed power," is the only way to stop the reliance on "power-over," and create space for consent ([1933] 1973, 100). In such a setting, the powers of everyone are pooled together to achieve the goal of that situation. Everyone's power and role are necessary to the execution of the work to be done.

Since "Dialogue demands vulnerability," for people to confidently engage in dialogue across power dynamics, they must know that there is a process in place to address harm that may occur (Denial 2024, 6). There must be a public measure of accountability. I recommend this take the form of a Chain of Communication or a Resolution Pathway.[6] This tool includes at least one other human alternative to the person in power in the room, as well as applicable hotlines and resources for the organization. Information about the process should be included in contracts, handbooks, etc., and posted if possible.

- The final word **Consent** when coupled with "Working," opens the idea of committed engagement and embodied action occurring all throughout the process of creating the work, by everyone involved. Consent is an ongoing process requiring the continual commitment and presence of all parties in performance and performance training spaces, as every moment of creating theatre and/or dance requires the full engagement of all collaborators.

In Working Consent, consent encompasses not only contact, but all the ways bodies interact with, and are affected by, both content and context in learning and art-making. Consent in this definition requires a dialogue between all parties, offering specificity and clarity around power dynamics, expectations, goals, and outcomes. It exists in and between bodies in a working relationship.

While Working Consent does not eliminate power differentials within existing systems, it does seek to transparently and continuously address them and highlight the need for equity in collaboration. Working Consent means that everyone gets to hold, and uphold, their own power. In the second section of this book, there are examples in each chapter of Working Consent in the movement classroom.

REFLECTION SECTION: Power's relationship to consent

How have I experienced power dynamic(s) influencing my agency, boundaries, and/or ability to give consent?

Can you think of a moment that you felt the influence of power dynamics in a way that made "yes" your only option? Or "no" too costly or risky an option?

_____

_____

_____

_____

How have I seen power dynamics affect performers' and/or students' ability to give consent in spaces I lead?

This can be a tough one to sit with, because I know you don't want to be someone who coerces others into doing something they don't want to do. Remember it's not you, it's the power dynamic. You may be able to mitigate this power dynamic.

_____

_____

_____

_____

What do students learn about themselves when I use power dynamics to shape my pedagogy?

_____

_____

_____

_____

What are ways I am already implementing or considering that enable consent in the classroom?

"I don't know" or "none" are valid answers. The second section of this book provides tools to help you do exactly this.

_____
_____
_____
_____
_____

Trauma-informed pedagogy

There are many excellent books and resources for understanding how trauma occurs and the neurological and psychosomatic responses to it.[7] This is not what we will be spending our time on in this book. Instead, we will examine why "trauma-informed" contributes to a care-full movement pedagogy. We will develop practices that mitigate harm and center humanity.

In *Equity-Centered Trauma-Informed Teaching*, Alexis Shevrin Venet writes, "This is perhaps the most literal sense of being trauma-informed: when our thought processes and teaching methods are *informed* by trauma" (emphasis original) (2021, 67). To be trauma-informed teachers, we must recognize that trauma exists, has been experienced in some form by every human, and therefore affects the students, and possibly their ability to learn, in our spaces.

I wrote for *Dance Geist*:

> Dancers, from a young age, are part of a toxic system. One that values certain types of bodies, hierarchies, and binaries. One that values particular behaviors, like obedience, quietness, and perfectionism. This system can traumatize the young people in it, physically, or mental/emotional. So, how might we alleviate harm as much as we can? (2022, 24)

It is asking questions like this that leads to trauma-informed, care-full teaching methods.

In a workshop I was leading a few years ago on consent-forward spaces for acting teachers, in a rather famous US-based acting program, we touched briefly on the intersection of trauma-informed work with consent-forward work. One of the teachers, rather famous herself, responded that sometimes acting students are experiencing trauma or the reactivation of a trauma in the acting class, and they just need to "push through it, come out the other side, and use it to make them better actors." I suggested to her that "if someone is experiencing trauma or a trauma response in your classroom, they are not actually learning. And, if they are not learning, you are not actually teaching. So, then, what are you doing?"

When someone is experiencing a trauma response, they cannot consent. A trauma response allocates all of one's mental and biological resources to fight, flight, freeze, or fawn—to survival. In such a response, one is considering how best to stay alive—they are running on instinct, not carefully considered choices. When in a trauma response, one cannot focus on the work to be done, they cannot engage in dialogue, and they are not fully present in their bodies or the current moment; therefore, they cannot consent.

One of the most challenging aspects of developing a trauma-informed approach to teaching or creating is the truth that trauma does not look the same on everyone. Because trauma is about the response to an event, not the event itself, it is personal (Schenk 2021). When I teach teachers about trauma-informed approaches, I tell them there is no one universal sign that lets you know someone in your space is experiencing a trauma response. Rather, it is noticing changes in attitudes and behaviors and being responsive to those.

Just like there is no checklist to know if someone is experiencing trauma or having a trauma response, when it comes to trauma-informed teaching, "there is no perfect implementation or checklist to be completed. Instead, trauma-informed practices should evolve continuously as our understanding evolves" (Venet, 16).

There are, however, some good guidelines for knowing that a practice is trauma-informed. The Substance Abuse and Mental Health Services Administration (SAMHSA) qualifies care as "trauma-informed" when it accounts for:

- Safety
- Trustworthiness and transparency
- Peer support
- Collaboration and mutuality
- Empowerment, voice, and choice
- Cultural, historical, and gender issues (2014)

This section of the chapter defines each through the relationships of power, trauma, and consent. The next section of the book will offer practices explicitly tied to supporting these points.

1. *Safety*
   Trauma responses, like fight, flight, freeze, fawn, were developed for human survival. Dacher Keltner writes in *The Power Paradox*:

   > The human stress response is a dictatorial system, shutting down many other processes essential to our engagement in the world....
   > ...the chronic stress associated with powerlessness compromises just about every way a person might contribute to the world outside of fight-or-flight behavior. (2017, 151)

Actively causing or allowing trauma is not a learning tool. Amy C. Edmonson explains in *The Fearless Organization*:

> Fear inhibits learning. Research in neuroscience shows that fear consumes physiologic resources, diverting them from parts of the brain that manage working memory and process new information ... Hierarchy (or, more specifically, the fear it creates when not handled well) reduces psychological safety. (2019, 14)

When we are simply surviving, we do not have the energy to give to learning, deepening understanding or nuance, or creativity.

Fear not only inhibits safety, but it also inhibits consent. Students who fear displeasing their teacher, because of the power dynamics inherent in that role, may acquiesce to the demands of the instructor, whether or not those requests fit within their boundaries, because to violate their own boundaries and choices feels safer than to violate the relationship of teacher to student by saying "no."

2. *Trustworthiness and transparency*

   In being transparent about the power dynamics of the classroom, we invite conversations around how to deal with them in healthy ways. Another opportunity for trust and transparency involves the expectations of the situation that we all agree to by being in the room, how we will progress through that work, and the consequences of (not) meeting those expectations. The next chapter deals explicitly with creating trust, or psychological safety, in the classroom.

   Time is also a component of trust. Trust is earned, not rushed. Early and clear communication can alleviate a lot of anxiety and harm that arises from the fear of the unknown. In addition, early and clear communication allow the time and specificity needed to consider consent.

3. *Peer support*

   Trustworthiness also needs to happen among students. Experiencing peer support is difficult in a studio space that upholds hierarchies and competition mindset. Power dynamics among peers (experience, a clear skill division between members of the class, some who are on a performance team or not, etc.) can contribute to distrust, heightening anxiety and reactivity. Again, transparency and dialogue are helpful.

4. *Collaboration and mutuality*

   Collaboration validates different skills and perspectives we all bring. When we collaborate, the things that make us different are celebrated. If we are really addressing power dynamics and creating spaces for people to be in and use their power, which means operating with consent, we have a more collaborative space.

Of course, a key to collaboration is to keep the focus on the work we are there to do, not the personalities at play. When personalities get involved, power dynamics can roll right back in, opening opportunities for abuse and harm. Focus on the work helps us keep forward momentum toward a shared goal, rather than dwelling on something that may be going wrong. We acknowledge the problem and then work together to fix it.

5. *Empowerment, voice, and choice*
In the same *Dance Geist* article quoted above, I wrote, "Folks who have experienced trauma had their opportunity to choose taken from them. Therefore, opportunities to make choices, and have those choices upheld, can be crucial to healing and moving forward" (24). No one chooses trauma. So, each opportunity to make a choice, and practice your power, even around seemingly insignificant scenarios such as, is the turn a double or a triple, selecting your own scene partner, or whether the rehearsal room door is open or closed, are opportunities to validate someone's agency and autonomy. Practicing consent to a touch, an exercise, a situation, or even a grade is a beautiful way to put into place trauma-informed practices.

There is no teacher I know who wants to actively perpetuate violence in their classroom. And yet, this is what our traditional, hierarchical, kyriarchical, transactional models of education, even in movement settings, do: the teacher deposits the information into the student, and the student deposits the information back onto a test or replicates it in execution. Freire reminds us that, "Any situation in which some individuals prevent others from engaging in the process of inquiry is one of violence ... to alienate human beings from their own decision-making is to change them into objects" ([1973] 2006, 85). Not only does transactional education enact violence, as the last line of the quote highlights, it divorces students from their ability to choose and create.

6. *Cultural, historical, and gender issues*
Cultural, historical, and gender issues happen because of our bodies and/or the situation we find ourselves in in those bodies. Movement training is all about connecting to our bodies and using our bodies to connect to others. Therefore, as responsible educators, we must be aware of cultural, historical, and gender issues, and the kyriarchy created by the bodies in our space. As we know, trauma is an embodied response to an event. We cannot separate our bodies from their

context, and we cannot separate our trauma from our bodies. All of this is tied together.

Venet puts it clearly, "Trauma-informed education means centering our shared humanity. Dehumanization causes trauma. ... Healing requires being fully human, with all the mess and complexity that entails" (14).

The last two points, choice and full humanity, are keys to collaboration, as well. Throughout the rest of the book, we will be developing strategies and practices for mitigating the possibilities of trauma responses in the movement classroom, and curating tools for dealing with those responses if, and likely when, they occur.

REFLECTION SECTION: Trauma

What is my definition of a "trauma-informed" movement classroom?

_____
_____
_____
_____

Are there ways I have seen movement pedagogy contribute to the trauma or dehumanization of students?

_____
_____
_____
_____

What are ways I am already implementing or considering that create a more trauma-informed classroom?

"I don't know" or "none" are valid answers. The second section of this book provides tools to help you do exactly this.

_____
_____
_____
_____

Which of the six factors of trauma-informed care do I feel I am already bringing to my classroom? Which would I like to add? Which feels challenging?

_____
_____
_____
_____

Conclusion: The intersection of trauma-informed and consent-forward pedagogies

I find that trauma-informed and consent-forward teaching are not a Venn diagram—they are the same circle. They both involve addressing power dynamics, communicating with openness and specificity, and focusing on the humanity of students, which means honoring their agency and power. With trauma-informed approaches to work, my goal is to let students know that they have agency or power within. When work is consent-forward, I use my power to create opportunities for students to practice their agency, their power to. Chavez writes:

> Every student deserves the opportunity to trust their creative impulse. Every student deserves the opportunity to exercise their own authentic voice. Every student deserves the opportunity to uphold their own convictions. (132)

When we create space for that to happen in our classrooms, we create collaboration.

Collaboration asks all of us, teachers and students, to bring our power, our creativity, and our humanity to the work we share—learning and making art.

A care-full pedagogy centers the full humanity of students, including their power, and recognizes all the elements that may inhibit that. As educators, we cannot know everything that may activate everyone in our space. We can, however, take steps to make our spaces as welcoming to risk-taking and the practice of power to as possible. We can adjust our content and methods to not retraumatize or cause a trauma response in someone an additional time. Care-full pedagogy is compassionate teaching of complicated humans.

Venet offers, "To recover from trauma, we first need to reestablish a feeling of safety, emotionally and psychologically" (xv). Creating physical and psychological safety should be our first priorities as movement educators. Psychological safety is the subject of the next chapter.

Chapter reminders

- We do not truly have consent in classroom or performing arts spaces.
- The best we can do is "Working Consent," focusing on the work, with continued dialogue, aiming for collaboration.
- Collaboration requires consent, power, and full humanity.
- Fear inhibits safety and consent.

- Opportunities to make choices, and have those choices upheld, can be crucial to healing and moving forward.
- Trauma-informed work and consent-forward work overlap, as they both require mitigating power dynamics to foster dialogue and agency.

Notes

1. See the "Honor Yourself" part of the Honor Triad in Chapters 5 and 6.
2. Boundary exercises for class are offered in Chapter 5.
3. See video linked in the "Resources" section.
4. There will be more on accommodations in Chapter 6.
5. All of these are specific examples offered in Chapters 7 through 10.
6. There will be templates for a Chain of Communication or Resolution Pathway in Chapter 6.
7. Some of my favorites are included in the "Resources" section.

4
Psychological safety: Creating spaces for learning and art-making

Building psychological safety

Before we can continue the work of dismantling power dynamics and building collaboration by creating opportunities for students to be in their power, they need to know that it is *safe* for them to do so. School is not, traditionally, a safe place for students to be powerful. Similarly, dance and theatre are not, traditionally, safe places for performers to speak or hold boundaries. Our work, in creating psychologically safe spaces for learning and creating, is not only doing so in our own rooms, but, asking folks in less powerful positions in those rooms to believe us that it is safe, even when decades of their past experiences will tell them otherwise!

You may have heard about "safe spaces" and "brave spaces," which have been talked about in both art and academia, specifically since 2020. In her 2023 article "Safe and Brave Spaces Don't Work (and What You Can Do Instead)" on Medium, Elise Ahenkorah, founder of the Global Inclusion Factor writes:

> A safe place is a place or environment in which a person or group of people can feel confident that they will not be exposed to discrimination, criticism, harassment, or any other emotional or physical harm. … Unfortunately, safe spaces are impossible to create because you can't predict people's behaviours and thoughts.
>
> …
>
> A *brave space* is a space where participants feel comfortable learning, sharing, and growing. Brave spaces are inclusive of everyone, including racialized, people with disabilities, Indigenous, women, and gender and sexually diverse lived experiences. Brave spaces highlight the importance of being brave enough to enter spaces where you can be your authentic self and share personal lived experiences.
>
> In short, brave spaces are exhausting.

Instead of these terms, I seek to design and engage in practices in the classroom that allow students to experience a level of psychological safety.

"Psychological safety" is a term created by Amy Edmonson in her book *The Fearless Organization: Creating Psychological Safety in the Workplace for Learning, Innovation, and Growth*. She defines psychological safety "as a climate in which people are comfortable expressing and being themselves" (2019, xvi). Psychological safety, in work and learning spaces, refers to the broad application of the term psychology, as defined by the Merriam-Webster dictionary, "the mental or behavioral characteristics of an individual or group," and does not refer to a particular type of analysis or a diagnosis. Rather, "psychological" puts us in mind of both the thoughts and experiences of a person. It is one thing for us, as educators, to declare a space "safe." But, for a space to be "psychologically safe," it must be experienced as such by students.

I'd put these definitions together this way: psychological safety is a personal experience of safety in being and/or expressing oneself and/or ideas. This may seem like the same as the definition of "brave space," but to me, these are not the same thing. A brave space requires that those entering "be brave," so they can have safety. In the classroom, that would mean that those in the less powerful positions, the students, are tasked with the responsibility of showing up bravely. That is a very vulnerable position to be in! A psychologically safe space requires that the one holding the space, the person with the power, in our cases as instructors, us, be responsible for creating a space where safety can be experienced.

You will notice the heading for this section says, "Building psychological safety." This is an active, ongoing, challenging job. Psychological safety, like Working Consent, is not a destination or a one-time achievement. Rather, it is something we are always working toward and creating together. Edmonson designates psychological safety as "a feature of the workplace that leaders can and must help create" (13).

Creating psychological safety is necessary to foster learning and growth. Alfie Kohn writes in *What to Look for in a Classroom*, "Only in a safe place, where there is no fear of humiliation and punitive judgement will students admit to being confused about what they have read and feel free to acknowledge their mistakes. Only by being able to ask for help will they be likely to improve" ([1994] 1998, 78).

Fear inhibits psychological safety. Edmonson cautions, "Hierarchy (or, more specifically the fear it creates when not handled well) reduces psychological safety" (14). A traditional classroom, reliant on power-over, is a place where hierarchy operates, and therefore can be filled with fear. She continues:

> More specifically, when people have psychological safety at work, they feel comfortable sharing concerns and mistakes without fear of embarrassment or retribution. They are confident that they can speak up and won't be humiliated, ignored, or blamed. They know they can ask questions when they are unsure about something. ... When a work environment has reasonably high psychological safety, good things happen: mistakes are reported quickly so that prompt corrective action can be taken; seamless coordination across groups or departments is enabled, and potentially game-changing ideas for innovation are shared. (xvi)

All these characteristics of a psychologically safe workplace can apply to classrooms as well. If I were to list characteristics of psychological safety in learning spaces, I would use Edmonson's descriptions as inspiration.

In the psychologically safe classroom, students feel safe to:

- Ask questions.
- Fail.
- Share their needs, opinions, and ideas.
- Work together.
- Challenge the status quo.

The psychologically safe classroom values:

- Growth and change over being right.
- Supporting each other over competition.
- Creativity and curiosity over perfection.

I imagine psychological safety in the classroom like putting up a scaffold; one level must be in place to construct the next level. Like using one on a construction site, using this scaffold helps lessen risk, while increasing access and connections. Also like a construction scaffold, it is used for work. Creating psychological safety will help us develop collaborative relationships and do our work fully. As Edmonson describes it, "Psychological safety sets the stage for a more honest, more challenging, more collaborative, and thus more effective work environment" (18). This sounds like a place ready for learning and creativity!

REFLECTION SECTION: Psychological safety

Would I define my classroom as a "safe space," a "brave space," or a "psychologically safe space?"

_____
_____
_____
_____
_____

Why is psychological safety important for a classroom?

_____
_____
_____
_____
_____

Levels of psychological safety

Timothy R. Clark's *The Four Stages of Psychological Safety* (2020) split the umbrella of psychological safety into four specific levels: inclusion, learning, contributing, and challenging. When I read Clark's book, I realized that what he described as levels of psychological safety would build a scaffold, not only of safety, but from Power Within to Power To to Power With. This scaffold gives us platforms on which to share power and create collaboration.

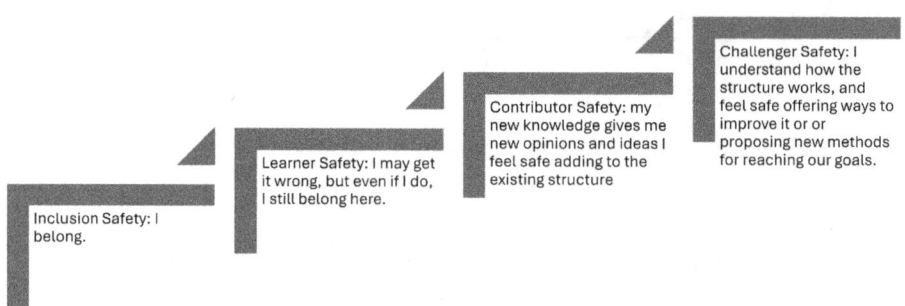

Figure 4.1 The Four Levels of Psychological Safety. Created by the author, 2024.

As I, as an educator, built the levels of safety in my own classes, I witnessed students experiencing and practicing levels of power. I started teaching these levels as steps to building collaboration with students in workshops in 2021. The dance and movement educators enrolled shared that this format helped them feel that power-with, or collaboration, was something they could plan for and facilitate, rather than just hope would happen. Creating psychological safety creates a space ready for collaboration.

In this chapter, I will define the stages of psychological safety, as well connect them to consent-forward and trauma-informed teaching. Exercises and tools to support each stage will be explicitly described in further chapters.

Stage 1: Inclusion safety

The first step in creating a space where people can learn or create is to ensure that everyone experiences a sense of belonging. In *The Fearless Organization*, Edmonson writes that psychological safety means, "diverse perspectives are more likely to be heard" (2019, 201). If a person does not feel that they belong in a space, they will be unable to take risks, which includes being creative.

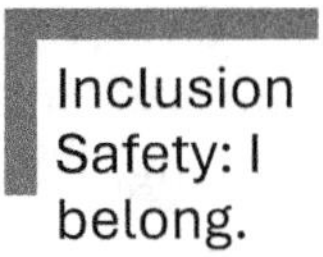

> Inclusion
> Safety: I
> belong.

Figure 4.2 Building Psychological Safety Step 1: Inclusion Safety: I belong. Created by the author, 2024.

When French and Raven recognized the Social Power of Referent Power, they were recognizing the safety of fitting in. By creating inclusion safety in our classrooms, we can change this power dynamic to be more positive, as we demonstrate care and acceptance for myriad experiences, ideas, bodies, etc. With inclusion safety, a student does not feel pressured to "fit in," because they are already welcomed as they are.

This also diffuses the possible cult mentality of belonging to a group, as the individual identities in the group are still honored. Inclusion safety supports students' Power Within, or ability to see themselves as powerful beings. Recognizing one's Power Within is the first step to being a collaborator or developing power with others.

One of the steps of trauma-informed care, as highlighted in the last chapter, is "Trust and Trustworthiness." To know that I am safe to be myself, to experience inclusion safety, requires trust. We cannot build even the first level of psychological safety without trauma-informed practices; it would be unsustainable.

Making sure students feel like they belong in our classes should be a priority of a care-full pedagogy. This includes addressing peer dynamics and student-to-student relationships, as well as the learning space as a whole. Building this sense of belonging starts on the first day of class and continues through the rest of the semester or year. Nel Noddings reminds educators, "Achieving inclusion is part of teaching successfully, and one who cannot practice inclusion fails as a teacher" (1983, 67). The next chapter offers several tools and scripts for creating inclusion safety.

Stage 2: Learner safety

In *The Fearless Organization*, Amy Edmonson declares, "By now it should be clear that psychological safety is foundational to building a learning organization" (187). She describes "A learning mindset" as one that "blends humility and curiosity," and "recognizes that there is always more to learn" (167–8).

Admitting that there are things I do not know makes learning inherently risky. In addition, as I learn, I run the risk of making a mistake or even failing. For those engaging in learning, Edmonson says there is "particular importance of psychological safety ... because they necessarily have to take risks and confront failure before they achieve success" (40).

Learning requires vulnerability. As teachers, we constantly ask students to be in this state of learning. As students are learning movement, they may feel even more vulnerable as their bodies and choices are often on display to the whole class. Turning in a test or paper does not have this same kind of vulnerability! So, we need to provide a level of learner safety, where they know it is acceptable to make mistakes.

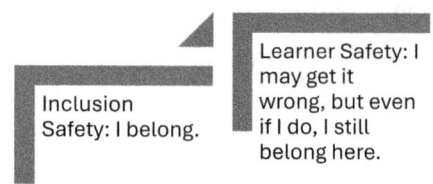

Figure 4.3 Building Psychological Safety Step 1 to 2: Inclusion Safety to Learner Safety. Created by the author, 2024.

This is why inclusion safety is foundational for learner safety. We must create learning environments where students can risk failure without a fear of losing belonging. When students know they will still be welcome and accepted, not judged or punished, they are able to take risks.

Since we are all in this space to learn, perfection should not be a requirement. However, failure tends to be a dirty word in education, including in dance and movement. As movement educators, we encourage students to develop performance-ready skills, as well as get good grades. But we all learn not only from our successes, but our failures. Failures and mistakes show us where our skills need more development. It was simply a failure of an attempt, executed in that time and space, with those methods. It is not a failure of the person.

In my dance technique and movement classes my syllabus reads:

> This course is structured as a lab in which you are both the scientist and your own (no one else's, including mine!) experiment. In this metaphor, I'm the director of the lab, whose job it is to make sure our experiments are safe and ethical, while still pushing us to new discoveries. I am a co-investigator, with my own experiment of my body and creative practice.

In a laboratory, failure is an expectation; so is safety. My job, as the professor, is to make a space where it is safe to risk, because it is safe to fail. Edmonson cautions, "unless a leader expressly and actively makes it psychological safe to do so, people will automatically seek to avoid failure" (160). To feel safe to risk or fail, students must know that they belong, unconditionally. If a space is not psychologically safe, built with care for the whole person and grace for failure, learning cannot take place. As we teach, we can reframe failures as opportunities to connect with students as autonomous humans and reinforce their own power over their learning.

Errors in the learning process could heighten students' awareness of the Reward Power of grades. Constant measuring or evaluating can inhibit psychological safety. Kohn writes, "Never grade[1] students while they are still learning something and even more important, do not reward them for their performance at that point …. If it is unclear whether students feel ready to demonstrate what they know, there is an easy way to find out: ask them" (79–80).

Besides setting the expectation that errors are a natural part of learning, we can demonstrate learner safety by:

- How we respond to mistakes.
- How we ask students to respond to mistakes.

When students err, we can offer reassurances that these missteps are part of growth. Then, we can guide reflection to what they learned during the experience, and how that can shape the next attempt.

Edmonson reminds us, "beginning in elementary school, we are taught to seek the right answer instead of learning to learn from mistakes as a pathway to innovative and independent thinking" (111). When we, as educators, accept or even encourage failure, we are asking students to go against a decade or more of previous dance and education experiences. This is where trust is so important—do we really act as if mistakes are normal, or even beautiful, opportunities for learning?

In doing this, we model for students that mistakes are not cause for judgment, mockery, or giving up. We do, however, expect them to be a cause for reevaluation and growth. Students are not removed for making mistakes, or ostracized. They are validated that they are doing the work they are there to do—try something and learn from it. In this, students trust their Power Within and experience the power to do.

Stage 3: Contributor safety

Timothy R. Clark describes the experience of contributor safety as being in a place where "Simply knowing that your vulnerability will not be exploited encourages you to be brave and contribute to the generative process" (114–115). Once I know that I belong, as I am, and that I will *still* belong, even when I make mistakes, which are inevitable and an accepted part of learning, I can feel confident to share my ideas and opinions about what we are learning.

Clark calls contributor safety, "asking for autonomy" (100). On this level, students get to "show what they know," and how that knowledge has created new ideas or skills for them. Edmonson emphasizes, "For knowledge work to flourish, the workplace must be one where people feel able to share their knowledge" (xiv)!

When students experience contributor safety, the structure (the curriculum, the exercise, etc.) remains the property of the instructor, but they bring their own perspectives and choices to the daily work. Students' power to do has developed, and they are ready to join with others to create power-with, or collaboration.

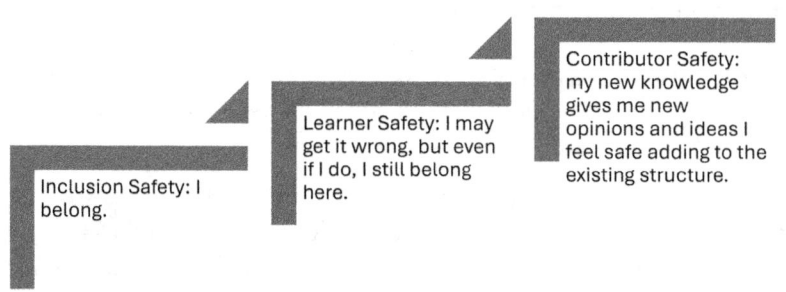

Figure 4.4 Building Psychological Safety Steps 1 through 3: Inclusion Safety to Learner Safety to Contributor Safety. Created by the author, 2024.

Edmonson reminds us, "Speaking up is only the first step. The true test is how leaders respond when people actually do speak up" (157). Just like in creating learner safety, how we respond to students is the proof that safety exists.

When I build opportunities for students to contribute, I honor their agency and choices. Students may discover, in sharing their ideas, that others disagree, that there are factual, historical, or anatomical reasons that do not bear out their conclusion, that they are missing some needed information or skill, or that their idea is only one of many ways to do something. When this happens, we are back on the step of learning safety, supported by inclusion safety. As educators, we can emphasize that these contributions are still learning opportunities. They may even be so for us, as student contributions may point out places where our instructions have been incomplete, or we have not been as clear or detailed in our communication of information as we thought we were!

Or students may follow their contribution through to a successful conclusion. They demonstrate that they have learned and are able to apply what they have learned themselves! In both instances, students have felt safe to trust their own choices, interests, or needs, and have been provided a safe structure within which they can explore them.

Stage 4: Challenger safety

The final step in the scaffold of psychological safety is challenger safety. While contributor safety maintains the existing structure, as set by the person or system in power, challenger safety asks everyone involved to create a new system, one in which we all share power.

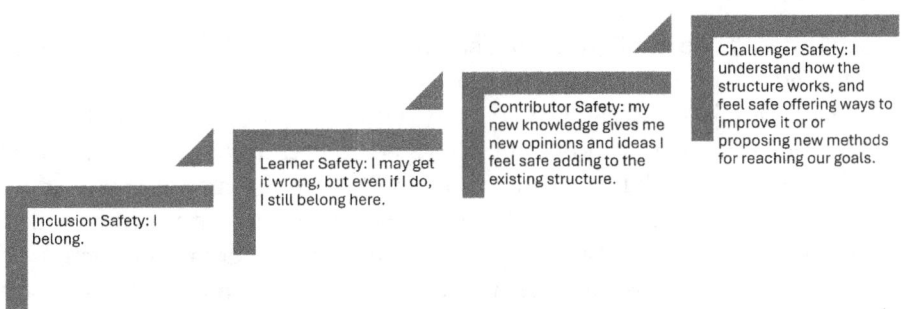

Figure 4.5 Building Psychological Safety Steps 1 through 4: Inclusion Safety to Learner Safety to Contributor Safety to Challenger Safety. Created by the author, 2024.

Challenger safety is supported for students by the knowledge that they belong in this space, this is a safe space to take risks, and their ideas are welcome. Only with consistent practice and experience of the first three levels of psychological safety will students be able to confidently create something new.

Clark warns, "The creative instinct propels us to challenge the status quo out of a desire to create and improve things, but doing so is unnatural in an environment that we perceive to be unsafe" (99). In classes that require students to generate movement, dances, or characters, we want them to be creative. We hope students will design movement and moments we have never seen before that come directly from their experiences and bodies. When they do so, we can reinforce not only have they learned in the structure provided, but they have transformed their, and our, experience of that structure. When students fully lean into not only their own Power Within and Power To, but also trust that they are safe to use their power with you and others to create something new, design a new way of looking at a problem or character, or point out an issue or idea we never saw or connected before, they have moved beyond transactional or regurgitative education, and are attempting to transform themselves and their world.

Challenger safety can be extremely scary for both teachers and students. When a challenge is made, we are all moving beyond what we know.

Challenges can feel like pushback or resistance to receive as educators. These new ideas and options may require us to change how we are thinking about or doing things in our classes. They may require us to let go of what we thought we knew or what we've always done. Fostering challenger safety means that we must encourage questions, be prepared to not know the answer, or even be wrong in the answer ourselves, and to give up our Expert Power in the room.

Clark states, "The challenge with challenger safety is that it takes time to create and no time to destroy" (116). As stated in the earlier chapter on trauma, trust takes time, and there really is no substitute for time in developing relationships. You will not get from students on day one the same level of creativity and confidence you get at the end of the semester. And yet, all the previous levels require trust. This is why consistency and accountability when we make mistakes (and we will) as the power holder in the room is so important. We demonstrate trust in the students as much as we ask them to trust us.

On the other side, challenges may make students feel that they are being defiant, "difficult," or "bad" if they make them. But, in creative pursuits, such as dance and choreography or embodying a character, we are asking students to make something new. So, we must also help them be confident in creating and challenging.

You may be saying, "But Nicole, I have had a student who has challenged me, and everything about the class, from day one!" I hear you, and I suspect these students are *not* experiencing challenger safety, based on a foundation of safe encounters of inclusion, learner, and contributor types. In fact, they are acting this way likely because they do *not* feel safe; they do not feel they as an individual, or their mistakes or ideas, are welcome in this space.

I want to reassure you that this likely has nothing to do with you (unless it does, in which case, please apologize to the student), but much more to do with the over decade-long experiences in the education system, as well as arts training programs, that have not been safe spaces for errors, explorations, or difference, that students come in with. Experiencing challenges from students before challenger safety has been built is all the more reason to start with inclusion safety. Failures to be inclusive, to accept errors, to listen to multiple perspectives, or quick judgments or punishments will only prove that, as they suspected, the classroom is not safe.

REFLECTION SECTION: Psychological safety

In the psychologically safe classroom, students feel safe to:

- Ask questions.
- Fail.
- Share their needs, opinions, and ideas.
- Work together.
- Challenge the status quo.

What are ways I can measure these markers of safety in my classes? Are there things I would add to this list?

_____

_____

_____

_____

_____

The psychologically safe classroom values:

- Growth and change over being right.
- Supporting each other over competition.
- Creativity and curiosity over perfection.

Do these align with my values for my classroom? Are there things I would add to this list? How do students know these are my values?

_____

_____

_____

_____

_____

Psychological safety

How do students know they are safe to fail, and that failure is part of learning?

_____
_____
_____
_____
_____

How do students know they are safe to speak up, and that their ideas and questions are valuable (to their own learning, that of the class, and my own)?

_____
_____
_____
_____
_____

What level of psychological safety (inclusion, learner, contributor, or challenger) would I use to describe my classroom, and why?

_____
_____
_____
_____
_____

Below are exercises or practices I currently use in class that fit the categories of psychological safety.

It's OK if some are blank! You're going to get a lot more tools and templates in the following chapters.

Inclusion Safety	Learner Safety	Contributor Safety	Challenger Safety

Conclusion

Students in a psychologically safe learning environment will be able to enter collaboration, and experience both their personal power and agency and power with each other and their instructor. Power-over and authoritarian control are enemies to psychological safety and collaboration. Edmonson writes:

> The belief that people may not push themselves hard enough without a clear understanding of the negative consequences of failing to do so is widespread and even taken for granted by many in management roles, along with just as many casual onlookers contemplating human motivation at work. What many people do not realize is that motivation by fear is indeed highly effective—effective at creating the *illusion* that goals are being achieved. It is not effective in ensuring that people bring the creativity, good process, and passion needed to accomplish challenging goals in knowledge-intensive workplaces. (57)

Or, I would say, in classrooms. As Kohn writes in *What to Look for in a Classroom*, "We may be able to force them to complete an assignment, but we can't compel them to learn effectively or to care about what they are doing" (256). Psychological safety is much more effective and ethical for both motivation and collaboration than Reward or Coercive Powers.

To experience psychological safety in the classroom, power dynamics must be mitigated, consent and agency must be facilitated, and trauma-informed practices must be in place. In this, we see the importance of care, and that having care necessitates an understanding of power dynamics and establishing practices to center consent, diffuse trauma, and promote psychological safety.

Amanda Stuart Fisher defined care as:

> a term that has many interconnected dimensions: it has a practical and emotional elements (how we practically engage with other people); it has an ethical and political dimension (disclosing values that determine how we should act in the world and within the limited resource we might have available to us); and, crucially, it has an aesthetic component (determining how artistry and the feeling evoked by an engagement with the arts frames interhuman relationships in solicitous ways). (2020, 6)

Power, care, and creativity are all experienced in relationship. Consent, trauma, and our sense of psychological safety impact how we "practically engage with other people" (Stuart Fisher, 6). This is why "care-full creativity" was coined—to encompass it all.

The rest of this book offers the structures and methods to support spaces of psychological safety for the risky work of moving, collaborating, creating, and performing. The tools and exercises offered in each chapter include the level of psychological safety they are meant to build.

Chapter reminders

- Psychological safety is a personal experience of safety in being and/or expressing oneself and ideas.
- Timothy R. Clark's *Four Stage of Psychological Safety* are:
  - Inclusion.
  - Learner.
  - Contributor.
  - Challenger.
- Psychological safety is like a scaffold, one level builds on the other, to create more access and connections as we get the work done.
- Inclusion safety means I belong in this space.
- Learner safety means it is safe to fail, because if I get it wrong, I still belong here.
- Contributor safety means it is safe to offer my ideas and opinions to the existing structure, because I have learned.
- Challenger safety means it is safe for me to ask questions, create something new, and even challenge the existing structure.

Note

1. There will be more on this in Chapter 9 regarding assessment and grades.

Part 2
Praxis

5
Practices for ensemble building: Creating inclusion safety

Inclusion safety as ensemble building

Much of the work of dance and theatre, even in learning, happens in a group. Group dynamics and community care impact both the creative process and the final performance. This is why building inclusion safety, so each student knows they belong in our space, is so important. I sometimes call inclusion safety "belonging safety." Another phrase for inclusion safety could be "ensemble building," or helping students develop an "ensemble ethic." This chapter offers the following six tools for the first day(s) of class to help create individual and group belonging:

- Land Acknowledgements.
- Class Contracts (Community Agreements).
- Needs for Learning.
- Boundary Conversations.
- Introduction Letters.
- Observational Practices.

These tools are presented in the order in which students encounter them in my classes. The first two are mechanisms for creating group identity, while the last four highlight the connections of the individual to the group, all of which serve to strengthen students' sense of ensemble or inclusion safety.

Land Acknowledgements

A Land Acknowledgement is a statement that recognizes the Indigenous peoples who originally stewarded the land on which we are. Land Acknowledgements place us in a larger story—they connect us to the past, to traditions, to each other. This may be a surprising way to create inclusion safety, but they can serve as a point of connection. I use our Land Acknowledgement time to remind students that wherever they come from, whatever their history or culture, this land the university currently sits on, its history, and honoring the violently displaced peoples affected is now a shared responsibility by all of us in this space.

The Land Acknowledgement I use is a version of the one I wrote for Momentum Stage in a workshop with Joseph Cloud, a member of Cherokee Nation.[1] In a previous class, one student shared in her Introduction Letter that her mother is descended from one of the tribes mentioned in the Land Acknowledgement. This had been a recent discovery and conversation in her family, and hearing it mentioned in the Land Acknowledgement was very exciting to her and helped her to feel validated and included with her identity. It was a moment of personal belonging.

The intent of a Land Acknowledgement is to provide inclusion safety for students, as well as to help create community and accountability around shared place. However, it may challenge some students who have not participated in a Land Acknowledgement, or whose worldviews do not include right relationships with Native people, displaced people, the land, and/or our nonhuman kin. By situating our shared experience on the land occupied by our institution, I reinforce the ideas of connection and community, without requiring immediate personal buy-in. Instead, Land Acknowledgements, like the Class Contracts we are about to engage in, are part of the "law of the situation" of our class.

Class Contracts

Most educational settings, including dance and movement ones, have rules and expectations that are set by the instructor, for the students to follow. Recently, Community Agreements have become a part of arts and academic spaces. Instead of one person (in the case of a classroom, the teacher) setting out the dos and don'ts for the room, everyone contributes. Community Agreements decentralize power by having the expectations for behavior in a group created by the group. These also include the behavior of the teacher in their expectations. Ideally, this mitigates some of the Legitimate and Reward and Coercive Powers of the teacher, and also promotes community and ensemble ethic, as the group has created the rules themselves.

I choose to call these Class Contracts, as the definition of contract implies that all parties have responsibilities and commitments that must be upheld

Practices for ensemble building: Creating inclusion safety

for it to operate and be effective. A contract binds us to each other, not just the students to me, as a traditionally hierarchical classroom would imply.

If you have created a Class Contract before, you were likely met with one of two common scenarios (or sometimes, both!):

1. Students look at you blankly, offering nothing, and creating an awkward silence instead of a robust conversation and community connection.
2. Students say multiple versions of the same thing. For example, "Don't be mean," "Keep your hands to yourself," and "Don't gossip." are all offered, but they really could have just been collected under "Be kind." Plus, we took a lot of class time to get there.
3. Sometimes, scenario one becomes scenario two, after some brave soul gets things started.

I went into my first class in which we would create a Community Agreement in the fall of 2018 with great expectations of conversations and connections. This is not what happened—I got scenario three. Let's talk about why these scenarios are so common.

We have already touched on the reason scenario one occurs as a reason that psychological safety can be hard to implement—students don't believe us! For many students, this is new. And, as we are doing this on the first day of class, it is also likely that the context, including the people involved, are new, too. So, by asking students to contribute, we're asking them to skip ahead to the third level of the scaffold (contributor safety), when they don't even know if they belong here yet (inclusion safety) or if it's safe to make a mistake in this place (learner safety)! Silence is a safety mechanism; it is not a sign of disinterest, confusion, or laziness.

In scenario two, students are talking and contributing! We're getting towards our goal of creating community! And, in our best efforts to do so, we likely try to hear from *everyone*, so we take a lot of time for this. But, for the time that we put in, we don't really get a lot of useful information. Students tend to offer the same thing in a variety of different ways ("be kind," "don't be judgmental," etc.).

In this scenario, a Class Contract may not feel "worth it" because it "costs" time, and the payout is lacking. In this case, echoing is the safety tactic. If someone said, "be kind" and got good feedback, I can say something similar, reasonably assured it will be received well. One courageous person jumped to contributor safety, but everyone else is still testing the waters of inclusion safety. Class Contracts, as a practice in a group of humans who are mainly new to each other, ask us to take too many risks, too early. We have not earned each other's trust yet, so we cannot expect bravery or authenticity.

For Class Contracts in my courses, I show up on the first day with the following in the syllabus and on a slide.[2]

Class Contract

Our Space

Each Other   Ourselves

Figure 5.1 The Honor Triad. Created by the author, 2024.

I call this "The Honor Triad," adapted from New York City-based Fight Director and Field Instructor at NYU Tisch School of Drama Lisa Kopitsky's "Do No Harm Triad" that she uses in workshops and rehearsals. I learned this from Lisa in 2019, in an intimacy director workshop we were both in. I explain the triad as, "In this class we will honor ourselves, each other, and the space, and that is the contract we have with each other." I then proceed to give some examples of each point.

- Ourselves
    - You don't have to ask me to go to the bathroom. Part of this class is learning and honoring your body, so if your body needs that, just go address that need and come back!
    - If you are injured, please let me know so I can offer modifications, or feel free to make modifications for yourself. Sometimes, this may mean that you don't do an exercise and instead observe and listen so that you can apply that learning the next time you are able.
    - I may be the subject matter expert, but you are the expert in your body (see how I snuck some power dynamics language in there?)!
    - I also use this dot point to talk about access and learning needs.
- Each other
    - Just like you are going to honor yourself, we are going to give others the grace to do the same. We won't make up stories or assumptions about why someone is leaving the room, sitting out, etc.
    - Since no one else can know what is being done with an electronic device (tablet, phone, etc.), do not use it during class. Recording is a consent issue. Please not give anyone cause to think their consent has been violated.[3]

- o   We will assume everyone is here to learn, and we all have different starting points and goals for our learning journey.
    - ■ This is a key point to this Class Contract working. Everyone must operate with their best intentions, and assume that everyone else is, too.
  - o   Because this is a class, we are learning together, in ensemble. Your presence and contributions are necessary to the group, so we all learn from not only from our own classroom experiences, but from sharing them with others and hearing about the experiences of others.
- The space
  - o   The "law of the situation," as defined in Chapter 2 is part of our shared space. Adherence to class days, times, content, and outcomes can all be communicated as honoring our shared space.
  - o   This is a space of learning; we enter without distractions or things that may cause physical or emotional harm. That means:
    - ■ No phones.
    - ■ No dangly or chunky jewelry.
    - ■ Fidget toys during lectures are acceptable.
    - ■ Music played cannot contain any slurs towards a person's race, gender, sexuality, etc. (See the section on Class Playlists in the Introduction Letter heading.).
  - o   Only water in the studio.
  - o   No street shoes in the studio.

I choose my examples specifically to build inclusion safety for different bodies and experiences and to emphasize the ensemble nature of learning.

Then, I say, "What questions do we have about these?[4]" or "Do we need to clarify anything about these?" After that, I ask, "Do we need to add anything to these that you feel specifically should be addressed?" Sometimes students have offerings, sometimes they do not. This format for a Class Contract doesn't require students to jump to contributor safety. If students do choose to contribute, there is a level of safety, as the structure and questions are clear.

When the class contract is not upheld

After any questions or contributions, I guide the conversation to the "contract[5]" part. I remind students that honoring ourselves, each other, and the space are expectations we *all* have of each other in our room, including them of me. If any of us hear something or see something that feels dishonorable, we all get to say "____ behavior doesn't fit with honoring ____." To both my delight and chagrin, I have also had students use this on me. In one university modern dance class, I said something sarcastic. A student looked me straight in the eye and said, "Ms. P, that was not honoring." He was right, and I apologized.

When we create the contract, we also create the expectations for the class, including what happens if someone does not adhere to the contract. Here's where this gets tricky, as to not rely on the Reward and Coercive Power to ensure compliance. Alfie Kohn writes in *Punished by Rewards*, "Whatever the real problem is, it remains unsolved if our intervention consists of promising a reward for an improvement...or threatening a punishment if there is no improvement" (2018, 61). I have recently started talking about "outcomes" instead of consequences, because "consequences" always feels like a punitive word.

Just like I propose the template and offer examples, I propose these outcomes and open it for conversation. The outcome I propose for failure to adhere to the Class Contract is a personal chat with me (or, in the case like the one above, a personal apology from me!). In that conversation we will discuss expectations, timelines, and next steps that could occur from not meeting those expectations. There is nothing here regarding grades, participation, removal, etc. All those punitive measures may address a symptom, but not the cause, of failure to meet the class expectations.[6]

In large classes, we create a collaborative document for the Class Contract. When I taught middle school, I was able to post this on the wall. Students signed it with their favorite color marker, and it became a beautiful visual representation of their commitment to our class. With it on the wall, if someone was behaving in a way that violated the contract, I didn't even have to say anything; I could just go tap the sign.

Now, the institution's learning management system (LMS)[7] becomes my wall. I start a class discussion thread with the Triad image, and everyone virtually "signs" by commenting with their name, a smiley face, etc. It is an accessible, easily referred to visual of our commitment to ourselves, each other, and the space.

The Class Contract makes clear the expectations of all of us in the accepted situation of our class. We all agree to the work that we are here to do—we are all here to learn, and learning requires teachers and students. We each have a responsibility, in creating power with, to fulfill our roles. We also have a responsibility, in our ensemble, to meet each other's needs.[8] Through the next two exercises, we add more detail to our Class Contract, as we find ways to strengthen our learning community.

Practices for ensemble building: Creating inclusion safety

REFLECTION SECTION: Land Acknowledgements and Class Contracts

What are ways my current Land Acknowledgement:

1. Situates us, as a class, as part of a larger story?
2. Helps to build inclusion safety by emphasizing connection and/or community?

If you don't have a Land Acknowledgement yet, you can use this space to write one!

_____
_____
_____
_____
_____

What format or language could I use for a Community Agreement or Class Contract to create inclusion safety?

_____
_____
_____
_____
_____

How can I share this with students?

_____
_____
_____
_____
_____

How can I communicate about the outcomes of not upholding the contract in ways that encourage community, not compliance or promote honor rather than penalize?

Needs

I couple the crafting of Class Contracts with a discussion on Learning Needs. I use a form of the Needs Inventory, available for free from the Center for Nonviolent Communication that I have modified for classroom use.[9] As I introduce these, I say "we all have a lot more needs in our life than these, but I'd like you to think about what you need to be able to do your best creative work and learning in this class."

I then link to, share on a screen, or hand out, the following:

PHYSICAL NEEDS	INDIVIDUAL NEEDS	CONNECTION NEEDS	LEARNING NEEDS
Air	Authenticity	Acceptance	Awareness
Food	Autonomy	Appreciation	Celebration
Movement/exercise	Beauty	Belonging	Challenge
Rest/sleep	Choice	Closeness	Clarity
Safety	Communion	Communication	Consciousness
Shelter	Ease	Community	Competence
Water	Equality	Companionship	Confidence
	Freedom	Compassion	Contribution
	Harmony	Consideration	Creativity
	Inspiration	Consistency	Discovery
	Honesty	Cooperation	Efficacy
	Humor	Empathy	Effectiveness
	Independence	Inclusion	Growth
	Integrity	Mutuality	Hope
	Joy	Nurturing	Participation
	Order	Respect/self-respect	Purpose
	Peace	Security	Self-expression
	Play	Stability	Stimulation
	Presence	Support	To matter
	Space	Trust	To understand and be understood
	Spontaneity	Warmth	

If the class is small, we will do this next part together. In a large class, I will have them split into small groups.

1. We discuss some of the words that seem similar, yet different, like: "Authenticity is the ability to be myself. Honesty is when I speak truthfully to others. Integrity is when I make choices that align with my values."
2. Individual students identify their top five to ten needs for being able to learn and create successfully. They should be able to articulate why it is important to them, as a student, to get that need met.
3. If we are breaking into small groups, I have students discuss their needs and be able to report back to the whole class what the group decided was their top need(s).
4. If we are one large group, I ask someone to give me their top need. Then, I ask how many other students had that on their list as well.
5. As needs are shared in the whole class, we discuss:
   a. What it looks and/or feels like to have that need met.
   b. What we can do, as a class, to help meet that need.
   c. What we should not do, as a class, because it would mean we were ignoring that need.
6. I write the needs on the Class Contract, or a document I can upload to the LMS as part of the Contract, and meeting these needs becomes an expectation of the class.
7. Students are also encouraged to include these needs in the Introduction Letter, especially if they are ones we did not discuss in the full group.

As students learn about each other's needs around learning environments, they become more aware of learning differences, and ways they can support their peers in class. Sharing learning needs are ways to build inclusion and learner safety, as well as give students an opportunity to practice Working Consent, as they decide what to share.

In a previous Movement for Actors class, that occurred late in the afternoon and was a double block of time, two common needs shared were food and rest. Students were coming to my class as their last class of the day, many having had two other movement classes before it and going into rehearsals after. To meet those needs, we established a couple of supports:

- Even though class started at 3 p.m., the somatic check-in (see Chapter 7) would always be first and take 2 minutes. Since eating and resting serve a somatic need, if they were doing one of those things, they were not expected to be in the room until two minutes after the hour.

- Since class was a double block, there would always be a 10-minute break at the 80-minute mark, as if we were following Equity rules. We built in rest as part of our learning time. If students needed to order food, they could do so at that time for after class, or even have it delivered for that time.

With these expectations set on day one, students knew that I saw their well-being as a necessary part of being able to learn. I referred to our contract to honor ourselves—getting enough sleep and nourishment is part of how we do that. As the power holder in the space, I was willing to make reasonable accommodations to support them, because I wanted them to be able to learn. But they were also expected to commit to meeting that need for themselves outside of class, or during breaks, so they can do what we needed to do in class.

Other conversations have been psychological, as students have reiterated a need for authenticity in learning spaces, or creativity and self-expression as we work in movement. With these, we referred to our contract to honor each other by releasing judgment, giving grace for failure, etc.

With the Class Contract and Needs Inventory discussions on the very first day of class, I strive to build inclusion safety, so that as we enter the work of the semester, students know that this is a space that is safe for learning, attempting, growing, and even failing. This is a space where they are seen as humans, with needs that must get met in order for them to do their best work. As this is a learning space, we are also committed to supporting each other in doing the work of learning.

REFLECTION SECTION: Needs

Use the Needs list above to complete the following.

If I were to think back to being a student in a movement class, what would be my top five to ten needs for my learning? Why are they important to me?

_____
_____
_____
_____
_____

What are some needs students may have I am already supporting/meeting in class? How am I doing that? How can I bring these into early class conversations?

_____
_____
_____
_____
_____

Are there some needs students may have I am not supporting/meeting in class? How might I do that?

_____
_____
_____
_____
_____

What are some needs students may have I cannot support/meet in class? Why? How can I bring these into early class conversations to manage expectations?

_____
_____
_____
_____
_____

Boundaries in movement classes

I continue the language of "needs" as we discuss boundaries. My colleague at Intimacy Direction in Dance, Sarah Lozoff, and my training in Nonviolent Communication brought this important addition to my vocabulary in 2023. I now use boundaries and needs pretty interchangeably in conversations with students. My definition of a boundary is: "A need I have, that must be met, in order for me to do my best work." If that need is not met, I cannot work, or at the very least, the work that I do will not be my best.

Many performers do not use the word "boundary" (although, thankfully, since the implementation of the intimacy choreography protocols in many arts training programs in recent years, young performers are using this more), but they do recognize they can have needs. Students in movement classes are used to saying, "I need to sit out or modify ____ because of my injury," and having those requests met with respect and accommodation from teachers and/or choreographers.

Boundaries operate in the same way. We are requesting a modification to participation or an exemption from participating in a certain way and/or due to a certain circumstance, so that we can do the work of learning as best as possible. Having a boundary does not mean that a student doesn't want to do the work, but that they are simply looking to get a need met to continue in the work. All the boundary exercises and conversation included in this section are ways I bring Working Consent into the movement classroom.

Baseline boundaries

I include in our Class Contract our Baseline Boundaries. Baseline Boundaries are a statement of what is always "off the table," as well as what is always "on the table." Just like the Class Contract itself, I start with an offering, and students provide additions, or ask clarifying questions. For movement classes, the Baseline Boundary offering I often begin with is:

Always Available	Always a Boundary
Arms (from shoulders to hands)	Genitals
Palms of hands	Glutes

In the past students have added "feet" to Always Available (ballet classes in particular ask for this) and "hair" and "face" to be added to Always a

Boundary. We clarify that anything that is not one of these gets a conversation. These additions and/or clarifications can happen in conversation or in a collaborative document. Regardless of how these boundaries are communicated, I make sure they are documented somewhere, either that collaborative file or our Class Contract. I also reiterate that even when parts are "Always Available," it's still a good practice to check in.

Facilitating boundary knowledge

When I frame boundaries as needs, it also opens the idea of "boundaries" to move beyond choreography, touch, and/or the body. When I talk about boundaries with the classes I lead, as well as workshops I facilitate for professional performers or as part of educator professional developments, I ask everyone to think of boundaries in regard to:

- Content
- Context
- Choreography[10]

Content boundaries

While teaching middle school dance in 2020–2021, I realized that young people were often engaging in emotionally challenging content in their conversations, TV shows, and even the dances they wanted to make as part of class. For some young dancers, those choices were cathartic. For others, they were dangerous. Likewise, college students in dance or acting programs are often asked to perform or create around sensitive topics.[11]

So, I ask students to ask themselves,

- Is there content I am unwilling to engage with, for my own wellbeing?
  - Not every story is right for every performer to tell, nor every character the best choice to bring into their body and/or psyche.
- What is the story in this piece?
- Who is this character?
  - What do they do onstage?

Similarly, not every story is safe for every audience member to witness. I do believe content advisories have a place not only in performances, but in classwork as well. If our spaces are safe for students to create and explore emotionally challenging content, we also need to create spaces where it is safe to not engage in that. I ask students sharing choreography or scene work that contains sensitive topics to state this before sharing, so their peers can choose to remove themselves or remain.

Context boundaries

The idea of context as an area of boundaries became clear to me across multiple performer workshops in 2021 and 2022. As we would work through the idea of boundaries, I kept hearing that "trust" in their scene partner[12], their director, and/or the ensemble, was a big factor in determining what those boundaries would be.

In an academic setting, the work a class is interested in exploring at the end of the semester may be vastly different from the beginning, not only in terms of skill levels, but in terms of relationship. If we care-fully scaffold psychological safety in our classes, students are more likely to be willing to take risks because they trust they will experience safety from us as teachers and power holders and from their peers. Everyone agrees to work and learn, and support others as they do, give grace during failed attempts, and celebrate growth.

Relationships and time are not the only contextual factors that can impact boundaries and needs. Space and location can determine these as well. In my career I have taught movement classes in studios, gyms, and classrooms with the desks shoved back. In a studio, where the floor is sprung, I feel safer to take physical risks than I do on a tiled classroom floor. In a gym, where other people who may not appreciate or know anything about the art I am working on can see me clearly through floor to ceiling glass walls, I may not want to take as many risks as I would in a space where most everyone is an artist, or no one could see me. Similarly, in performance spaces, there are those in which the audience is hundreds of feet away from the stage, and some where performers and audiences practically share breath. All these things contribute to a student performer's consideration of their boundaries and needs in the moment and should be discussed and upheld with the same intentionality as physical boundaries.

A discussion of Context Boundaries may be a good time to revisit "the law of the situation." There are some parts of our context that we cannot change, like the schedule. I have had this come up in a rehearsal context, when students ask to add a conflict, and think that they can tell me that spending time with a visitor that weekend is a boundary, because it will let them do their best work the next weekend. If a student has a conflict with the schedule, it is not a boundary; it is an inability to engage in the situation we agreed to, an inability to do the work (and it affects other people's ability to do the work!).

Boundaries, as we discuss them, are about being able to engage fully and confidently in the work, and that work happens in each given situation, aka, "the law of the situation." In addition, failure to abide by "the law of the situation" means that others can't do *their* best work, because you aren't there. In a class, like a rehearsal process, our work affects the work of others, so we must be committed to upholding our shared situation.

Prentis Hemphill, a somatic practitioner and podcast host, defines boundaries in this way: "Boundaries are the distance at which I can love you and me, simultaneously" (2021). When we remember that our relationships are affected by more than just our bodies but are also affected by the context we are a part of together, and the content we engage in together, we are reminded that boundaries are about relationship; boundaries are ever-changing ways that we relate well to one another.

Some questions students can ask themselves regarding Context Boundaries are:

- What factors make an atmosphere, both physically and psychologically safe for me to engage in risky or challenging material or actions?
- What factors signal un-safety?
- What is the level of trust between collaborators?
- Who am I demographically in this room?
    - It can be very challenging to enter vulnerable work if I am the only person holding a certain marginalized identity in the room.

Choreographic boundaries

Finally, we are at the part of the examination of boundaries you may have been expecting from the top—touch, bodies, and consent! In having these conversations regularly with students and performers for the last more than five years, I have discovered that there are a lot of nuances to be parsed here as well. Instead of saying "what boundaries do you have around your body or touch," I try to get students to dive more deeply into these instances, to help them clarify their needs:

- What are they willing to have their body do?
    - That is, what physical actions will they perform or, in the case of simulated and/or stylized sex or violence, be seen as performing?

- What are they willing to consent to have done to their bodies?
  - That is, receive touch, be lifted, etc.
- What are they willing to have their bodies do (with consent) to the bodies of others?
  - That is, give touch, perform a lift, etc.

I offer a personal example that as an "old dancer," I am no longer willing to kick above ninety degrees on my left side. Could I? Sure. But I am not willing to experience the pain that would occur from my chronic injury to my labrum, nor the recuperation and possible physical therapy that would be required to deal with aggravating it. As I mentioned before, dancers readily identify injuries as "allowable" boundaries. So, I use this example, as well as those included in my questions above, to state clearly that *all* physical boundaries are valid, not only the ones that come from injury.

Helping students separate discomfort and unsafety

Facilitating boundary knowledge may bring up a concern that students simply do not know the difference yet between discomfort and pain, or between something that is simply "out of the comfort zone" and a boundary. In 2020, while teaching a section of *The Ethics and Pedagogy of Teaching with(out) Touch* course for Momentum Stage, I realized the need for a tool teachers could use with students to help sort out some of these differences. So, I created a graphic[13] exploring the range that exists between someone's "Confidence Zone" and their "Boundary Zone."

This graphic uses the framework of "Growth Mindset," coined by Carol Dweck to promote the idea that there is always room for change (2007). Growth Mindset, as a theory, can be harmful, as it puts the onus on the individual to create change, and does not take into consideration systems of oppression that may be affecting them. However, in the idea of creating individual boundaries, I find that assessing where we are now, as well as where we may want to be in the future, to be helpful.

The graphic uses colors and terms to examine various feelings and/or experiences a student may have when encountering new material or a new activity. Teachers may ask students to describe their feelings about an action or piece of content with one of the colors or one of the statements or words on the graphic. Or they may choose to designate sections of the room as each zone, for students to move themselves to when offered a new activity.

- *Confidence Zone*: colored deep green. A student feels confident in the activity or material, as well as the directions they are receiving and the space in which they need to perform the activity. They might describe the activity as "easy" or feel "stable" or "secure" in the moment.
  - The teacher can step back and watch them perform with confidence!
- *Stretch Zone*: colored a lighter green. This zone is a mix of confidence and discomfort. I introduce this zone to students by asking them to demonstrate their favorite stretch. I remind them that a "stretch" is inherently uncomfortable. That's how we know change is occurring—it isn't what our body is used to. However, in this area of discomfort, the student must feel confident in their ability and/or opportunity to learn the material or action being requested of them. In fact, they are willing to engage in the discomfort, even seek it out, because they want the change, the outcome, that comes after the work. They may need guidance, or encouragement, but they are ready to put in the work. Most new things in movement class are a stretch—challenging and uncomfortable at the start, but something students want to be able to do.
  - The teacher may be needed for a moment, but for the most part, the student simply needs to know that someone is there to help if it's needed, but that they are trusted to learn.
  - In time, what feels like stretch should become something the student feels confident in.
- *Risk Zone*: colored orange. This section covers both things that are inherently risky (for example, being lifted or suspended) and things that feel beyond uncomfortable and have entered the unsafe range. A key feature of this zone is that the student can ask for what they need to feel safe and confident, whether that is more time, a spotter or a mat, or something else. Even though this is challenging material, the student does feel ready to take the risk. However, they need explicit support in doing so. This ties back to Clark's learning safety tier. Learning is risky because it requires vulnerability in the possibility of failure. However, there is the underlying safety of belonging in the space.
  - The teacher should be able to provide that support, so that students can feel confident in taking a risk. Or, they should clearly state that the needed supports are not available and ask if now this becomes a boundary.
  - Some things, like lifts, flying on stage, staged violence and intimacy, are inherently risky because of the reality of the situation. In these cases, the goal is not to make the risk disappear, because we can't! Instead, we are transparent about the risks and how we are mitigating them (rehearsal time, spotters, fight call, etc.), and allow the

student to evaluate whether those mitigations are enough for them to feel confident in performing the action.
- *Boundary Zone*: colored red. This zone means that a student is feeling unsafe about everything—the activity or material, the directions, and the space in which they are being asked to do them. They are filled with fear and self-doubt.
  - At this point, teachers should respect this choice. They may ask a clarifying question to ensure students understand the difference between boundary and risk like "Is there any condition that may help you do this, such as: more time, a spotter, etc.?" If the student does have a condition that can be met, teachers can offer that perhaps this is a risk, and not a boundary. However, students' boundaries should always be respected.

The goal with actions that fall within Stretch or Risk Zones for students is to have an honest conversation about what it would take to move that action to the Confidence Zone, or to know that it is in the Boundary Zone. We go back to dialogue as an important tool for care-full creativity and pedagogy, so that actions do not stay in the Stretch or Risk Zones forever.

Doing this deep assessment does take time. But that is also part of its power. In the past, a middle school-aged student who learned this tool through a training with the Dance Education Equity Association, relayed back to us that using it helped them know that they were not "overreacting" or "being dramatic" when they had a need or a boundary, but that they had carefully evaluated it. I encourage you to place this graphic in the room or LMS and invite students to think about their "comfort zones" in these more nuanced ways, so they make choices that help them learn and progress in healthy ways.

Facilitating boundary communication

For conversations between peers, or as a tool those in power can offer those not in power, I have developed a three-step boundary conversation formula I share in workshops and use in my movement classes.

Early in class, day one or two, I have students practice this conversation with the below script. While actors are often confident in speaking using scripts, or even improvising, dancers often are not. Historically, dancers do not speak in class or in performance, so the concept of their voice being welcomed in space may be difficult for them to embrace at first. I find a script, even if it feels stilted, helps students who are afraid to speak be more confident in it, as the words are there for them.

When introducing this script, I offer examples students might give around touch and/or types of touch, such as "I don't want contact to my face," "If the contact is to my waist, I need a Strong touch, not a Light one," or "You can use your full hand, but please don't poke me with one finger."

Boundary conversation for known boundaries[14]

1. Know that you can. Everyone has boundaries and has a right to expect them to be heard and upheld in the workplace (which our classroom is).
2. Ask theirs first. I model this as "Hey partner. I know we're doing this work together today that requires some contact. I was wondering if you had any boundaries or needs I should know about?"
    a. By asking theirs first, I have centered their humanity. I have made evident that I believe boundaries are normal, and I expect people to have them.
    b. I also demonstrate that I want to be a good collaborator. I want to create work we both feel confident in.
    c. By including "or needs" in the ask, I may stop the conditioned response many performers have of "I don't have any boundaries," and cause them to think about their situation in a nuanced way.
3. Share mine. Hopefully, after I complete step two, my scene partner will follow up with, "Do you have any boundaries?" But even if they do not, I still have an opening to say, "Thanks for sharing that with me. Here are mine."

As an aside, I also find that the way in which I address partnerships in class can help build inclusion safety, rather than foster competition mindset. Partner work in class is a place that power dynamics between peers can sneak in. To help alleviate these, I try to remove the power dynamics from the language used in the set up.

- Instead of calling partners "A and B" or "1 and 2", which implies rank and hierarchy, I use "Lemon and Lime" or "Blueberry and Raspberry." Even when I do small groups, I name them fruits!
- I often let students choose their own partners, but if I see cliques developing that exclude others, I may:
    o Say "this time your partner must be someone who:
        ▪ You have never worked with before."
        ▪ Has the same color shirt as you."
        ▪ Etc.
    o Change from partner work to small group work.

I start this language in these boundary conversations early in class, and then continue it through the rest of the semester. In this, not only do I remove language of rank from class, but I also continue to create inclusion safety.

Boundary conversation for boundaries we may discover in the moment

Performers are often asked to do things they have never done before, or didn't even anticipate were possible. Therefore, it is unlikely that performers, especially students, will know all their boundaries to communicate them when asked. A second boundary conversation formula reinforces the idea that boundaries may be encountered "in the moment," and can be addressed quickly and respectfully.

Just like the first conversation, there is a script students can use to practice saying "no" or asking clarifying questions in new situations.

1. Students return to their partner from the previous conversation. This time, they are "mid-work," and a new possibility arises.
2. One partner says, "May I _____?"
    a. I model this first in two ways:
        i. "May I use the back of my hand to lift your elbow into second position, since this is what the aesthetic of ballet requires of us?"
            1. This example is incredibly specific. I tell my partner what body part of mine would contact what body part of theirs, and why.
            2. The "why" is important, because it shares that it is not just because I want to, or that it would please me, the teacher. It is related to the work we are doing. This calls back to "the law of the situation."
        ii. "May I put orange cheese puffs between your toes?"
            1. This is my example for a thing that could come up that we would never anticipate! It's silly and extreme. But it encourages students to practice saying "no" or asking clarifying questions.
    b. The response can come in one of four variations:
        i. "Yes" or "No."
            1. These are pretty straightforward.
            2. The requesting partner then does, or does not, do the thing asked.

Practices for ensemble building: Creating inclusion safety

    ii. "Yes, if …"
        1. "Yes if …" creates expectations. I give the example of "Yes, if you use your pinky finger and not the back of your hand."
        2. The asking partner then confirms the parameters or container for the action, and once confirmed, may do it.
    iii. "No, but …"
        1. "No but …" is a counteroffer. I demonstrate with "No, you cannot put orange cheese puffs between my toes, but you can try to balance one on my nose."
        2. The asking partner then confirms the new action, or says, "no, thank you."
  c. After an action is completed, each partner asks the other "did that meet your expectations?" This important question was added by Sarah Lozoff of Intimacy Direction in Dance when we taught this conversation on a recent podcast and is also something we model at Intimacy Professional Education Collective when we teach about boundaries[15]. This question is important for helping students understand:
    i. Different embodied perceptions and experiences.
    ii. The importance of clarity in communication.
    iii. For example, a student may respond, "no, actually. When you said the touch would be on my arm, I imagined it on my bicep. Then you touched my forearm. It was totally fine, but it was not what I expected." Both students now have more information about how to phrase a request and how to ask clarifying questions.

When I introduce the Boundary Conversation with students making offers, I like to remind them that this is a way to honor their own creative impulses. But it is in no way compulsory, especially in the professional world. It is the director's or choreographer's job to come up with the creative solutions to story-telling if a performer has a boundary or need that creates a "no."

I tell students that as a choreographer, I love getting a "no," because it makes me be creative. The thing I offered first, I already had in my head. It's an easy answer. But, when I get a "no," I must find a new way. What a creative gift I have been given!

However, dancers and actors, because they are the ones in the bodies telling the stories and are also artists, may have ideas of how the moment could go, that would honor their boundaries. If so, they may want to make an offer. This exercise and script give them opportunities to practice doing so, with the reminder that it is never solely their responsibility.

Boundaries build inclusion, not excuses

In workshops with educators, someone inevitably raises a hand to ask, "But, what if students decide *everything* is a boundary, and they will do *nothing?*" My advice, should a situation like this occur, is to go back to the Confidence Zone graphic, and see if you can ask clarifying questions about what needs would have to be met to help this activity feel like an acceptable risk or stretch to attempt.

Students refusing to engage in everything has honestly not been my experience of college dance and acting students, or even the students I taught in middle school. Many dancers and actors are truly interested, eager to learn more about their artform, and ready to push themselves, creatively and physically. I am willing to say I may have been very lucky with students, but since this has been my experience across ages and institutions for almost a decade, I suspect students who say "no" to absolutely everything are the exception, not the rule, when given opportunities to state boundaries. In fact, it has been my experience that having boundary conversations make them more willing to try, to say "yes," and to explore, because they know it is safe to say "no," to change their minds, or to have a different need.

Teachers may also be resistant to having these conversations, as having to modify or substitute an exercise or experience requires time and creativity. For some teachers, this will mean reexamining an activity that has "worked" for decades. However, I find that time and creativity, willingly invested in the psychological safety of students, leads to trust, which in turn leads to creativity and collaboration.

As educators, we are not encouraging collaboration or power with when we expect or assume the "yes" of everyone in the room: *Yes, they can be touched by the director, pas de deux partner, scene partner, and everyone in the ensemble. Yes, they want feedback not just on their execution, but on what that execution says about them as a person or about their body. Yes, they want to engage in every possible opportunity and exercise offered to them.* Just because folks have said "yes" to being in a class (that they may not have even had a choice about because of major requirements, schedule, etc., which takes us back to consent not being able to be truly revocable in academia, see Chapter 3) does not mean they have agreed to harassment, injury, conflict, or to have no boundaries or needs. Simply because a student is in a class does not mean that they are ready to adhere to any and all requests I as their teacher, a person in power over them, would make. The idea that students and performers do not have, or should not have boundaries, so that they can be a vessel to the art, is dangerous and inhumane. We cannot assume someone's age, gender, experience, sexual orientation, manner of dress, or any other outwardly observable factor determines their willingness to engage in touch, staged intimacy, difficult or traumatic content, physical activities, or any other specific performance-related action.

In fact, Timothy R. Clark wrote in *The Four Stages of Psychological Safety*, "if you make any excuse for not extending psychological safety, you're choosing to value something else more than human beings" (2020, 123–124). When we normalize boundaries and boundary conversations, we humanize our pedagogy. Care-full work and pedagogy normalizes boundaries and agency, putting people at the center of the artistic process.

REFLECTION SECTION: Boundary conversations

Complete the questions or use the worksheets in the "Resources" section for Content/Context/Choreographic Boundaries and Zones of Action for yourself.

What new insights did I have about my own boundaries? About the distance and nuance between discomfort and unsafety?

_____
_____
_____
_____
_____

What sensations or feelings in my body did I notice when thinking of activities in the Confidence Zone? Stretch Zone? Risk Zone? Boundary Zone?

_____
_____
_____
_____
_____

How can I introduce these concepts in my classes?

_____
_____
_____
_____

Practice the initial Boundary Conversation script with someone.

How did it feel to have this conversation? What new insights or questions do I have about boundaries?

_____
_____
_____
_____
_____

Practice the second Boundary Conversation script with someone.

How did it feel to have this conversation? What new insights or questions do I have about boundaries?

_____
_____
_____
_____
_____

Introduction Letters

In both the Land Acknowledgements and Needs section, I have referenced Introduction Letters. Introductions Letters are ways to facilitate my connection to students, bolster individual belonging, and they provide the baseline for the ungrading practices[16] used in the course.

The first assignment students have in all my courses is to write me an Introduction Letter. This is the prompt that appears in the LMS:

- Name you would like all class participants to use in our space.
- Pronouns if you would like to share them.
- Where you are from the world, if that feels safe to share. And if you know your land acknowledgement, please include that! If you don't, but you want to, check out this site.[17] They also have an app.
- A little bit about your past dance/movement/performance experience (if you shared some in our class intros today, please give me more depth here).
    - Do you enjoy creating and/or improvising your own movement?
    - What is your experience in making choices in movement (aka improvising or following impulses)?
- What is exciting to you about this session (may relate to this class or not)?
- What is concerning to you (that feels safe to share) about this session (may relate to movement or not)?
- Any needs you have for our learning environment from the needs list.
    - If you do need accommodations for this class, this is a space to articulate those.
- Your five goals for the first half of the session from the Movement Experiences Guide.[18]
- Song suggestions for our class playlist.
- Anything else you think I should know.

These letters offer students a way to be seen as individuals. In dance technique courses that emphasize unison and uniformity or large general education appreciation courses, these communications humanize the learning process for both me and them. The letter is also an opportunity to follow up on their needs for a learning environment, as well.

Class playlists

In each class, I have the students submit songs for the playlist in their Introduction Letter. In theory or lecture courses, the playlist is on as students are coming in and sometimes during group activities. In movement classes, I use the playlist for the somatic check-in, the warm-up, and during experiments or group work.

Creating a class playlist is a way of building inclusion safety. When students hear "their song," they get excited, and have tangible proof that their contributions and choices have been heard. This collaborative song list (because I have choices on there as well) is also a way of sharing power. My aesthetics and choices are not the only ones present, but students craft the soundscape of our class. This is also a great way for me to learn about new music or artists and have different creative inspiration. For safety, I do have one rule for the submissions: they cannot contain any slurs against people's race, ethnicity, gender, ability, etc. Personally, I do not mind cursing in lyrics, but you or your institution may wish to make that rule as well.

Observational practices

Belonging, or inclusion safety, creates a foundation from which we can explore what we don't know, with a sense of security. An early way I do this is asking students to examine what they think they already know and see what they are missing. When I teach, particularly Modern Dance, Dance History or Dance Appreciation, or Movement for Actors, I offer inroads to this awareness through quotes, videos, and exercises. Brian McLaren, a theologian and podcaster, titled one of his episodes, co-hosted with spiritual writer Richard Rohr and the Reverend Jacqui Lewis, PhD, "What you focus on determines what you miss" (2020). I couple it with the ancient Egyptian proverb, "We were so focused on the snake; we missed the scorpion." I offer these to students as cautionary statements against assuming we see all there is to see, or assuming that we are seeing anything other than our own preferences when viewing and interpreting art.

For students to know themselves, and to engage responsibly in group discussions, they also must be aware of the lenses they constantly wear because of their own cultural context. For these self-examinations, we use selective attention tests,[19] and an exercise I call Story People. In Story People, first I model the exercise for students. I share a 3D rendered image of two people,[20] engaged in an action, but fairly devoid of context.

I tell students that first we will "objectively" or "clinically" describe what we are seeing. For example, one person is on a low level, the other is at a mid-level. They both have a hand extended, one is supported by the ground, etc. No interpretation is allowed at this point, only observation.

After that is completed, we enter the narrative phase and write or record a short story or other creative piece about what is happening. They are encouraged to create context, and to be as specific, and creative, as possible. Students are then asked to do the same two steps with a new image.

After following these steps, I ask a student or two to share their story. They often interpret emotions from body positions, even though there are no facial expressions, as well as ages and genders for the images. For example, for the image described above, some students see the standing person offering help to the person on the ground, while others seem them as mocking them. Students are frequently surprised how deeply their assumptions have affected them, as I point out that these images are blank canvases. Any story that includes emotion or identity, they have created themselves, based on their worldview.

I use this exercise to demonstrate to students that they have a worldview and a cultural context that constantly influences their interactions, and interpretations of those interactions, with others. Felicia Rose Chavez tells her writing students, "you are but one voice among many. Your valuable insights spring not from immoveable truth, but from biased perspective; your body, culture, class and privilege influence your knowledge construction" (2021, 116).

In all these experiences, I remind students that what we are learning in class gives us a vocabulary to enter conversations with others, to get curious about what we see, and how it fits into both our world and the worlds of others. Movement and body language should not be used to make assumptions about the intentions, purposes, or desires of others. As Suzie Gablik wrote about art, "In these terms, to know oneself becomes an end, instead of a means through which one knows the world" (1992, 25). Rather, viewing movement can be used to engage in knowing them more deeply, as we ask questions about their meaning-making and context. I leave my students with a quote from Captain Michael Burnham of the starship, *Discovery*, "We cannot interpret their intention from our own cultural context" (Goldsman 2021).

With these tools, we have set the stage not only for learner safety, but contributor safety as well.

REFLECTION SECTION: Introduction letters and observational practices

What assignments or activities do I include early in class to create a sense of individual belonging for students?

_____
_____
_____
_____
_____

What assignments or activities do I include early in class to create a sense of communal belonging for students?

_____
_____
_____
_____
_____

Complete the Observational Practices for yourself. The links to images and videos can be found in the Resources section.

What did I notice? What did I miss?

_____
_____
_____
_____
_____

What sensations and feelings are coming up for me as I consider how my worldview and/or assumptions around movement may affect what I see?

_____

_____

_____

_____

_____

Conclusion

Inclusion safety is a level of psychological safety that is required for learning. Building inclusion safety means establishing that our space is welcoming for individuals, as the humans they are, and for what they bring to the group.

Inclusion safety begins on the first day of class as the teacher demonstrates care for both the individual students and the ensemble, by communicating clearly about expectations, and offering students time to know themselves and their needs, as well as the needs of those they are learning and working with. Practices for inclusion safety let students know that they are valued for who they are, and that they belong in the classroom community as they are.

In this way, creating inclusion safety is an antidote for competition mindset. When we are all valued and belong, we do not see others as obstacles to our success. Rather they are collaborators and co-learners. They are teammates and all our successes depend on each other.

Chapter reminders

- Tools for inclusion safety and ensemble building include:
    - Land Acknowledgements.
    - Class Contracts.
    - Needs Inventory.
    - Boundary Conversations.
    - Introduction Letters.
    - Observational Practices.
- Collaboratively created Class Contracts help define the situation of each class.
- A boundary is a need I have to have met, in order to do my best work.
- Having a boundary does not mean that a student doesn't want to do the work, but that they are simply looking to get a need met to continue in the work.
- Boundaries are normal, human things to have.
- If our spaces are safe for students to create and explore emotionally challenging content, we also need to create spaces where it is safe to not engage in that.
- Boundaries are often much more nuanced than we think.
- Knowing our boundaries takes time.
- Presence is not an implied "yes."
- We all see through our own lenses.
- Inclusion safety can disperse competition mindset.

Notes

1. See my Land Acknowledgement linked in the "Resources" section.
2. See more on syllabus language in Chapter 6 and access the template for the Honor Triad in the "Resources" section.
3. If you teach in certain institutions, you may be required to allow recordings. I had to remove this language at one point. There is more on phones and recording in Chapter 6.
4. You will find more information on this phrasing in Chapter 7.
5. A contract is not traditionally a tool of consent, as it comes from one party, to the other, so the party who issued it has more power, as they set the terms of negotiation. That is, in fact, what is happening in Class Contracts, when I come forward with the template as describe here. However, as I am transparent about this, and the power involved, and invite student feedback, it is an early example of trading my power-over for power-with students.
6. We do set some "immediately no" behaviors like, calling someone a racial or sexual slur in class with the outcome of immediate removal and a discussion with the chair.
7. A gross title I have some thoughts about but are likely for another book ....
8. Calling back to the last chapter and the citation from Ahenkorah, a Class Contract creates a space that is not brave or safe, but rather "accountable."
9. Links to both my version and theirs are available in the "Resources" section.
10. A handout for students, with all these questions, is included in the "Resources" section.
11. With those middle school students and with university students creating work on sensitive topics, I also have them create a closure practice for themselves and/or the dancers they are working with. These were challenging conversations to have with middle schoolers, but they are ready for them if they are ready to make art about sensitive topics. Therefore, I know these conversations and practices can become a common part of university-level work.
12. I want to be clear that boundaries are about me, and my work. They are not about the other person. A boundary could be "I don't want to work on intimate scenes in the first week of rehearsals or have contact in the first week of classes so we can build trust that supports the work" is a boundary. "I don't want to do _____ with that person" is not a boundary because it is about their identity, not my work. "Boundaries" should and do not cover harmful biases and prejudices.
13. Available in the "Resources" section.
14. The full color handout of this formula is available in the "Resources" section.
15. Links to these are in the "Resources" section.
16. Chapter 9 will include an in-depth discussion on the whys and hows of ungrading.
17. Linked in the "Resources" section.
18. Also included in Chapter 9. An abbreviated form of this guide is used for goal setting in non-movement courses.
19. Linked in the "Resources" section.
20. See the images in the "Resources" section.

6
Practices in the syllabus: Setting the stage for learner safety

I love writing my syllabus. I truly do. I get excited about the start of a new class and what we are all going to learn from each other.

In the nonprofit world, there is a saying, "A budget is a moral document," meaning, where we spend our money says a lot about who we are. In academia, I would suggest the saying is, "A syllabus is a moral document." What we present as requirements, how our policies support (or don't) students of all abilities, genders, races, etc., and how this is communicated says a lot about who we as educators believe education is for and what success in learning looks like.

Syllabus as tool for creating learner safety

As I present the syllabus to students, I do so as a values and vision statement for our class. This document is the first time a student encounters me, my values around teaching and learning, and my hopes for our time together. With transparent and accessible communication, clear expectations, and explicit supports, the syllabus offers a guide for learning in community. It is my hope when students encounter my syllabi, that they feel confident in not only being in our learning community, but in how they can find meaning and success through it.

Format

Much of my syllabus, and likely yours too, is a copy and paste boilerplate of legal jargon and necessary statements from the institution. However, if you have a lot of flexibility over how your syllabus is presented, I recommend exploring visual syllabus options, for both accessibility and ease of use.

Anne-Marie Womack wrote a definitive essay on accessible syllabi, "Teaching is Accommodation: Universally Designing Composition Classrooms and Syllabi" for *College Composition and Communication* in 2017, that is available for free on the Accessible Syllabus[1] website. The site offers theory and reasoning for creating accessible syllabi, including creating a visual syllabus, as well as examples and resources. Her work greatly informed my own format and language for syllabi.

I was able to do a visual syllabus previously and found it much more engaging for all students, as well as accommodating neurodiverse students. Pictures and smaller blocks of text made it easy for me to turn it into a presentation to accompany our discussion. However, in the institutions that most recently employed me, I had to use an organization-wide template that did not allow for formatting choices.

Power dynamics

Creating an accessible, transparent, well-communicated syllabus is part of building inclusion and learning safeties. I do not try to hide what is required or expected from students, nor obscure it with academic speak or hope they will find it for themselves. Womack writes, "Time spent on inclusion is worth it educationally and ethically because learning depends on access" (2017, 521). This is why I do take class time to go over the syllabus, and do not simply assign it. I believe this time is necessary to care-full pedagogy as it lays bare the power structures of the room, the expectations of the class, and my invitation to collaboration, creativity, and agency.

In the previous section of this book, we acknowledged that as educators, we do, in fact, have power. We can use those powers to attempt to control students, or to help students practice and experience their own power. In her essay, Womack quotes Diann Baeker, another researcher focused on the syllabus as a communication tool, who says, "A balanced syllabus is not one in which power is shared, but rather one in which power is made explicit ..." (512). I explain and name the powers over that students may be used to experiencing in a class. I acknowledge that students are likely feeling pressures from power dynamics that will influence how they engage in the class. I also state that I hope our class can be a place where they can practice their own powers of choice, creativity, and autonomy.

Every section below is one that I read, display on a presentation, and/or ask students to find in their document or the upload on the learning management system (LMS), and give time to discuss or question. Going over the syllabus, instead of assigning it or hoping students will read it does take time. However, it is time that sets the tone for our learning environment. I can start it with dictatorial orders or not being clear about expectations; or I can start it with access and communication. Creating transparency around power dynamics is a necessary part of using Working Consent in the classroom.

Because so much time is spent in conversation around the syllabus, students have opportunities to ask for clarity around expectations early. Since I demonstrate early that I value communication and want students to be successful in learning, I believe students will continue to ask for what they need.

I mention to students that they may be used to a learning environment where the teacher is the keeper of all knowledge and the arbiter of success. This is due to a society that values hierarchies, in which only one person can be in power. I tell them that the syllabus is not a document on how to please or appease me as a singular power holder. Rather, the syllabus will guide us on how we can all work and learn well and successfully, together.

This chapter offers sample language from my syllabi, as well as the consent-forward, trauma-informed, and/or psychologically safe reasoning for my statements.

Syllabus statements for inclusion and learner safeties, and beyond

- Classroom Expectations and Community.
- Student Outcomes versus Guiding Questions.
- Dress Code.
- Artificial Intelligence (AI) Use.
- Electronic Devices.
- Conflict Resolution.
- Attendance and Participation.
- Course Outline.
- Important Resources for Learning.

Much like the tools in the previous chapter, these statements are presented in the order in which students encounter them in the syllabus. I have used my most recent syllabus as the template for this chapter. You will notice there is nothing about touch and contact in class, nor grading and/or late work in this section. While included in my syllabus, these topics are addressed in depth in Chapters 8 and 9, respectively.

Classroom expectations and community

This is perhaps the most important part of the syllabus to me. If I am not required to use a template, this appears first. I do believe a class is a community; we have gathered here because of some shared interests or goals, but we are all unique individuals with needs, boundaries, perspectives, and experiences. Because of this, care is needed.

My syllabus statement on Classroom Expectations centers on the idea that we are all here to do the work of learning:

> This course is structured as a lab in which you are both the scientist and your own (no one else's, including mine!) experiment. In this metaphor, I'm the director of the lab, whose job it is to make sure our experiments are safe and ethical, while still pushing us to new discoveries. I am a co-investigator, with my own experiment of my body and creative practice.
>
> This course is (re)designed on a continual basis to meet the needs and requests of participants. This syllabus is a living document, as changes may be made during the semester to meet special interests and talents of the group, or if conditions on campus change. Also review our learning management system on a regular basis, as that site will be regularly updated to reflect what is occurring this semester.
>
> OUR CLASSROOM COMMUNITY AND VALUES
>
> In order to discover answers to the course questions, your consistent, brave, and thoughtful engagement is desired. Please bring a paper and pen or electronic device in order to record information and/or insights you wish to think through.
>
> As movement and performance are most often community or ensemble pursuits, so too is the learning of them. Even a solo on a stage has required collaboration with a costume designer, lighting designer, composer, stage manager, etc. We need each other and must respect each other's role and contribution to the process. On Day 1, we will create Community Expectations, or a Class Contract, as a class.
>
> You are encouraged to speak up and participate during class meetings and in discussion threads. Everyone is an expert in their own embodied and lived experiences, and we can all learn from each other.
>
> Sharing your ideas and your work with others can be intimidating for even the most seasoned academic (it still is for me!), but we will work together to make it an inviting and supportive learning atmosphere. This sharing is an important part of learning in this class.

These expectations are key to creating and maintaining psychological safety.

Practices in the syllabus: Setting the stage for learner safety

We pause here to create our Class Contract and review the Needs list,[2] allowing us practice inclusion safety and build belonging. This time also sets the stage for learner and contributor safeties, as we discuss what it would take to feel safe bringing our ideas forward and how we can support that for each other. In this, we acknowledge that sharing is risky and has perhaps been traumatic or harmful in the past, but in our class, we are working to create psychological safety.

Perhaps my favorite line of this section is, "Everyone is an expert in their own embodied and lived experience," and I use this to reiterate that I am not the only expert in the room. I bring certain expertise in the subject matter and pedagogy, as well as more lived experience in it. However, I truly believe that each student contributes to our learning because of their unique experiences and embodiment. I make Expert Power nonexclusive, building learner and contributor safeties.

Guiding questions versus student outcomes or course objectives

Many courses list student objectives or outcomes. While these may be required by the institution (especially if there are multiple sections of the same course), to ensure graduation requirements are met or curriculum stays cohesive, these lists do not encourage student inquiry or ownership of learning. "Course Objectives" imply that the instructor and department already know what students will learn from a course, and center the content, rather than the people. "Student Outcomes," while it does emphasize that students are involved, portrays them as cogs in a predetermined machine. This may leave students who do not experience or achieve one of the outcomes feeling as though they are deficient as learners or movers.

The truth is, no course is "one size fits all." Some students enter a course having already met every criterion listed as an objective or outcome. That doesn't mean they shouldn't still engage in class or won't experience any learning. Some students may never achieve a certain objective or outcome. This doesn't mean their experiences and learnings from class are null and void. Language like "outcomes" or "objectives" tend to center one-time assessment or "mastery," rather than ongoing growth.

In my current syllabus, the institution has put in outcomes that I must (and do) include. I follow those with Course Guiding Questions. Guiding Questions are meant to inspire growth; to let students claim what they know and get curious about what they don't. By including these with the goals of the class, I demonstrate for students that the process is just as important as the product. The following is what currently appears in my Movement for Actors syllabus:

Course Guiding Questions

This course is an opportunity to build on what you already know of movement techniques and theories, as well as your own personal embodied experiences. In order to do so, we will engage with readings, videos, movement experiences, personal reflections, class discussions, and performance to examine questions like:

Embodiment and Somatics

- What is somatics?
  - What does a somatic practice and somatic knowledge offer my creative practice and performance?
- What are my personal movement preferences at this time?
- What are some of the movement preferences of others that differ from my own?
  - What new perspectives or ideas does this knowledge offer me?

Movement and Meaning

- How can I bring my personal movement preferences to others (collaborators and audiences) with clarity?
- What movement qualities and movement training do I need to be successful in performance?
- How does movement/physicality help me and/or my community find, make, and/or express meaning from experiences, observations and/or ideas?
- What new perspectives or knowledge have I gained from learning in a community?

Yours

- What questions do you bring into this space about movement as performance, pedagogy, embodied experience, history, etc.?

I shift the above vocabulary slightly to refer to a particular dance technique if that is valid for the class.

The phrasing of these Guiding Questions is also meant to inspire learner safety: to let students know that it is expected that there are things that they don't know, and that learning is a journey.

- "At this time" gives us space to revisit ideas and chart change and progress.

Practices in the syllabus: Setting the stage for learner safety 137

- "Personal movement preferences" and "preferences different than my own" imply that multiple points of view are valid and expected.
- "Others" and "community" are part of our inquiry, we learn from our classmates, as well as the teacher and ourselves.
- "What do I need" and "new perspectives" invite reflection on current and future learning opportunities.

These questions are part of Artist Logs, detailed in Chapter 7.

REFLECTION SECTION: Syllabus statements part 1

You may wish to complete these questions with your own syllabus in hand.

How would I describe my current syllabus? Is it a vision statement? A guidebook? An academic text?

_____

_____

_____

_____

_____

What purpose does the syllabus serve in my class? What does my syllabus say I value? I envision for our time together? I believe constitutes learning and/or success?

_____

_____

_____

_____

_____

Practices in the syllabus: Setting the stage for learner safety

Use the space below to examine and reimagine your syllabus.

	What my syllabus currently says about:	**How I might change this to encourage a level of psychological safety and/or Working Consent:**
Power		
Accessibility		
Community		
Expectations		
What and how we will learn		
The purpose of learning		

Dress code

Dress codes in movement classes serve to ensure physical safety, as well as support the instructor's ability to give accurate anatomical feedback. However, for students of marginalized genders, dress codes can be a source of worry or even oppression.

My current syllabus reads:

> Dress appropriately for movement work: clothing you can move confidently in, such as work-out clothes (i.e. sweatpants and t-shirts, NO jeans, khakis or dresses [unless with shorts]).
>
> - Including socks/ballet slippers/jazz shoes. No street shoes may be worn in the studio.
> - You do NOT need to buy any of the things linked here, but this site[3] and list are resources for your reference.
> - Your clothes and accessories should help you (and your classmates) focus on the work.

The above was for a Movement for Actors class. For a dance technique class, I would specify shoe type and that if students did not have those, they would need to purchase them. As I do not teach in any conservatory programs, I do not require leotard, tights, or any particular color schemes.

By removing binary gender categories and examples, and by showing pictures of a variety of body types in the link, my dress code helps build inclusion safety. In the past, I have even included photographs of previous classes dressed appropriately, without their faces. By stating that the purpose of the dress code is to help students move confidently and focus on the work, I give space for their choices, while also reminding them that we are here to learn and engage in embodied practices.

AI use

One of the most surprising (at least to me) inclusions in my syllabus is a statement on AI use. Naively, I thought students in movement classes would be unaffected by these tools, as our emphasis is on embodied experiences.[4] However, in a world that emphasizes technology, I was wrong! My current policy, given below, emphasizes creativity, and considers AI to be a hindrance to students' developing of creative skills.

> The use of ChatGPT and/or other AI tools as the exclusive source of composition constitutes plagiarism and is a violation of academic

Practices in the syllabus: Setting the stage for learner safety 141

integrity. AI can be a tool but should not be the source of your writing. In fact, for this class it should be impossible for this to be true, as all assignments require reflection on embodied experiences from that week's class. See more on this in our Assignments and Grading sections.

Tools like ChatGPT, Claude, and similar are LANGUAGE models, but not LEARNING[5] models. AI doesn't actually know or learn anything. These programs just regurgitate the already existing knowledge. As artists, we are moving beyond what exists and trying to create something new.

I believe AI is a tool. However, it is not creative. One of the goals for this class is to build your creative impulses and learn to respond creatively. **Do not dismiss your own creativity or artistic choice by relegating it to AI.**

Since the language highlights learning and contributing in the classroom, I must build learner and contributor safety for students.

My policy is supported by how I word my assignment prompts,[6] as alluded to in the first paragraph. These questions ask students to relate embodied sensations and tie them to specific class experiences and vocabulary—things AI will be unable to answer. Instead of explicitly banning AI tools, I ask students what it means to consider their own creativity to be the priority.

I have an AI engineer as a life partner. When a new tool comes out, I know about it. Our dinner table conversations often include the ethical issues raised by AI tools, particularly for artists. In fact, in 2024, he, a filmmaker colleague, and I received a grant from the Doris Duke Foundation to develop a product, *Totentanz*,[7] to protect dancers and choreographers from unauthorized AI access and use of their movement. It is the second arts and technology grant we have been awarded.

I share all of this with students so they understand that my technical knowledge, or ability to gain that knowledge, is quite high, and that my policy is well-considered. It isn't borne of fear, ignorance, or a belief that AI is bad or useless. Rather, my perspective is one that strives to protect and promote creators and creativity, more than technology or even efficiency. In a classroom where we are creators and developing those skills, I am always going to ask us to prioritize creativity and autonomy.

Electronic devices

Electronic devices like phones and tablets fall into the category of tools as well. Again, I take a different tact than outright banning of use. First, these are adults, and I should trust them with their own possessions. Second, in movement work there are times that recordings are very helpful. So, I ask students to consider electronics from a consent-forward[8] and trauma-informed standpoint.

The syllabus reads:

> There may be times I ask you to use your phone or device, or you wish to do so to record a movement sequence. While your phone can be used for educational purposes, it should not be used otherwise in this class.
>
> Recording is, to me, an issue of consent. If you need to record your group work for your own memorization (particularly of movement experiences), please communicate your need to your group, and/or those near you, to see if they have any needs around recording. Please honor their boundaries around being recorded.
>
> I also encourage you to get curious about your phone use, or the desire for it. When do you find yourself reaching for your phone?
>
> - If you need a fidget to occupy your hands to help you focus, get one from me as you come in, and return it when you're done!
> - If your phone is an escape, get curious about why:
>   o Are you bored?
>   o Are you stressed or overwhelmed?
>   o Do you need a break?
>
> Any of these may occur in a learning scenario. But, using your phone or other device to meet these needs during class can be disrespectful or distracting to the people around you.
>
> Please communicate with me if you are feeling bored or overwhelmed by the course and/or the content. If you need a break, refer to our community agreements.

I have taught in institutions that require that students be allowed to always record lectures. In that case, the first paragraph of this statement in my syllabus has read:

> You may use your phone or device to record lectures presented by me in this class.

The rest of the statement reads as above. This makes sure other students and guests are given the opportunity to consent to recording.

Technology policies can inadvertently harm neurodiverse students or students experiencing a flight-type trauma response by punishing classroom phone use. I recognize that phone use may be a way students are demonstrating activation or a trauma response or dealing with a symptom of their neurodiversity and encourage them to notice the same with the above questions.

Instead of shame or frustration at their phone use, I offer conversation and other resources like fidget toys.

Framing phones as a consent issue builds learner and contributor safeties for all, as well as incorporates Working Consent into the classroom. Students are expected to be responsible consumers and users of technology in our class, and to use it in ways that support their own creativity and learning, as well as the safety of others.

Conflict resolution

Part of the values of a psychologically safe classroom is a straight-forward and transparent way of dealing with conflict. If we want students to contribute, and even challenge us, the curriculum, performance traditions, etc., in the classroom, we must be able to hold conflicts that will arise from contrasting ideas.

Conflict, and even harm, is inevitable in teaching and creating because we are complex, fallible humans working with other humans who are equally as emotionally involved, all with equal possibilities of making mistakes. The latest statistics, published by Swedo, Aslam, and Dahlberg, et al in 2024, from the Department of Health and Human Services show that over 63% of US adults have had at least one Adverse Childhood Experience. It would be inaccurate to assume that we can avoid activating everyone's earlier trauma(s). We are humans and despite our best intentions we cause harm.

To pretend that harm will not occur in a psychologically safe space is a ridiculously false premise. What makes the space psychologically safe is not a lack of harm. It is safe because we value the humanity in the room, meaning we know that harm will occur, and we have a plan to deal with it humanely, with compassion and accountability. When it does occur, we follow this statement included in my syllabus:

> In any group of humans, conflict will arise. When it does, we will utilize a Resolution Pathway.[9]
>
> 1. If you feel confident in doing so, address the person with whom you have a conflict directly. Express which behavior you would like to see change, what change you need, and when you would like that change to happen.
> 2. If you do not feel confident in having that conversation, or your request is met with disrespect, please see me or email me at [my email].
> 3. If your concern is with me, I invite you to bring it to my attention. Your success in this class is important to me, as is your wellbeing. I

am well aware that I make mistakes, and I never want those to cause harm or a loss of learning.
4. If you feel you cannot address an issue with me, please contact the chair/program director/etc. at [their email], or one of the other resources included at the end of the syllabus.
5. The goal of conflict resolution is always maintaining or restoring the community. We will always speak and pursue change with that in mind.

The last statement is of particular importance to me and is one I highlight with students. The purpose of addressing harm and engaging in accountability is to restore community. The purpose is not to punish or shame. If we believe we are all a community, we are all responsible for each other's learning and we need each other to do our learning, we will be invested in restoring our community. After a conflict, restoring community often means creating some change in behavior, speech, and/or expectations. Sometimes a simple apology will suffice. We also must acknowledge that sometimes, community cannot be restored. But those moments are rare and being accountable to create change to honor and/or support each other is something that comes up far more often.

Because of all these factors, the journey on the Resolution Pathway takes a differing amount of time and leads to different locations for each situation. When a student begins the path, the first thing I do is ask what the desired change(s) and/or action(s) are that they wish to see. I also reassure them of my commitment to helping restore our classroom community. As we continue down the path, I update the student on:

- When a conversation will happen with the other party(ies).
- When changes/action can be expected.
- When they will be receiving a follow up conversation.

This transparency and commitment to communication helps keep more harm from occurring, as could when someone doesn't know what is happening with their concern, or where to go from where they are.

I demonstrate through the Pathway that I want students to experience class as a place where we can have hard conversations, and I invite them to start those when necessary. I also recognize that sometimes students don't feel safe or able to have those conversations and need support. With this statement, we build toward all levels of psychological safety.

If a student uses your Resolution Pathway, although it may not feel like it, it is a good thing. It means that the students in your space believe you when you say you care about their consent and agency. It is an opportunity to practice our care-full pedagogy.

Practices in the syllabus: Setting the stage for learner safety

REFLECTION SECTION: Syllabus statements part 2

You may wish to complete this question with your own syllabus in hand.

Are there places in these policies where I have inadvertently been ableist? Neurotypical? Sexist? Hierarchical or authoritarian?

_____

_____

_____

_____

_____

Are there places in these policies where I have inadvertently made assumptions about students?

_____

_____

_____

_____

_____

How could I address these inadvertent harms?

_____

_____

_____

_____

_____

Use the space below to examine and reimagine your syllabus.

	What my syllabus currently says about:	How I might change this to encourage a level of psychological safety and/or Working Consent:
Dress code		
Bodies		
Gender identities		
AI and other technological tools		
Conflict resolution		

Attendance and participation

Attendance and participation policies are often some of the most dehumanizing, ableist, sexist, neurotypical, and punishing statements in education. I believe these policies are not meant this way, but are well intended, as much of what we want students to learn happens in class, especially for movement courses. However, many policies do not consider the complex humanity of students including living off-campus, part- or full-time jobs, visible and invisible disabilities, and more. Therefore, many of these policies do not build inclusion or learner safety.

Jessica Zeller, PhD, believes that punitive and harsh policies also devalue students' Expert Power. She writes in *Humanizing Ballet Pedagogies*:

> Fostering an environment in which trust is supported is an ongoing process. Teachers' explicit disclosures are important here: stating aloud, repeatedly, that students are experts with the most comprehensive knowledge of their own persons and bodies; and explicitly trusting students to autonomously determine how to best care for themselves and their bodies. Dealing forthrightly with, or even subverting, and policies that might hinder this care is important—attendance, participation, or grading, for example. (2024, 56)

In movement classes, we want students to learn their bodies. As an educator, I want students to know themselves. I can support this type of embodied learning by having attendance and participation policies that recognize that because students have needs and priorities outside of the classroom.

Attendance

I often say, as I introduce my attendance policy, "Your attendance is about your priorities." Every student has their own priorities—for some, getting to class is high on the list, for others it is not. It is not anywhere in my job description as an educator to make them place my class, or any class, higher on the list. It is my job to educate them, which includes helping them see how their decisions affect their short- and long-term successes in the field. So, instead of a punitive attendance policy, I crafted one that helps build the life skills of setting priorities and being accountable to our choices.

My most recent institution did not mandate attendance, leaving me free to craft my own policy, which you can see here.

> An absence must be communicated to me, via email. This should happen before class if possible. If this is not possible, an absence must be

communicated within 24 hours. Your communication should also include HOW you plan to make up the work missed in class, as class participation is required for each week's Artist's Log. Failure to communicate will result in an "incomplete" Artist's Log for that week, which will affect your grade bundles. If you have 3 absences, we will have an honest conversation about your ability to complete the learning in this course.

The policy helps students develop the life skill of professional, timely communication. Many jobs, including in the arts, allow for flex time and/or absences. I make it clear to students that class is important, it is a commitment and an expectation. However, we all have other needs and expectations, so our responsibility to each other is that we will communicate when we cannot fulfill our commitment.

In the past, I have been part of institutions and/or departments that have had policies regarding attendance that my own classroom procedures had to uphold. In those cases, the department or school had a stated number of unexcused absences that would result in a grade penalty. Then my syllabus read:

> An absence must be communicated to me, via email, for it to be excused. This should happen before class if possible. If this is not possible, an absence must be communicated within 24 hours. Your communication should also include HOW you plan to make up the work missed in class, as class participation is required for each week's Artist's Logs. If this communication does not occur, your absence will be unexcused and count towards the school/department policy of (number here) of unexcused absences resulting in a grade penalty and (number here) of unexcused absences resulting in failing the class.

In this case, I do communicate the punitive power of attendance, or lack thereof, but it is only when professional communication is not upheld. Absences are "excused" or "unexcused" based on communication, not based on the reason. The expectation is still professional communication, not perfection or my judgment of what a "good" or valid reason is.

Birdwell and Bayley, two scholars who taught English in higher education settings call for caution in these instances:

> What's clear, however, is that professors and authors frequently make assumptions about their students' reason for missing class that are implicitly ableist …. Worse, these attributions come with implicit moral judgements, since we frequently link hard work to worthiness and value. (2022, 229)

I have had colleagues who have asked for doctor's notes or even obituaries from students to "prove" that their absence should be excused. These are not trauma-informed practices, and do not allow for autonomy, privacy, or inclusion safety.

I have also had colleagues who say "well, they will just take advantage." Yet, I fail to see what advantage students gain by not coming to class. They are missing the learning and not building their skills. They are missing the community.

If students have priorities that are not learning and community, my class probably isn't the right place for them, anyway. If a student has three absences, I call them in for a conversation, and we go from there. I suspect colleagues who fear students are taking advantage actually fear they will lose control in their classroom. As I see a classroom as a space of co-active control, or collaboration, to start with, I have nothing to lose with a care-full attendance policy.

Participation

Being present is only part of the equation. Participation in class is key to success in movement courses. Students may be unable to participate in class because they are absent, or because of an injury or a boundary. My class policy continues:

> Ungrading[10] only works when we all enter with our best of intentions, and with integrity to our community (this class). As a community, we learn together, so everyone's participation is needed. Accountability to ourselves and to each other is expected. Therefore, your attendance and work engagement are expected. The Learning Management System will only be used to track attendance, not its effect on your grade, so please keep on top of your attendance.
>
> **You absolutely will not be able to complete the Letters, Logs, or Showings without excellent attendance.** This will affect your grade.[11]

In participation, I call back to our Class Contract and Community Expectations. Students are not only here to learn, but they are also here to help others learn. There is also the reminder that getting a good grade, even though it is an "ungraded" course, depends on doing the work, and in movement classes that happens in the room.

You will see there is no discussion of lateness in the policy. I removed late penalties from my syllabus and classes in 2022, before I changed the attendance policy fully, as I realized penalizing lateness was punishing the behavior

I valued, coming to class! When I saw that not penalizing lateness did not cause excessive lateness to occur, I took it a step further to full attendance.

If a student shows up late, they often bust through the door saying, "I'm so sorry I'm late!" Which I meet with, "I'm glad you're here." And I am. I am delighted that through whatever stressors or mishaps their day threw at them, getting to class was still on their list of priorities.

I do not believe penalizing lateness accomplishes anything. If a student is shamed, they are not experiencing inclusion safety and will not be able to learn at their best. If they are unable to participate because a late policy excludes them from doing so after a certain time, they are not learning.

I deal with each instance of lateness separately. Sometimes I say, "go warm yourself up," and return to the rest of the class. Other times, I tell them to take a breath and get themselves together, and then jump in where we are. And there are times where I give them an observational task, so that even if they cannot engage physically with the material, they are focused on learning.

Attendance and participation conclusion

Venet tells readers of *Equity-Centered Trauma-Informed Education*, "An overarching question to ask about any policy is, 'Does this support a culture of care or a culture of compliance'" (150)? I think this is especially true about attendance and participation, because this determines the culture students will expect and contribute to when they are in the room. Are they in class expecting to give and receive care, or having to give up their humanity and expect others to do the same? Rewriting our attendance and participation policies to "support a culture of care" can bolster students' sense of Expert Power and their feelings of inclusion safety. Both build students' trust in themselves and our class experiences so they can enter more freely into learning and risk-taking.

Practices in the syllabus: Setting the stage for learner safety

REFLECTION SECTION: Syllabus statements part 3

You may wish to complete this question with your own syllabus in hand.

Are there places in these policies where I have inadvertently been ableist? Neurotypical? Sexist? Hierarchical or authoritarian?

_____
_____
_____
_____
_____

Are there places in these policies where I have inadvertently made assumptions about students?

_____
_____
_____
_____
_____

Are there places in my syllabus or policies where I have inadvertently implied that work and worthiness as a human are intertwined?

_____
_____
_____
_____
_____

How could I address these inadvertent harms?

_____
_____
_____
_____
_____

Use the space below to examine and reimagine your syllabus. Some of the categories also appear other places, but you may have a new insight based on the above examples.

	What my syllabus currently says about:	How I might change this to encourage a level of psychological safety and/or Working Consent:
Attendance		
Participation		
Lateness		
Accessibility		
Privacy		
Priorities		
The humanity of students		
Accountability to ourselves and others		

Course outline or timeline

Part of consent-forward teaching is including as much information as possible, so people can make the choices that are best for them. I do this in a course outline. I have had two institutions in the past require this and some that have not. It is a feature of my syllabus, regardless, because of my focus on consent. My current outline in my syllabus looks like this:

> Below is the current anticipated work of our course*. Besides exploring movement and movement concepts in class, I will try to give you some time each week to simply handle "business"—prep large assignments, turn in assignments, give feedback, ask me questions as a group, etc.
>
> | Week number | Topic | Guiding questions we will be working to answer | What is assigned | What is due | Anything special about this week: a guest, a need for a certain item, a dress code change, etc. |
> |---|---|---|---|---|---|
> | | | | | | |
>
> * The contents of this outline are subject to change based on class interests and progress, and at the discretion of the instructor.

This format sets the stage for learner and contributor safeties.

I use the asterisk to reiterate to students that their interests and skills matter. If we need to take more time on a skill or topic because they need extra support or because it is really piquing their interest, we will! I remind students that the questions they bring to our work and around how the learning in class can support their artistic work are welcome. This is a space where it is safe to fail, learn, and question, and the schedule can accommodate all these realities. By offering that the schedule may change, I even challenge the structure of the class.

Important resources for learning

We are educators, not therapists or doctors. Our job does not include treating or diagnosing the people in our spaces. Instead, we can offer resources and life skills for the development of resilience, healthy coping, and personal expression. The last few pages of my syllabus include support resources for students. I believe one of the worst feelings in the world is knowing that you need help, but not knowing how to get it. Helplessness can feel overwhelming and providing a "one stop shop" where students can go to find assistance on a variety of issues can remove a lot of stress and/or embarrassment from the process of seeking help.

While syllabi traditionally include information like how to get support for academic writing and/or the registrar's and department chair's emails, I also try to include resources that support students not only as students, but as humans and artists. Venet writes, "connection means that we look to connect our students to the right people and resources for support, being humble that this may not be us" (117). In helping students access the resources they need to engage fully in learning, and decentering ourselves, we reinforce inclusion and learner safeties and students own Expert Power and agency. My current syllabus includes:

- Hotlines.
    - 988 and its website for mental health support.
- Title IX and important clarifications.
- Institutional support.
    - Writing and/or academic assistance.
    - Student services including:
        - Food insecurity assistance.
        - Housing assistance.
        - Health services.
- Local resources.
    - Food insecurity assistance.
    - Housing assistance.
    - For those experiencing domestic and/or sexualized violence.
- Industry.
    - Discounts.
    - Reporting.
    - Networking.

I provide some more details on some of these sections below.

Title IX

In the section regarding Title IX, I include the school-mandated information, as well as contact numbers and links. However, because of the Title IX rules that went into effect on July 1, 2024, I also include the following statement, adapted by Dr. Nicole Bedera,[12] a scholar and educator whose research focuses on campus sexual assault reporting, advocacy, and efficacy:

> All faculty and staff are now mandatory reporters. This means that if we learn about something that might be sex discrimination (e.g., sexual harassment, sexual assault, intimate partner violence, stalking, pregnancy discrimination, LGBTQ discrimination), then we must report what we know to the Title IX Office. Usually, reports will only leave a record of concern, but sometimes, a report can be escalated into an investigation without a victim's consent. Mandatory reporters are expected to share information learned in all settings, including during class activities, assignments, office hours, and outside of class. Please be thoughtful about what you disclose to me.
>
> How to Seek Help: Sex discrimination can impact your education. I recognize that you may need to seek help from me, even if you do not want to report. If you need assistance in class or help navigating available resources, you can always ask me. You do not need to tell me why you are asking for help for a friend, another student, or yourself. I will respect your privacy and I will help you.

In our discussion of this section, I make it clear to students that I will follow the law, as my position requires. I also point out the resources that can support them that do not include reporting.

Local and industry-specific resources

- I include a link to a spreadsheet I created of local support resources.
    - I initially created this as an intimacy professional, and often included it in my presentation resources for casts. However, I quickly realized how important this was for all folks to have at their fingertips.
    - I have not included this in this book, as mine are likely different than yours, but I encourage you to take the 15 minutes to make one if you can and share it with colleagues.
- I include industry-specific reporting tools[13] like:
    - Lighthouse Reporting for Actors' Equity.
    - SAG-AFTRA hotline.
    - AGMA hotline.
    - Theatre Advocacy Project hotline.
    - JDoe.

While JDoe is a third-party anonymous app that anyone can use, the others do have some restrictions. I include these here so that students are aware that not only is harassment and abuse illegal in school, but they are also illegal in the industry as well, and there are a variety of resources to deal with these issues.

Finally, the syllabus includes local industry organizations and groups that I feel students could benefit from. They may offer discount tickets, weekly newsletters of events including auditions, or networking opportunities. If I say I value community and belonging, that also means I must value the larger arts community and want students to be a part of it. Including this information is building community.

REFLECTION SECTION: Syllabus statements part 4

You may wish to complete these questions with your own syllabus in hand.

Are there places in these policies where I have inadvertently been ableist? Neurotypical? Sexist? Hierarchical or authoritarian?

_____
_____
_____
_____
_____

Are there places in these policies where I have inadvertently made assumptions about students?

_____
_____
_____
_____
_____

How could I address these inadvertent harms?

_____
_____
_____
_____
_____

Use the space below to examine and reimagine your syllabus. Some of the categories also appear at other places, but you may have a new insight based on the above examples.

	What my syllabus currently says about:	How I might change this to encourage a level of psychological safety and/or Working Consent:
Time and urgency		
Expectations		
What and how we learn		
Community		
The humanity of students		

Conclusion

Clarity on and clear communication of "the law of the situation" keeps a pedagogy of care from turning into a pedagogy of chaos. The work we are there to do, and the given context of its schedule, expectations, etc., remains—we simply believe and act like our students are fully equally human as they do it. Work parameters, like schedule and deadlines, are part of the work itself. If we have consented to be in the situation, we have also consented to the terms of the situation. For example, in class, on syllabus day, I say, "This is the situation in which we find ourselves: a graded ballet course at an academic institution. Therefore, there will be aesthetic and technical expectations according to the aesthetics of ballet, due dates, and accountability that in my role as teacher I must report back to the institution."

But, if the syllabus is truly going to be a guide to success, it must discuss more than the situation. It must lay bare the powers we all hold, share, and expect from each other. It must be inclusive, and it must promote psychological safety. Success that comes at the expense of mental, physical, or emotional well-being is not actually success. I have attempted to write all parts of my syllabus with student success, both in the class and in their lives, in mind. Womack writes, "Ability and independence, though, depend on accessible environments" (497). If we are truly looking for ways to be trauma-informed and consent-forward, so all students can practice their agency and power, accessibility is required.

Inclusion safety, because it values each person as they are, requires accommodation. I have heard teaching colleagues state that creating inclusion, even on the syllabus, does not provide rigor. Womack provides one of my favorite perspectives on this, "Inclusion and rigor are only incompatible opposites when rigor is defined as exclusion and inflexibility" (497). Unfortunately, what many educators call rigor is not inclusive.

I would consider my syllabus very rigorous; my approach to our learning structure and student success is well-examined and meticulous. The syllabus is long, usually around twenty pages, and thorough, because it includes all the above statements. Since I do go over the syllabus fully, as well as take the time to build Class Contracts and answer questions, all of which promote consent and psychological safety, "syllabus day" can sometimes turn into a day and a half or two days. But, by the end of this time, students are aware of the expectations I have of them, and they can have of me and each other. Our environment is not harsh, but it is exacting.

A rigorous syllabus and approach to syllabus day focused on creating as much student access and success as possible is a humanizing, inclusive, and care-full approach to teaching and learning. Taking this time could cause concern for a "loss of instruction time." Then, I recall Womack's words in her conclusion to "Teaching is Accommodation," "Time spent on inclusion is worth it educationally and ethically because learning depends on access" (521).

Despite this attempt at thoroughness, I have not always been able to include everything in my syllabus that I wanted to share with students because of institutional requirements. In the past, I have made additional documents with resources and uploaded them to the LMS. I have also simply worked statements into discussion. Taking the time to discuss the syllabus on day one (and sometimes into day two) allows for any or all of these scenarios.

You don't have to, and maybe even cannot, make every change or inclusion you'd like on your syllabus. You may disagree with some of my statements or know better ways to say them for your institution and/or students. Please do what is right for you and the students you work with.

REFLECTION SECTION: Syllabus statements part 5

What new insights do I have about my syllabus? About what my syllabus could be?

_____
_____
_____
_____
_____

If I am going to make some changes to my syllabus, who else do I need to talk to get information and/or permission?

_____
_____
_____
_____
_____

If things can't be added/changed in my syllabus in the ways I would like, do I have other methods of communicating these ideas to students?

_____
_____
_____
_____
_____

Chapter reminders

- A syllabus is a vision and values statement for class.
- A syllabus gives students a guide to success.
- Accessibility and inclusion start on day one and start on the syllabus.
- "Inclusion and rigor are only incompatible opposites when rigor is defined as exclusion and inflexibility."—Anne-Marie Womack
- "… learning depends on access."—Anne-Marie Womack
- You don't have to, and maybe even cannot, make every change or inclusion you'd like.

Notes

1. Linked in the "Resources" section.
2. Instructions for these are in Chapter 5.
3. Linked in the "Resources" section.
4. For lecture classes like Dance History or Dance Appreciation, that may be more susceptible to AI use, I have an entire lesson I present. It is linked in the "Resources" section for your reference, in case you may find it useful!
5. This policy was written in Fall 2023 and shared through the Fall 2024. By the time this manuscript reaches publication, the abilities and applications of AI may have changed. But I really hope this line remains true ….
6. Examples of these are provided in Chapter 9.
7. Learn more about this project from the link in the "Resources" section.
8. See also page 100.
9. For your syllabus you can use this statement or try the Resolution Pathway Guide given in the "Resource" section.
10. More on this in Chapter 9!
11. Chapter 9 deals exclusively with assessments and ungrading.
12. Her website, with many helpful documents, is linked in the "Resources" section.
13. All of these are linked in the "Resources" section, as well as information on how to use them.

7
Practices in class: Structure, language, and experiences for learner safety and beyond

The daily business of class is where "the rubber meets the road" for all the grand visions in our syllabus and pedagogic theories. The first day of class sets the tone for the semester, but it is the everyday occurrences that create or destroy students' sense of inclusion and learner safeties or their experience of care. In the introduction to his book *Care Aesthetics*, James Thompson (2023) writes:

> Care aesthetics is an idea that makes a double claim. …. It argues that we need to think how the making of art can be an act of care. Care is not a context, a theme or a set of protocols governing practice. Instead, … through the process of working with people, materials, and places, care happens: as a game is played or as we rehearse and stage a performance, care takes place. The second claim flips this first one. It says that caring, … can be an aesthetic practice: that is, it has a certain craft and involves the creation of sensory, embodied experiences. (12)

The structures and practices that make up our regular learning environment demonstrate our commitment to consent-forward, trauma-informed teaching and student success. How each class starts, how each student is addressed, and how much choice is available during a class can provide psychological safety for students in the risky acts of learning and creating. This chapter will offer practices to support a care-full pedagogy in each of those areas.

Starting class with check-ins

When I teach workshops on consent-forward practices for classes and rehearsals, a daily check-in is the first tool I offer. In class, we often have this time built in to take attendance, but a check-in expands that to serve several purposes:

- Gauge the energy level and needs in the room.
- Ask students to begin class in touch with their bodies and boundaries and develop their somatic awareness.

DOI: 10.4324/9781003596301-10

- Provide context for the day for students to make informed choices around their boundaries.

Check-in for building somatic awareness

I begin the check-in process by providing two-ish minutes for students to make a choice about what they need somatically to be able to enter class. The time is a bit arbitrary; sometimes I give the length of whatever song is playing, sometimes I set a timer. I find two minutes is good because it allows time for students to settle and tune into their bodies, but not so much that I will run out of time at the end of class.

Drawn from the work of Molly W. Schenck, particularly her Autonomic Color Wheel workshop and *Trauma-Informed Teaching Practices for Dance Educators* (2023) book, I ask students to decide if they need something to bring their "energy up" or their "energy down," so that they can best engage in learning. They then spend this time giving themselves what they need. The goal of the somatic check-in is to engage in an activity that will help bring awareness to their bodies, regulate their nervous systems, and allow them to work in class with presence and attention.

During the first week of class, I share with students a brief overview of trauma, overstimulation, and stress, and how they affect the body. My goal is not to provide a deep scientific grounding for trauma and/or regulation work, but to resource students for addressing their own needs.

I give examples of situations in which they might want to bring their energy up, like, this is their first class of the day, the class is right after lunch, or they feel sluggish or less focused. My examples for times when they might want to bring their energy down are they got up late and/or couldn't find parking and had to rush here, they just had a fight with a loved one, or they are feeling scattered or distracted.

In the first few weeks of class I offer one exercise each day for "energy up" and one of "energy down."

Energy Up Exercises	Energy Down Exercises
Walk around the room at a brisk tempo, trying to take up space and bring your heart rate up.	Walk around the room at a slow tempo, really noticing your body and/or the space.
Pilates 100	5-4-3-2-1 grounding tool[1]
Dance burpees	Sit and breathe; maybe include a mantra or goal for class.

After providing these examples, I remind students that they know a lot of exercises and movement practices that would fit one of these categories. Beginning in week 3, students are left to choose how to spend these two minutes for themselves.

This somatic check-in builds inclusion safety, as students know that their full selves and experiences are welcome in class. They learn to appreciate their bodies and the differences in needs in their own bodies and those of others from day to day. Their power within and power to are reinforced as they connect to themselves and make choices to address their needs. It lays the groundwork for learner safety, as this time helps prepare us all to enter the work we are going to do together. In addition, because it is two minutes at the top of class, it creates a little grace period for people to be a few minutes late and not miss class content.

Check-in for context

After the timer goes off from students' individual somatic check-in, we move to a group check-in for class. I use this time to take attendance and to tell students where we are going in class today. I do not take attendance by just calling student names and having them respond "here," instead I use provocative questions. In the first few weeks of class, I use "icebreaker"-like check-in questions[2] to help build inclusion safety as everyone gets to be heard and students (and me!) get to know everyone else in the room as people, not just as dancers or actors and students. These personal questions are also great later in the semester when we are all getting a little tired and need something fun to jumpstart the class. Other frequent check-in questions are "Tell me something you are still carrying with you from the last class," or "Is there a question you have from the last class?"

Between their answers and the choices they made during the somatic check-in, I can get a pretty good sense of the energy level and needs of the room. Sometimes that leads me to modify the plan of the day, or simply address what I am noticing, as we move into the next section of our check-in, providing the layout of class. This usually sounds like:

- "In our last class we ...."
- "So today we will ...."

OR

- "Today, the plan was .... But because I'm noticing .... We're going to ...."

THEN

- "By starting with …."
- "Then …."
- "And by the end, we will …."

Being able to share this information at the top of class does mean that I have spent time planning my class, and that I am willing to let that plan go to better serve the students. This sharing supports neurodiverse learners who need a sense of security from the ability to plan. This time also allows for students to consider boundaries around the content of the class. If touch or contact are planned to occur, they can then make choices that meet their needs.

Check-in for boundaries and establishing communication

We discussed in Chapter 4 that consent requires information, and we can best know, state, and hold our boundaries when we have complete information. So, the above step provides a critical foundation for students being able to communicate their boundaries and needs for class. This communication can be incorporated as part of a check-in process, via props or discussion.

Props for boundary communication

When I was still using corrective touch in teaching,[3] I used props to help students quickly communicate their interest in receiving corrective touch that day. Perhaps you have seen a picture on social media at back-to-school time of green, yellow, and red rubber bracelets that students can pick up in class to show that they want contact (green), do not want contact (red), or are open to it with a discussion (yellow). I have also seen photos of buttons with "yes" and "no" on them. These may be a great choice for your class.

I used Yes/No Cards.[4] I was teaching middle and high school students at the time I developed these tools. I made two versions: cardstock 5 × 7 cards that students could put on the floor either in our Check-In Circle or at their spot on the floor, and foam door hangers, with a slit cut at the knob opening, so it could hang over the ballet barre. I had these in a basket or bag at the door, and students grabbed one on the way in. Both the cards and the barre hangers had "yes" on one side and "no" on the other with pretty designs.

It was important that "yes" and "no" looked the same, so there was no aesthetic reward or punishment in choosing one over the other. The options are also on the same object so that students could change their minds with ease. If they were on different cards, students would have to miss part of an exercise to go change and may even feel exposed in making a change. Part of enabling consent is ensuring that "no" is an equally valid option to "yes." My design choices for the cards were made to make either choice feel equally available.

The cards foster autonomy and consent, as well as inclusion and learner safeties. Students were reminded every day that their bodies and boundaries were important to their learning, and that this was a space where they should expect their bodies and boundaries to be treated with respect.

Dialogue for boundary communication

Now, I use this time to set up dialogue for students with each other around boundaries and needs. If I mentioned earlier in the flow of the day that an exercise may use contact or touch, I ask students to consider how they feel about that and then have a boundary conversation[5] (which we have already practiced) with a partner they will work with during that time. I may also remind them of the baseline boundaries we have set as a class, so that the boundary conversations can be as focused as possible.

While I, as the teacher, have given permission for contact, only the two people doing the action can have consent. By providing time and context for student conversations around touch, boundaries, and consent, they can practice their power within and to. Inclusion and learner safeties are built as their needs are respected so that they can engage fully in the learning process.

REFLECTION SECTION: Check-ins

Do I already have a typical Check-in process for class?

_____
_____
_____
_____

How does the Check-in build Somatic Awareness? Provide context?

_____
_____
_____
_____

Does this Check-in provide time for consideration and discussion of boundaries and consent?

_____
_____
_____
_____

Which part of the Check-in process would I like to add/build more? How will this support inclusion and/or learner safety in my class(es)?

_____
_____
_____
_____

Language

As I sought to add consent-forward and trauma-informed practices to my classes, I quickly realized that my language had to change as well. Removing "you guys" as well as "ladies" (often in dance classes) required slowing down and being conscious of my speech. I believe my switch to "folks" and "dancers" is much more inclusive. Other gender-neutral greetings like "y'all" also foster belonging. Other language that builds inclusion safety is using students' proper pronouns.

Language for learning and contributing

I have shifted my language during the giving of directions for combinations or experiments. I have tried to remove cues that would encourage a student to say "yes" to me, like adding an "OK?" or "Right?" to the end of a statement or set of instructions.

This is one I struggle with, as "right" tends to be a filler word for me, but also a way to check in with students and see if they are following. I am working to eradicate this, particularly in lecture settings. I aim to ask more open-ended and engaging questions. Like we discussed with boundaries, students are conditioned through power dynamics to respond in the positive and we move on, without discussion or addressing any questions they may have.

Instead, I try to ask, at the end of a lengthy description of a theory or a set of instructions, "What questions do we have about this/these?" This implies that I expect there are questions. This phrasing is purposeful, as it:

- Gives students permission to ask. I do not say, "Do we have any questions?" but "What questions do we have?" This phrasing implies questions are expected.
- Demonstrates my willingness to be wrong and learn in front of students. If I assume that there are questions, I am also assuming that I did not provide the information or instructions perfectly to everyone.

With this phrasing I ask for learner safety from the class, while at the same time, extending it to them.

Language for equity and collaboration

Another way to consider language is in terms of possession or bodily control of student collaborators. Possession, rather than collaboration, is a practice of colonialism, as well as a denial of autonomy. "My dancers," "my students," etc., deny the agency of the student collaborators in our spaces. Directors and choreographers often use similarly possessive pronouns. These phrases do not acknowledge the Power Within or Power To of others.

We should encourage students to try their own choices, or to seek knowledge from a different genre of movement or a different teacher. We cannot both possess students and see them as equal collaborators, with their own power, agency, and creative choices. A challenging, yet effective mindset shift can occur when we acknowledge full humanity by leaving out ownership and simply speaking of/to them as dancers, students, performers, etc. By relinquishing our "ownership" of students, we also release a belief that our way is the right or best way. I have tried in this text and its reflection questions to remove possessive language around people, to help reinforce this concept.

Language for context and decolonization

Language also plays a role in colonization and erasure of marginalized people, and this shows up in the movement classroom as well. I have worked concertedly over the past few years to remove a reliance on ballet terminology from the Modern, Jazz, and Movement for Actors classes I teach.

Ballet is an imperialist, kyriarchical art form and is structured as such. But "ballet vocabulary" is not the same as "dance vocabulary," and by diversifying how I speak about movement, I can help create inclusion and learner safety in the classroom.

Modern dance was created to be the antithesis of ballet. Its early concern was with personal expression and exploration, rather than adherence to rules or a previously held structure. And yet, many modern choreographers did use ballet steps and vocabulary in their work. I have chosen not to, whenever possible.

In Modern classes, I use anatomical actions, describing a plié-like movement as "hip flexion, knee flexion, ankle flexion", or a tendu-like movement as "stretching the leg from the glutes through the toes." Since I teach somatics-based modern, the emphasis is on the body of the dancer, so the anatomical language also upholds the goal of helping dancers connect to their bodies. If I was teaching a specific technique, different vocabulary may need to appear to honor the creator. As modern dance is also about the dancer's inner life, I also use a lot of imagistic language, as well as asking students to notice sensations, rather than outside form.

Jazz dance developed from social and ritual dances of enslaved African people in the Americas who had to use movement and music to communicate with each other, because they did not always share the same verbal language (Guarino and Oliver 2015, xv). It did not grow out of ballet, as is sometimes assumed by students (and I'm sure some teachers!). In Jazz class, we spend the first two weeks of class looking at historical African American dance steps and discussing jazz dance's musical and social roots. I emphasize the importance of relationship, to both music and other people, to truly call a dance a jazz dance. These concepts are often different from how students have experienced Jazz in a studio setting.

Brenda Dixon Gottschild's *Digging the Africanist Presence in American Performance: Dance and Other Contexts* (1996) as well as Lindsey Guarino and Wendy Oliver's *Jazz Dance: A History of the Roots and Branches*[5] (2015) provide much more context on why language in jazz is important and how to speak of movement in Jazz class. Fusion forms like musical theatre jazz and lyrical jazz did borrow ballet steps and terms, and so I use ballet terms where appropriate when teaching these styles. Latin jazz uses vocabulary from Latin dance, and I use these terms where appropriate if I am teaching this genre.

Martial arts, often incorporated in Movement for Actors or Stage Combat classes, far predates codified ballet. Yet even in these settings, I have heard ballet vocabulary.[6] I suspect some of this comes from a desire to make it choreographed, so students understand we are learning these movements for the stage, not actually engaging fully in the discipline, and so we use "dance terms." But reducing "dance" to ballet vocabulary is inappropriate, ahistorical, and Eurocentric. Reducing the rich traditions, cultures, histories, and vocabularies of different martial art forms to ballet terms erases important cultural representation and context of nonwestern movement forms.

Honoring the true roots of movement styles like jazz dance or martial arts is important for building inclusion safety for students who find their culture represented in those forms. Dance and theatre in the academic sphere tend to be biased towards European techniques and traditions. Using language to support the bodies and peoples in our spaces, and that are specific to cultures, aesthetics, and histories that influence our movement builds inclusion safety. As we demonstrate respect for traditions and offer appropriate context and representation, we encourage students to do the same.

I am transparent with students about why I do not solely use ballet terminology in these classes, as it is often a huge shift from how dance classes are often experienced in a commercial studio setting. While the language adjustment was initially challenging, and there are still times I struggle (I cannot find a concise, yet descriptive alternative for pirouette in Jazz or Modern, for example), it has become a normal part of class instruction for me. When I share with students my struggles with the vocabulary, or say, "In Ballet, we call this _____, and I can't find a good way to communicate this yet in this class," I demonstrate that I am experiencing learner safety in our class. I know that this is a space where I can risk being vulnerable, and even "failing" at the task of communicating the way I would like. Changing the traditional vocabulary is also an example of contributor and challenger safeties, as I bring my own ideas and descriptions to challenge the typical dance vocabulary that stems from ballet. I hope that my demonstration of these higher levels of psychological safety encourages them to risk and create.

Sandra Styres (2019), a Canadian educator of Indigenous, French, and English descent, quotes Marie Battiste (2013), an Indigenous scholar focused on protecting and promoting Indigenous knowledge systems and education, "in order to effect change, educators must help students understand the Eurocentric assumptions of superiority within the context of history and to recognize the continued dominance of these assumptions in all forms of contemporary knowledge" ([186] 33). Tuck and Yang, in their foundational text on decolonization, "Decolonization is Not a Metaphor," write, "The settler positions himself as both superior and normal ..." (2012, 6), and this is often what happens to ballet in dance studio settings—it is considered a baseline for other genres, rather than its own form, drawn from its own cultural context. In every class, students are encouraged to find the appropriate cultural context from which to consider their situation, and our class.

REFLECTION SECTION: Language

How do I already practice inclusion safety in my language? How can I offer more inclusion through my language?

_____
_____
_____
_____

Where is my vocabulary not supporting students' Power Within or Power To?

_____
_____
_____
_____

Where can my language encourage questions or demonstrate my own willingness to be wrong?

_____
_____
_____
_____

How do I already offer cultural and historical context through my language? How can I offer more?

_____
_____
_____
_____

Choice

Often, in our classrooms, we settle for inclusion or learning, but we could be offering opportunities for, in the words of Timothy Clark, "contribute to" or "challenge" the structure in which learning is done (2020, ix). In other words, we can offer students opportunities to make choices around how they learn and how they demonstrate their learning, as well as, as "the law of the situation" allows, what they learn and what is valuable to them about their learning.

As I mentioned in Chapter 3, no one chooses trauma. So, each opportunity to make a choice, even around seemingly insignificant scenarios such as: is the turn a double or a triple, selecting your own scene partner, whether the rehearsal room door is open or closed, is an opportunity to experience agency and autonomy.

Differing modes of engagement

In workshops, when teachers express concern that students will use choice to opt out of experiences, I remind them that that is not the offering. According to Follett's "law of the situation," we have all agreed to be here, and do this work (Ballet class, Acting class, rehearsal, etc.). Therefore, the care-full pedagogic tools, like choice making, are to help students stay engaged in the work and/or the learning outcomes, in ways that are accessible to them.

A tool I use to help keep students involved in and contributing to the process of learning is "Zones of Participation" (ZoPs), which I learned from Colleen Hughes and Cara Rawlings in a class called "Consent in the K-12 Classroom[7]" at Intimacy Directors and Coordinators in 2020. ZoPs offer students different modes of engagement, while still staying connected to the work to be done. This choice allows for different learning and communicating styles and meets the 2024 CAST Universal Design for Learning Guidelines for "Multiple Means of Engagement." These choices are also a way to bring Working Consent into the classroom.

These offerings may look like,

- You can be an Active Observer during this movement experiment, observing for Energy, Levels, etc.
- You can be an Active Participant, and choose to perform the movement solo, with a partner, or in a group.
- You can be the DJ, timekeeper, prop person, or participate in other tasks that will support the experience.

Teachers in high school or middle school theatre will recognize the modes of engagement structure as ways to involve folks in performance who are not ready to be, or interested in being, onstage. By giving them experiences as crew, understudies, marketing and promotions assistants, and/or front of house staff, students stay engaged in the work to be done.

If the goal of the experience is learning, I want students to be in the room and engaged in the activity in a way that keeps them focused on the learning outcome. That does not mean they all need to be doing the thing, in the same way. For example, if I want Modern students to understand weight shifts and weight sharing, I can provide options for them to experience that:

- Back-to-back with a partner.
- Back to a wall and sliding down and up.
- Using an exercise ball.
- By observing all these different performances and noticing what is happening in the bodies performing, and in their own bodies, as weight shifts and shares.

Movement for Actors students working on incorporating physical concepts with a monologue may be given the opportunity to:

- Perform for the whole class.
- Perform for a small group.
- Perform for a partner.
- Perform just for me.
- Record their performance and share with me.

All students gain a better understanding of the concept and meet the expectations of the class, yet no one was asked to participate in actions that felt unsafe to them.

As another example, when I do the "yes/no game," sometimes called "The Consent Circle," in boundary and consent lessons, I offer that participants can be an "active game player" or an "active game observer." I then explain that a "player" follows the directions given for the game, and that an "observer" is to note their own somatic response to the answers given in the game, as well as count the total number of "nos" stated. I offer these options as equal and valid ways to engage in game; that is, I don't wait until someone opts out of gameplay to give them a task. I know that the goal of this game is to notice how difficult it can be to say "no," even in a low-stakes situation, and have crafted multiple ways for participants to experience that learning. We could apply similar options to many in-class exercises, including when a student must sit out due to an injury.

Choice in practice

Choice making is a time for students to experience learner safety, as they claim what they know, or what they are working on. It also gives students an opportunity to engage in Working Consent. In terms of practicality, I do not offer choices on every single exercise. Instead, I ensure that each section of class (the check-in, the warm-up, the technique work, the combination, the cool-down, and the check-out), has at least one opportunity for students to make a choice.

I have chosen to structure class this way for several reasons; including time and efficiency. However, the biggest one is relationships. Students likely have, for the previous nearly two decades of their lives, experienced both academic and dance and/or theatre settings that were highly structured, even to the point of authoritarianism. To completely upend that familiarity would likely cause them to not trust me, in terms of their academic rigor and physical safety. By balancing structure with freedom, their trust in me is allowed to develop, as well as their trust in their own embodied knowledge and creativity. Their trust in the class ensemble as a place where they can take risks and belong also increases. Some of these options for choice making are detailed below.

Warm-up choices

The warm-up follows the check-ins discussed above, which are practices with a lot of choice making for students. Because of this, and because my warm-up is geared towards that day's content, choices tend to be limited, so that I know students are physically prepared for the work ahead, whether we are in a dance technique class or a Movement for Actors course. However, I do encourage them in this time to modify levels or intensities to support injury or illness. I also give them time at the end to stretch or move in a way I didn't offer them that they feel they need. In these ways, students demonstrate their knowledge of their own body and its needs.

Technique instruction choices

During times of dance technique instruction, choice may look like giving the option for students to do a balance instead of a turn, choose the number of turns they attempt, or leave out the arms on a complex footwork pattern.

In all types of movement classes, I can remind students they can adjust levels in space to protect knees and backs, have boundaries, and/or make or request modifications.

By asking students to make choices early in the class, during check-ins, warm-ups, and technique instruction, I am asking them to listen to their body, and to claim their knowledge about it. Class is not just about "showing what you know" in terms of steps, rather, students are asked to demonstrate their embodied knowledge of self. I remind students that this means that they *should* be making different choices every day, because our bodies are different every day. The triple turn is not rewarded because it's "harder;" listening to the body and making the appropriate choice for the day is the goal. Students are encouraged to know their bodies and to know their own learning goals.

Choice in combinations/movement demonstration

As they execute movement and movement concepts, in both Movement for Actors and dance technique, I may offer students choices around how they apply their Effort Energy,[8] i.e., *Will the movement be Strong or Light? Free or Bound?* For challenging combinations in dance technique, I often give choices around tempo, i.e., *group Lemon will perform at tempo, group Lime will perform at half speed*. A basic choice early in the semester, or with beginning dancers may be *choose a shape to start or end the combination*. Students in Movement for Actors may be given a structure such as, *include two movements from today's warm-up or movement drills that you enjoyed or that you want to work on more*, or *include at least four different types of locomotors in four counts of eight*.

This is a time of learner safety as students in any class demonstrate their embodied knowledge or choose to work towards more. I try to encourage both versions of work as valid, worthwhile, and safe, with prompts like "include a movement that felt successful and one that felt challenging" or "what do you know about this type of movement and what is a question you still have about it."

A significant choice that impacts students' sense of safety is whether to share their work. Sharing requires vulnerability and not every student may be ready for this risk. Choices can be made in combinations everyone is doing at once, with me as the only observer. Or I may say, "would you like to show each other your choices," and leave the performance as a consent-based opt-in. This is also an excellent time for "pair and share," so students share with just one other person, rather than the whole class.

Under the next section, "Choice as Practicing Power To or Bodily Autonomy," I offer directions for specific movement exercises created for students to move beyond learner safety, and into contributor and challenger safeties with their movement choices.

Choice in cool-down/check-out

In both dance and movement classes, as we reach the cool-down, like the end of the warm-up, I leave time for students to include a stretch or movement they feel their body needs in the moment, that I didn't offer them. Finally, students check-out with the option to share something from class they are thinking about/working on. Schenck encourages a check-out as a partner to a check-in. In her *Trauma-Informed Teaching Practices*, she asks students to notice where they are, as compared to where they were. I still struggle with having that check-out time available in each class. It is part of my own work in creating learner safety to make this a more consistent part of class.

Choice as practicing Power To and bodily autonomy

Personal power should be experienced by students in dance and theatre classes in their bodies. Yet, bodily autonomy and personal agency are issues in dance and theatre performance, because teachers often exercise bodily control over students, in the name of modeling the discipline and/or technical precision. This authoritarian method of teaching denies students agency, consent, and power and does not offer inclusion or learner safeties.

There are some exercises I come back to in nearly every class I teach, because they provide opportunities for students to experience their own power and autonomy, which connects to the higher levels of psychological safety, contributor and challenger safeties. These are included below.

Experiments for building confidence in embodied knowledge and contributor safety

My most frequent studio exercise, regardless of the genre I'm teaching, is a "movement experiment." Since my syllabus calls our class "a lab," frequent "experiments" fit our language. Experiments are a chance to try something, based on existing knowledge, to make a new discovery. Sometimes they fail, sometimes they soar; however it works out, we learn.

Experiments are an opportunity for students to demonstrate current embodied knowledge or deepen it. I create the structure and ask students to bring their own ideas to it. Everyone has the same assignment, but the opportunity to interpret it as they desire; students can be creative and share what they know. I ask them to consider creating movement to fulfill the assignment from a variety of sources: *something they enjoyed doing in class and want to experience again, something that was challenging during class and they'd like another chance to review it, something they know and I didn't offer in class*, or *a creative way they've thought of to apply their knowledge and want to see if it works*. All of these are valid reasons to move. They are asked to be purposeful in their embodied learning.

- Ballet
  My Ballet classes are structured around exploring the elemental movements of the genre (*plier, relever, etendre, glisser, sauter, tourner, elancer*)[9] in ways appropriate to the class level. Two weeks are spent on each verb. Students are asked at the end of class (at least once a week) to complete the combination.

  In the first few classes, students are asked to complete counts seven and eight of a movement phrase with a pose or shape. Since our first two words are *plier* and *relever*, this works out well. Many ballet students are not used to being asked to improvise or create. Starting with shapes drawn from vocabulary they are familiar with can help them quickly build their confidence and feel safety in contributing their embodied knowledge to the class.

  As the semester progresses, I ask students to experiment more. They add a full 8-count phrase, and sometimes two, to the combination I've started, with the focus on the term we are exploring.

- Jazz
  The "experiments" in Jazz class are structured very similarly to those in ballet. In this class, I ask students to create movement that matches the style of my combination and demonstrates the concept we are focusing on during that two-week segment, (Contrariety, Polycentrism/Polyrhythm, High-affect Juxtaposition, Ephebism, or Cool), drawn from Chapter 2 of *Digging the Africanist Presence in American Performance: Dance and Other Contexts* by Brenda Dixon Gottschild (1996). We spend two weeks on each concept: we start with them adding two

counts to my six and work our way to them adding one or two eight-count phrases.

- Movement for Actors
  Movement for Actors, as I teach it, is a Laban/Bartenieff derived course. I regularly ask students to experiment with the different categories of movement. One specific example, early in the semester, uses Laban's Shape Forms with basic locomotor movements (walking, running, skipping, hopping, leaping, galloping, creeping, crawling). Students choose a character from any source (book, play, movie, etc.) and create the following phrase for them: enter with a locomotor, make a Shape Form, exit with a different locomotor. The experiment is repeated with a different structure: start in a Shape Form, locomote around the space, end in a different Shape Form. While the movement combinations come directly from the students, the structure of the experiment provides safety in its limited choices.

These experiments are designed for students to experience contributor safety. Engaging in these experiments requires that students feel included, and that risk and failure are acceptable. Their creative interpretations, their varied purposes, and their efforts are witnessed and held equally valid and worthwhile attempts at demonstrating or deepening knowledge.

Part of the safety structure for the experiments described includes gradually increasing the risk-level of sharing. When experiments are first engaged in, students do them in small groups in either an across the floor exercise or movement combination. While they are performing individually created movements, they are not performing their created movement alone. When students are asked to perform created movement alone, they share first with a partner or in a small group. Finally, students share individually created and performed movement with the whole class.

Movement creation class experiment for fostering consent, bodily autonomy, and challenger safety

In Modern class we examine somatics as a way of knowing ourselves, in a choreography/composition course we use the body as the inspiration for movement, and in Movement for Actors we explore the movement potential of our bodies. In all these classes, I ask students to name the metaphors and images they know for the body. Answers range from "a temple" and "an instrument," to "brain taxi" and "meat puppet," to *Star Trek: The Next Generation's* (1988) "ugly, giant bags of mostly water." These and other derogatory or objectifying phrases are how we often speak about and perceive our bodies.

I ask students to consider that many of the metaphors, idioms, and/or images we discuss put the body into object status, subjected either to their own mind, as the body is described as less valuable than thought or intellect, or to me, as an authority figure.[10]

An instrument or tool serves a purpose outside of themselves. They are also meant to be used by others; left on their own, they are not functional. A temple, while a place to attend to your spirit, delineates the body as separate from spirit. I invite them to think about what it might be like to be with and of their bodies, technically, expressively, and functionally.

We also discuss different cultural values on bodies, or body parts. These differing values can make it challenging to be present in our bodies and to be vulnerable in this movement space together. Through these conversations, we see the cultural implications and values of bodies through the language we use every day. And, by naming them, we are all able to examine if they are what we truly believe about bodies, and particularly the bodies we are in.

After discussion, we progress to the movement work. Scattered around the room on slips of paper, are idioms, metaphors, and imagistic language regarding the body.[11] I ask students to go find one that speaks to them—maybe the body part mentioned piques their interest, perhaps the meaning behind the phrase is relevant to them, or maybe it evokes a memory—and create movement not from the words on the slip, but the story it holds for them.

This is an early exercise (week two or three in Movement for Actors and Choreography/Composition, and about halfway through the semester in a Modern class) for students to begin bringing their own meaning-making to their movement choices.[12] It also reinforces their bodily knowing and bodily autonomy. This exercise is meant to be an experience of challenger safety as students design their own movement, based on their own meaning-making. Some are also challenging the messages they have received about bodies, from their family or society.

Having a conversation about bodies can be seen as an opportunity to build and experience challenger safety, as well as inclusion safety, as these conversations bring up individual emotions and experiences, as well as cultural and societal norms and expectations. Navigating and guiding these types of conversations can be tricky as an educator but can also build a deep appreciation and understanding between students of their different experiences and values.

Final thoughts on incorporating choice

I bring us back to the brilliant mantra of Felicia Rose Chavez once again:

> Every student deserves the opportunity to trust their creative impulse. Every student deserves the opportunity to exercise their own authentic voice. Every student deserves the opportunity to uphold their convictions. (132)

The experiments described above for movement classes are ways for students to explore different choices so they can find what they believe in, what they want to express, and what they want to create, and why. Isn't this the purpose of learning?

REFLECTION SECTION: Choice

Where/how do I already encourage choice-making in class?

Think of a lesson you teach consistently.

What is the objective of the lesson/what do I want students to leave understanding or embodying?

What are at least two other Zones of Participation a student could be in, or modifications I could offer, so that all students, regardless of needs, could gain this knowledge?

What choices do I offer that build beyond learner safety to contributor or challenger safeties?

One choice I can offer in each section of class is:

Check-in	Warm-up	Technique drills	Combination	Cool-down	Check-out

Conclusion

I recognize that you may be experiencing resistance to creating these changes, as changing our language and/or routines, and offering choices within exercises or experiences requires time and creativity. This may mean reexamining methods that have "worked" for decades. However, I find that time and creativity, willingly invested in the psychological safety of students, leads to deeper learning. I am brought back again to Clark's declaration, "if you make any excuse for not extending psychological safety, you're choosing to value something else more than human beings" (123–4). As care-full educators, we must humanize our pedagogy.

None of these offerings for establishing learner safety—check-ins, inclusive language, and choices—are ground-breaking pedagogic tools. And yet, for many students, this may be the first time they have been asked to communicate their needs, think about context, or contribute their own embodied knowledge or creativity to their learning, particularly in a routine, rather than in a one-off way. For students who have experienced trauma, particularly at the hands of teachers or creative leaders, these moments of ownership are key to their senses of safety and belonging. Chavez describes the process as, "By equipping them with choice ... and with craft ... and with the freedom to risk-take ... [students] demonstrated curiosity, inquiring, and a journey of thinking ..." (102). With the ability to gain new perspectives, risk, fail, learn, and grow, students have opportunities to practice their power and see the impacts of their power on their world.

Chapter reminders

- Check-ins:
    o Gauge the energy level and needs in the room.
    o Ask students to begin class in touch with their bodies and boundaries, and develop their somatic awareness.
    o Provide context for the day for students to make informed choices around their boundaries.
- Language of possession is not language of collaboration.
- Language that includes proper cultural and historical contexts creates inclusion and learner safeties and demonstrates challenger safety.
- Each opportunity to make a choice, even around seemingly insignificant scenarios, is an opportunity to experience agency and autonomy.
- Choice making is a time for students to experience learner safety, as they claim what they know, or what they are working on.

- Changing our language and offering choices within exercises or experiences requires time and creativity.
- "If you make any excuse for not extending psychological safety, you're choosing to value something else more than human beings."—Timothy R. Clark.

Notes

1. See full instructions for this tool in the "Resources" section.
2. A full check-in question list is available in the "Resources" section.
3. I no longer use touch when I teach. Touch is addressed in depth in Chapter 8.
4. The template for these is found in the "Resources" section.
5. For a deep discussion on jazz history and lineage, please see Guarino's books. Both are included in the "Resources" section.
6. However, if the combat being taught is fencing (or sword work drawn from fencing), which is French, the vocabulary is appropriate.
7. Unfortunately, this class is no longer available publicly. However, Hughes and Rawlings are currently writing a book based on this class. Be on the lookout for it if you are interested in more K-12 applications of consent-forward work.
8. Laban/Bartenieff terms are capitalized in this book, as according to the System.
9. For more on teaching ballet in this way, see *Creative Ballet Teaching* by Cadence Whittier. Full citation is in the "Resources" section.
10. This conversation and its resulting exercise were sparked by a conversation with Laban/Bartenieff Movement Analyst colleagues Halie Bahr and Sara Donahue.
11. See my list in the "Resources" section.
12. Having done the Story People and Observational exercises prior to entering this discussion and exercise is helpful for healthy dialogue.

8
Practices in class: Touch and contact

The ethics and practices of teaching with(out) touch

In the first section of the book, as we looked at the intersections of power with trauma, consent, and psychological safety, you likely realized that students have a difficult time saying "no" to a teacher because of the power dynamics at play. Touch can heighten these pressures, as contact brings the instructor into the personal space of the student. Because of this, they may feel the dynamics of Expert, Legitimate, and/or Reward Powers more tangibly. Touch as a teaching method, in both dance and theatre, calls for care-full pedagogy, as it deeply affects psychological safety. It is also perhaps the most obvious place to incorporate Working Consent in the movement classroom.

Students bring with them past experiences with dance and movement teachers' treatment of their bodies. Some have positive ones, in which educators deftly guided their bodies to new shapes, validated their boundaries, and/or honored embodied difference. However, some students bring with them traumatic memories of physical manipulation or abuse, negative comments on their bodies' shapes, sizes, etc. Some have had their physical boundaries violated by a teacher or experienced a teacher encouraging another student to violate their boundaries in a partnering exercise. This may lead them to being on "high alert" for unwelcome touch in a movement class and give them less energy to put toward learning. A simple awareness of the facts that not all students will learn through touch, and some may even be harmed by it, is reason enough to explore alternatives.

Even a successful use of touch in instruction has harmful potential, because of the power a teacher holds. Venet cautions, "Putting on hands on students in any way can cause long-lasting distress" (2021, 37). In Alfred J. Deikman's examination of cult thought and behavior in America he writes, "By promoting the idea that the leader or the in-group have special information and expertise, they remove themselves from criticism ..." (1990, 145). Edmonson agrees, "Excessive confidence in authority is a risk factor in psychological and physical safety" (2019, 97).

A touch from a teacher that results in correct execution or alignment may leave a student feeling that their instructor has "magic hands," imbuing them with a level of other worldly power that has potential for abuse. A touch that creates change, coupled with the endorphins of exercise, could also heighten a teacher's power to make a student feel "successful" or "good." These situations may make a student less likely to speak out when boundaries are violated or power abuses happen, because of the sense that those may be the "price to pay" for training with this teacher and/or gaining success. Even without the potential for abuse of power that exists in touch, if a student credits the teacher's touch with the change, they may abdicate their own agency in their education or feel unable to apply corrections or their own creative thoughts without an accompanying touch, creating a learning process centered on the instructor.

Even if a change occurs while a teacher's hands are on them, that does not mean the student has learned how to support their body in the new pattern of movement. A former student in a Jazz dance class wrote to me about her experience of learning via verbal cues and body sensations, rather than from corrective touch, "Describing not just how the movement should look, but how it should feel, gave me a frame of reference that I could keep coming back to instead of a momentary fix." Embodied sensations can provide "proof" to the student of their own learning, as it was a barometer for their ongoing progress, which is how they measure success in the classes I teach.

I have been teaching dance and movement for about twenty years. When I started, I taught as I had been taught—hands-on. However, once I began intimacy professional training, the complexities of touch and contact were exposed not only as an often-unexamined tradition, but as issues of power and consent.

After my first introduction to staged intimacy work in 2018, I began asking for consent to touch students. I made a concerted effort to ask in open-ended ways, like, "How would you feel if I ...", rather than putting an assumption of availability in the question with a phrase like, "Is it OK if ...." As time went on, I also tried to get very specific in the ask, with questions like, "How would you feel if I used the back of my hand to bring your elbow up into second position, since that is what the aesthetic of ballet is asking of us?" However, students likely still felt the pressure to agree to the touch because of the power dynamics of the teacher/student relationship. Now, in my teaching practice, I only use touch when it is requested by students (see the syllabus language on page 193).

In 2012, Fiona Bannon, a UK-based dance educator and researcher published her study of touch in UK dance spaces, as *Relational Ethics: Dance, Touch, and Learning*. In it, she states:

> The argument made clear in this study is that if we, as educators, diminish or become fearful and so do not teach with touch, we devalue one of our most formative and informative sensations. What is most appropriate is to redress the growing fear of touch through a renewed ethical ethos that promotes it as a safe way to learn. (2012, 38)

I echo this as you move through this chapter. The goal of this chapter, and the *Ethics of Teaching with(out) Touch*[1] course that I developed on which it is based, is for movement teachers to understand, and be able to articulate, why and how touch is a part of their pedagogy.

The goal of this chapter is not to have you decide that teaching with touch is wrong or bad. It is not to have to you decide that you will never use touch in the classroom again. The goal of this chapter is that you reflect deeply on your use of touch and its efficacy, as well as challenge your own assumptions and communications around touch, so you can better facilitate consent, mitigate the influence of power dynamics, and circumvent activation or harm that can be caused by touch in the movement classroom.

The use of touch in the movement classroom

In Bannon's study, she offers nine different categories for the use of touch in the dance classroom (8). In *The Ethics of Teaching with(out) Touch* course, I have reduced these to six, and explain them as follows:

- Touch to impart instruction or correction.
    - While sharing technical information to the student, the teacher uses touch to create accuracy and/or alignment in the body, or to assist in execution of new material.
- Touch to bring kinesthetic awareness or attention to detail.
    - Once the movement is being executed, more precision may be required, and the teacher's touch is meant to guide attention.
- Touch to offer physical support or safety.
    - While learning an acrobatic or other physically risky movement, "spotting" or a touch to ensure the safety of the student may be necessary in the early stages.

- o Partnering and lifts require this touch.
  - o Young students may require this touch for their own safety from themselves or others.
- Touch to offer emotional support.
  - o A teacher may offer a hug, high-five, or other physical contact as encouragement or congratulations.
- Student-to-student or self-touch.
  - o Students may contact each other in choreography, including partnering or lifts as mentioned above, but also for purely aesthetic purposes.
  - o Students may use touch for any of the reasons noted above in peer teaching situations.
  - o Self-touch may be encouraged for any of the reasons mentioned above.

In the "Reflection" section, I ask you to examine your current use of touch, and the context for that touch. The goal of this reflection is not only to bring clarity to touch, but to help us consider what else might be happening in our space. For example, we may intend our touch to be corrective to a student who we perceive needs it. However, that student may not know that intention and may feel targeted, or that their boundaries have not been respected. Conversely, students who do not receive a corrective touch, because we perceive they don't need it may feel ignored, or that they are not getting any feedback. In either case, because of a lack of transparency and understanding in teaching methods and purposes, the trust and safety of the room can suffer. In words used often in social justice circles, "Intent does not equal impact.[2]"

REFLECTION SECTION: Current use of touch

What was my experience of touch in movement class as a student? How did my instructors use touch? Explain their use of touch? How has this shaped my use of touch in the movement classroom?

_____
_____
_____
_____
_____

Refer to the six categories of classroom touch mentioned above.

What types of touch do I use in class? Are students aware this is the purpose of the touch? How do I know when/if the touch was effective at achieving its purpose?

_____
_____
_____
_____
_____

In thinking about the type(s) of touch I use in class, when do I tend to use it:

- I interact with every person this way.
- Only those that "need" it.
- Only those who do not seem to have gotten the information in other ways.
- When it is the quickest, most convenient, or "easiest" way to communicate.
- Other.

_____
_____
_____
_____

And are students aware of this reasoning for touch?

_____
_____
_____
_____
_____

What other "stories" might students be telling themselves about my use (or lack) of touch with them?

_____
_____
_____
_____
_____

Are there any settings I teach in, in which I do not use touch or use touch less than others? Are there any genres I teach in which I do not use touch or use touch less than others?

_____
_____
_____
_____
_____

Because of all the possibilities of loss of learning and/or harm that arise with touch, I choose to not teach with touch. My syllabus includes the following regarding touch and contact:

> Physical interaction is often a part of our learning in which people touch others while dancing, moving, and learning together. Students may have occasion to physically interact with each other during movement experiences. All containers for interaction (location, type of touch, purpose of touch, duration of touch) will be defined clearly before contact is made. Consent between partners is to be established before contact is made. This conversation will be modeled on the first day of class.
>
> Baseline Boundaries will also be created as part of our Class Contract, and they will always be in effect. You may revoke consent or change your mind about a boundary at any time.
>
> As the teacher, I will not initiate touch with a student, to correct or to interact. However, a student may request a corrective touch, and that touch will be discussed at that time.
>
> I may have cause to touch in the pursuit of safety, for example in spotting a lift. Your safety takes priority in this class.

These final paragraphs honor students who learn kinesthetically, and their safety. In this way, I center the students' learning and wellbeing above my policy.

With the classroom goals of learning and teaching, touch, and communication around touch, deserve care-full examination and communication. To be trauma-informed, touch must be consented to. This can only happen in a room where power dynamics are discussed, and students' boundaries and agency are respected. When students feel psychologically safe, they can take physical and creative risks, and truly embody the movements, characters, or concepts they are there to learn.

Effective and ethical teaching with touch

Once you have analyzed your use of touch and feel confident that it is a valuable part of your teaching practice, you can take steps to ensure that students understand that value. This looks like creating procedures and practices that create effective communication and support the consent-forward, trauma-informed, psychologically safe methods you have implemented in other parts of class. I offer three steps for this.

1. Create an "Ethics of Touch Statement."
2. Implement a boundaries practice.
3. Ask and approach.

Creating an "Ethics of Touch" statement

Above, I shared my syllabus language around touch and contact. You may have a departmental or organization statement you are required to use. If you can add to it, or are ready to create your own, sharing a statement in your syllabus or on your learning management system (LMS) regarding touch and contact in the classroom is a foundational way to create safety for conversations on these topics that are important for healthy, sustainable movement training. A comprehensive "Ethics of Touch" statement includes:

- Acknowledgment of power dynamics and that they influence students' ability to consent to touch from an instructor.
- Description of why and how you use touch (see categories and reflection questions above).
- Statement(s) on how consent-forward practices operate in the classroom. This may include:
    o Baseline boundaries (see the next heading and Chapter 5).
    o Regular boundary practices (see the next heading and Chapter 5).
    o In what scenarios asking for consent occurs.
    o That "no" is a valid answer and will be supported with alternatives.
        ▪ Similarly, that students can change their mind about their "yes" or their "no," and that will be supported.
- Chain of Communication or Resolution Pathway[3] for students who feel this statement has not been upheld.

There is space in the next "Reflection" section for you to start a draft of your own "Ethics of Touch" statement. Think about what is important for you to communicate to students about power, trauma, consent, psychological safety, and touch. Also think about what is practical for you to do consistently.

Your first draft may be extensive, if you feel compelled to write about every possible example of power and consent that occur. Go ahead and let it be long! Start to synthesize all your ideas around power, trauma, consent, psychological safety, and touch. Then you can edit. An effective statement is about a paragraph in length and is easily and consistently applied in your class.

When I teach the six-week course on "Ethics of Touch" to dance teachers, we create three drafts. I recognize that creating such a statement takes time, conversations with colleagues or supervisors, and maybe even consultation with legal advisors. And even when it is "done," it likely isn't. You can revisit this statement for different genres of movement, different settings of teaching, as institutional policies change, and/or as your own life experiences provide you with a different perspective.

Your completed version may become a part of your syllabus or posted in your LMS. It may be used in your class contract or in a production or departmental handbook. It should be easily accessible to everyone. Clear communication of the policy, and what to do if the policy is not followed, is important to disrupting power dynamics and creating trust.

Implement a boundaries practice (or several)

Ethical and effective teaching with touch necessitates the communication of boundaries. How can we know if our touch is achieving its purpose, in a way that respects every person in the room, if we do not know what their needs and boundaries are?

These practices[4] may look like:

- Creating Baseline Boundaries as a class.
- Teaching and practicing a boundary conversation with partners.
- Daily check-ins regarding the content of the day and ways in which touch may be used and providing props (cards, bracelets, etc.) or time for conversation to communicate boundaries and choices.
- Asking every time contact is going to be used.
- A combination of these things or something I haven't thought of!

Like nearly everything in this book, there is no one way to create a boundary practice. You may have entirely different ones for classes you teach in the same semester, or you may find a way that works for nearly every situation. The important thing is that we, as educators, normalize having, communicating, and respecting boundaries—between students and us, and between students themselves.

Whatever boundary practice you choose to institute in your classes, it is important to reiterate that "no" is always available, and that students can change their minds. As discussed earlier, students may not trust that this is the case early in their work and relationship with us. However, consistent respect for boundaries, coupled with support for "no," and teaching alternatives that still allow students to engage fully in learning will create that trust and safety.

Ask and approach

When I teach power and consent workshops for teachers, and the *Ethics of Teaching with(out) Touch* class, there is often more than one educator who is concerned that teaching in trauma-informed, consent-forward, psychologically safe ways is inefficient and will "take too much time." And while it does take time to have boundary conversations and to ask for consent, I see this time as a worthwhile investment in students' knowledge—of their bodily autonomy, what a care-full class and teacher can look like, and that there is a multiplicity of ways to teach and create. As mentioned before, students are not actually learning if they are experiencing a trauma response, so to not ask or to not uphold bodily autonomy in a class seems like a sure way to waste time, as at some point, some student will not be able to engage in learning because of an unwelcome or unexpected touch.

My solution for saving time includes the use of Baseline Boundaries (as noted above and in Chapter 5) but also to ask and approach. Whenever I see a student who needs a correction or assistance that fits with my use of touch as a teaching method, it is very likely that I am seeing them from a distance, as I teach a concept or move through the room observing. I formulate and make my ask from where I am, while still demonstrating or observing the whole room. I have not lost any time, as I am continuing in my previous task, and not anticipating a "yes." Also, since I am not in their space, the pressure of an assumed "yes," because I am right there to touch them is removed, as is the stress of saying "no" directly to my face!

These asks may sound like, "Name, how would you feel about me using my flat hand to align your foot in your anatomical second position?" Or "Name, what are your feelings about me using my forearm and Strong Energy to draw your attention to where your spine is behind your hips and causing a misalignment?" In both examples, I use a question that doesn't have a "yes" or "no" answer, short-circuiting the reflexive and conditioned "yes" of students and performers. I also let them know the body part of mine, touching the body part of theirs, its shape or quality, and its purpose. This language absolutely takes practice but removes some of the pressure to please me as the teacher. Then, if they consent, I move to them.

REFLECTION SECTION: Ethics of touch statement draft

Create a draft of a statement you could include in your syllabus or other classroom communication that includes:

- Acknowledgement of power dynamics and that they influence students' ability to consent to touch from an instructor.
- Description of why and how you use touch (see categories and reflection questions above).
- Statement on how consent-forward practices operate in the classroom. This may include:
  o Baseline boundaries if you choose to use them.
  o Regular boundary practices.
  o In what scenarios asking for consent occurs.
  o That "no" is a valid answer and will be supported with alternatives.
    - Similarly, that students can change their mind about their "yes" or their "no," and that will be supported.
- Chain of Communication or Resolution Pathway for students who feel this statement has not been upheld.

Who else do I need to discuss this statement with?

_____

_____

_____

_____

_____

How does this statement make me feel? What sensations do I notice in my body?

_____

_____

_____

_____

_____

How do I anticipate students might react to reading this in a syllabus or in other course materials? What questions might they have?

_____

_____

_____

_____

_____

Low- and no-touch alternatives for the movement classroom

Touch as a teaching method is simply taken for granted as "the way it's done" in many studios and classrooms because it has been the way we've experienced learning. However, we can choose to make things different for our students; to better support those with different learning styles, to honor their bodily autonomy, and to avoid trauma activation of those who have been harmed in the past.

Here is a list I bring forward in the *Ethics of Teaching with(out) Touch* of alternatives to traditional tactile teaching.

Corrective or instructional touch possibilities (from highest to least amount of contact)

- Hand-on-hand.
- Security hands.
- Goal hand.
- Hover hands.
- Framing.
- Energy touch.

Hand-on-hand

Hand-on-hand uses a student's hand and an instructor's hand. As the teacher, I may use my hand to place their hand on a body part that could benefit from some resistance or realignment. In this scenario, I am only touching their hand, and they are contacting another body part. This limited area of touch may feel much safer to students than granting a teacher full access to their body.

Or I may ask them to put their hand on mine, as I give them a corrective touch, like spiraling around the thigh for rotation. This could be particularly useful if the energetic quality of the touch is related to the energetic quality of the movement, and I want to highlight that for them. This could also particularly benefit students who are learning to teach, to distinguish different qualities of touch and how they communicate.

Security hands

The name of this type of touch refers to what we may experience at the airport. When a TSA agent is going to touch us, they say "I'm going to use the back of my hand to lightly brush (fill in the body part)." Which is a great example of specific information, at it gives us information about what body part of theirs is going on what body part of ours, and how. But it is not consent-forward communication, as there is no opt out!

In using this as a teaching method of touch, an instructor uses the back of the hand instead of the palm. One cannot grab a student with the back of a hand, so students may find it more appropriate and/or less activating to be touched in this way. This example was brought to an *Ethics of Teaching with(out) Touch Class* by dance educator and Laban/Bartenieff Movement Analyst Hannah Fisher, MFA.[5]

Goal hand[6]

The instructor puts a hand outside of the student's body as a "goal." This could be used for a *tendu* that is not in the right location, a misaligned pelvis or spine, or to encourage performers to send their energy beyond their physical body. They then ask the student to reach to it or for it, with a particular body part or movement. A goal hand puts the control of contact, if any, with the students.

When using this type of touch, I would say "you can extend the arm to touch my hand or stop when you feel you are close enough." If they choose to stop without contact, but in that choice have not gone far enough to make the correction, I repeat it, and simply set the goal hand farther away. In the case of misalignment, I could say, "If you touch my hand, you've gone too far!"

To keep this idea of a goal, but to remove the touch, a sticker on the floor (especially for younger students) or a prop instead of a hand maybe offer the same instruction.

Hover hands

As the name implies, in this scenario, the teacher's hand(s) hover over or around, but do not contact, the student's body. Unlike *Goal hands* where the hand(s) are placed where we would ultimately like the body part to end up, in *Hover hands* they are placed above (or below, or both, as the case may be) where touch would be applied; they hover over the area. In this case, our hands serve to draw attention to a body part or section of the body, and coupled with our words, help students know the correction to make. For example, a teacher's hand may *hover* above a student's shoulder with the verbal cue "release your trapezius muscles away from your ear." Or the hand may even gesture the sliding of the scapula down and back while floating outside the body.

Framing

Framing is very similar, but now, two hands are used to help channel or corral the body part or energy. In dance, this could be helpful for *retire* or other positions to the side of the body, or for postural alignment. In a Movement for Actors class, *Framing* could be used for spatial clarity in movement, or in the creation of tableaus or poses.

Energy touch

In Movement for Actors class, early in the semester we play a movement game I call "Element Bending." Students embody, through movement and sound, air, water, fire, or earth. We talk about the differences in quality in these elements. If I was trying to touch you with water, I could choose to touch you with a gentle springtime shower, or with a tidal wave—two totally different types of energy! Then students give and receive energy, through movement and sound with a partner, from across the room, changing up elements and the different states in which they could exist.

Similarly, Energy touch is contact that happens only through energy. I might say, "release your head to the floor like a waterfall is coming out of it," or "release your head to the floor like it is full of mud." I couple that imagistic language with movement, like I am sending that energy towards them or mimicking a touch from a distance. I do recommend if you are going to use this method of no-contact contact in class, that you play a few rounds of the game, so students get used to embodying and communicating about energy.

Other options

Some students may not want to be touched by an instructor, because of power dynamics, personal relationship, past trauma, or some other reason. However, that doesn't mean they are not open to other types of touch. In these instances, we have some other options.

- Self-touch.
- Partner touch.
- Props.

Self-touch

As the name implies, in self-touch, the student provides their own kinesthetic feedback. This is often guided by my words telling them about the quality of touch, or the purpose of the touch, so that they can reap the most benefit.

Partner touch

Students may work with a peer who will provide them kinesthetic feedback. I use this frequently in ballet class. I will describe where the hands are going on the body, what quality of touch should be used, and why this is helpful. This could particularly benefit students who are learning to teach, as they learn the why and how, not only of the movement, but of a correction.

Props

Props are one of my favorite teaching tricks! Props can create a barrier between me and the student, helping to mitigate power dynamics or diffuse a possible trauma response. Or, giving a student a prop during an exercise may put them into the position or help them embody the energy, because of the interaction. The right prop could offer a quality or image of movement. And they're just fun. Below is a list of prop possibilities.

- Feather.
- Massage ball/foam roller.
- Skeleton.
- Wall/floor.
- Chair.
- Exercise ball.
- Pool noodle.
- Scarf/fabric.
- Rope/exercise band.
- Jump rope.
- Hula hoop.
- Pen or pencil.
- Stability cushion/balance board.
- Yoga block.
- Meditation cushions.

- Pinwheel.
- Sticks or canes.

In the past I have used the wall to provide feedback to students regarding weight sharing, jumping through the feet, and aligning the spine. A skeleton is a great visual aid to anatomical corrections. An exercise band provides feedback on the quality of energy students are exerting. A band, stick, cane, or pool noodle can also assist in finding arm and shoulder placement. An exercise ball is also great for supporting contractions or extensions, and small ones can be held to feel the energy in the upper body. One of my favorites is a pinwheel for students to hold and make spin during pirouette drills or complex footwork sequences to make sure they are still breathing!

If a student is dancing with a prop, or using a prop in a scene, we may also be able to adjust their body by adjusting their prop. However, when a prop is being held, we should treat it like part of the student's body, as touching it will require us to be in their space and will impact their body. So, ask for consent just as you would if you were touching their actual body.

Final thoughts on no- or low-touch teaching

You may choose to make one of these your preferred method of touch or offering corrections. Or you may decide to offer these "low"- or "no-touch" methods as options during more traditional hands-on instruction. If it is the latter, please consider how you present these. Low- and/or no-touch options should be offered as equal and valid ways to engage in learning/receive instruction. Don't wait until a student says "no" to a corrective touch or asks if there is an alternative available. Present these methods as regular parts of learning and engagement.

REFLECTION SECTION: Low- or no-touch teaching

Think of an exercise, correction, or lesson you typically teach with touch.

Are there any low- or no-touch alternatives I could offer that will still help students obtain the learning objective? How can I offer this as an equal and valid way to engage?

_____

_____

_____

_____

_____

If I choose to keep touch in this exercise, correction, or lesson, can I be more specific in my quality of touch, my body part usage, and/or my purpose, to provide as much information as possible, so students can make their choices of consent? What would that sound like?

_____

_____

_____

_____

_____

With the list above of alternatives and props, what other ideas for low- or no-touch are sparked for me?

_____

_____

_____

_____

_____

How does the thought of teaching with no- or low-touch make me feel? What sensations do I notice in my body?

_____

_____

_____

_____

_____

Conclusion

As I wrote in "Trauma-Informed Approaches to Dance Class" for *Dance Geist*, consent-forward work and trauma-informed work share the same characteristics as, "They both involve addressing power dynamics, communicating with openness and specificity, and focusing on the humanity of students, which means honoring their agency and power" (25). In critically evaluating touch as a pedagogic method, teachers can incorporate more care into their classrooms. In failing to do so, they are also failing to see the full humanity of their students.

Chapter reminders

- Touch in movement pedagogy is an often-unexamined tradition. It deserves deep examination because of the connections of touch to power, consent, and trauma.
- Not all students learn through touch, and some may even be harmed by it.
- Our use of touch in the classroom can create unintended consequences to relationships and learning.
- A teacher's hands are not magic!
- Ethical and effective teaching with touch requires a clear statement of the whys and hows of touch in the classroom, uses boundary practices, and offers a Chain of Communication or Resolution Pathway for when or if things go wrong.
- For low- or no-touch teaching methods to be seen as valid in the classroom, they must be offered at the same time and with the same learning objective as touch-based instruction.

Notes

1. I created a course called *The Ethics and Pedagogy of Teaching with(out) Touch*, meant for dance and movement teachers, in 2020. I have taught this course through Momentum Stage, the National Dance Education Organization, and the Laban Institute of Movement Studies. Much of the content of this chapter is drawn from the materials from this course, as well as my own teaching experiences. I have taught this course seven times in just over four years (You can still take this course during summers at NDEO, and if you found this chapter stimulating, I hope you do!). In every class, teachers enter willing to examine their reliance on touch, yet fearing they will not be effective teachers without it. Without fail, in all previous courses, teachers left feeling confident in being able to adapt to the needs of their students, including their

ability to teach both with and without touch. I hope that happens for you as you read this chapter.
2. I attempted to cite this phrase, however there is not a clear first usage. The earliest written documentation is a commentary by Kira Hudson Banks written for the *Saint Louis Beacon* in 2008, however, the phrase has its roots in philosophical and social work research and writings of the late 1980s and early 1990s, as well as social justice movements, and was likely used in conversation well before this date.
3. More on creating a Resolution Pathway or Chain of Communication can be found in Chapter 6.
4. Revisit Chapter 5 for more on the boundary practice tools.
5. Hannah is a colleague from my CLMA program and has also done research on touch in teaching settings. Her website is linked in the "Resources" section.
6. In Integrated Movement Studies' (the Laban/Bartenieff Movement Analysis certification I hold) "Touch for Repatterning" curriculum, this is called an Attracting Touch.

9
Practices in assessment: Personal reflection and (un)grading

Theories of power and trauma as related to assessment and grading in higher ed movement classes[1]

You will remember back in Chapter 1 we were introduced to the "Bases of Social Power," as named by French and Raven (1959). In dance, theatre, and academia, Reward and Coercive Powers exist in reputation and grades. Grades, and the rewards they represent through recognition, validation, and/or pleasing authority, support the power imbalance of teacher over student.

A reward of grades can be the ability to be seen as "good", or "better than …". When this couples with a system that already values one party over another, competition cannot help but form. Grades often create a space where "being the best" is the goal, rather than growth or learning. Therefore, grades can stifle learning and inhibit collaboration. Jesse Stommel, an educator and pedagogue, believes, "Agency, dialogue, self-actualization, and social justice are not possible (or, at least, unlikely) in a hierarchical system that pits teachers against students and encourages competition by ranking students against one another (Blum 2020, 28)."

The Reward Power of grades also means that students with "bad grades" risk poor relationships with peers or with authority figures who may have ability to affect their academic standing for their institutional career. A lack of academic success, as represented by grades, may have consequences for students on scholarships or the possibility of a professional reference, creating levels of financial influence as well. While these factors may not consciously manipulate the behaviors of teachers or students, leaving the power of grades unexamined and unaddressed can cause harm, and even trauma, as students experience these impacts.

Trauma can erode trust in one's own power or ability to make good choices. As noted in Chapter 3, SAMHSA defines care as trauma-informed when it includes opportunities for choice (2014, 10). In *Pedagogy of the Oppressed*, Paolo Freire reminds us that, "to alienate human beings from their own decision-making is to change them into objects" ([1973] 2006, 85). Similarly, Stommel cautions,

> Grades are currency for a capitalist system that reduces teaching and learning to a mere transaction. They are an institutional instrument of compliance that work exactly because they have been so effectively naturalized. Grading is a massive coordinated effort to take humans out of the educational process. (27–28)

In implementing ungrading practices like those detailed in this chapter,[2] teachers can create opportunities for students' power and agency—their full humanity.

Even if a student has not experienced trauma, or is not affected by trauma in class, choices bolster creativity and intrinsic motivation for learning. In addition, educators Simon Cullen and Daniel Oppenheimer report, in one of the most recent publications regarding autonomy in higher education, "Choosing to learn: The importance of student autonomy in higher education" for *Science Advances*, "Autonomy-supportive policies empower students to better manage their complex lives (2024, 7)."

To diminish my Reward Power and practice trauma-informed teaching and practice Working Consent in the movement classroom, I try to bring as much choice to assessment and grading as possible. As a teacher, I had a gradual transition to "ungrading," by implementing assessments that center autonomy and growth over compliance or a single demonstration of mastery. Ungrading practices fit a "care-full" pedagogy—they ease the demands of power dynamics as meeting my expectations is not the standard for success. They are consent-forward as students have tangible agency over their grade and they are trauma-informed as they limit opportunities for harm that occur in systems built on power and hierarchies. In other words, ungrading promotes care for the complex humanity of students.

Practices of ungrading in higher education

As I worked to create a more care-full movement pedagogy, I set the goals of giving students more agency in assessments and alleviating the harm grades have potential to cause. I started back in 2018 by co-grading with the middle and high school dance and drama students on certain activities, using a rubric. In 2020, I did the same for dance technique and lecture courses in higher education. In both settings, while student evaluation mattered, the rubric, developed solely by me, was the arbiter of success. The evidence from student responses and classwork made it clear that they could take more risks and more deeply appreciate their learning when given opportunities to reflect on their growth, rather than working to please me or attain an outside goal. So, in 2022, I fully "ungraded" and gave students control of assessments and grades.

I wrote for *Dance Teacher* magazine[3] in October 2024:

> Ungrading is not a single practice of assessment, nor a simple matter of "just not giving grades." Instead, it's an umbrella term for practices that emphasize learning over assessing, process over product, and intrinsic motivation for growth over external rewards. Ungrading practices work to remove the control of the teacher, present in the rewards and punishments of grades, so that students can be more free to explore and question during class, without the fear of a "bad grade" or being a "difficult student." Additionally, ungrading practices provide a variety of benefits, including support for differentiated learning, anti-racist pedagogy, collaboration, community building, and body positivity.

My ungrading practices (laid out first generally, and then with specific class examples) are supported by a desire to mitigate power dynamics and extend consent-forward and trauma-informed practices beyond their usual applications of touch and contact.

Purpose of grades

When I introduce ungrading to students at that part of the syllabus on the first or second day of class, it is with a conversation question, "What is the purpose of grades?[4]" Often the answer is, "To know how I'm doing." I follow that with, "Do you really not know how you are doing in class without a grade?" Students quickly realize that they do, so it changes to, "To know how you (the teacher) think I'm doing." Which leads to the question, "Why should my opinion of your learning matter? Or matter more than yours?"

While grades can serve a purpose for personal validation, merit scholarships, or telling others "how you're doing," grades do not truthfully measure learning. Instead, I ask students to think of grades as simply a symbol, translated for the institution, of how they, the learner, measure the embodied learning done over a small period, in our shared setting. I also like Felicia Rose Chavez's definition of grades she provides students in her writing workshops,

"Read 'final grade' as 'commitment to your creative power'" (2021, 54). Instead of viewing grades as the purpose of being in class, we could tell students that grades are a translated symbol of how well they have upheld their commitment to their own creativity.

My syllabus, for both movement practice and dance studies classes introduces the concept of ungrading in the following way:

> Grades reinforce the hierarchical power dynamic of traditional classrooms, rather than encourage creativity, exploration, and risk-taking. In order to foster those qualities, grades are not the best way to represent learning. Rather, your full-bodied attempts at class work demonstrate your engagement with the material. Your reflection and conversations show your commitment to your own learning, and that of others. Your vulnerability and creativity in movement is valued over technical perfection.... Your personal growth cannot be compared to that of the person next to you.

> Ungrading only works when we all enter with our best of intentions, and with integrity to our community (this class). As a community, we learn together, so everyone's participation is needed. Accountability to ourselves and to each other is expected. Therefore, attendance and engagement are expected.

The main values of ungrading are that learning is more essential than the grade, the process is just as important as the product, and the student is worthy of trust and care.

With traditional assessments and grades, an "A" is not proof of learning, simply of knowledge. In classes like Dance or Theatre Appreciation or History, students with previous experience are likely to have more background knowledge, and do well on multiple choice tests, particularly if the class and assessments center Eurocentric forms found in many schools and studios. However, teaching a diverse and inclusive curriculum, encouraging personal process over final product, and offering creative assessments that allow students to work towards their own goals all create a more equitable learning atmosphere.

Every class that I taught at one university, even though it had a level in its title, was open to everyone. There were no prerequisites. This meant I had a student in the 400-level Modern class who has been dancing since they were two years old and used to compete, right next to a twenty-two-year-old who has never taken a dance class before. Grading these two students on technical proficiency alone would be ridiculous, not to mention extremely disappointing for the new student. Comparing and contrasting their abilities would not be a measure of learning, nor humanizing.

When I interviewed her for the *Dance Teacher* article, Dr. Alexia Buono, a professor in the Education Department at the University of Vermont, who teaches arts integration and dance education courses, call ungrading practices, "humanizing modes of assessment." I would agree; my ungrading practices not only decenter grades but try to emphasize autonomy and humanity and demonstrate care.

General ungrading practices for psychological safety

Late work and learner safety

Included in my syllabus in the grading section is my philosophy on late work. Penalizing late work, much like penalizing coming late to class, is a case of punishing the behavior I wish to see. I want students to do the work, which in my classes is reflection-based, as it is a time for them to see their own progress towards their goals, make connections between class material and their lives and/or creative practice(s), ask questions, and get personal feedback. Therefore, I want them in class, and I want them to do the work. So, I admit students late and accept late work!

My practices are created to encourage engagement, rather than compliance. Crafting a late work policy like this is not about punishing students who don't adhere to deadlines. Rather, it is about encouraging "doing the work," even under less-than-ideal circumstances. This helps to mitigate the Coercive Power of grades, while encouraging learner safety.

Like my attendance policy, late work does require communication. I use a "token" system, borrowed from Dr. Danielle Rosvalley, an assistant professor in the department of theatre and dance, University at Buffalo. With it, students start the course with a set number of tokens (for my classes usually two) they can use to excuse late work. If students are overwhelmed with work, or simply made an error on a deadline, they can redeem one token to request an extension of one week. Students must communicate before, or within twenty-four hours of the deadline, for this request to be met. If students miss that deadline, or they know they are not going to be able to do the work, they send me an email requesting to use the full number of tokens to excuse the assignment. Students can excuse an assignment up until the midterm for assignments in the first half of the semester, or the last day of class for assignments in the second half. If students do not have the full number of tokens[5] available, they are not able to use this option.

At no point are students asked to tell me why an assignment is late or needs to be excused. This would not be trauma-informed or filled with care for the student as a whole human. Nor would it demonstrate that I trust students to use their power to make the choices they need to make. The token policy leaves space for grace, the real-world situations many students experience of multiple classes with varying levels of work, jobs, caregiving, etc., and encourages an examination of priorities and a commitment to personal goals. I trust that students are making the decisions that best serve their life in that moment. All that is required is professional, proactive communication. This demonstrates that students are aware of the impact their choices have of their world and are taking responsibility to meet all their needs as best they can.

Reflection as learner and challenger safeties

I suspect that simply from the layout of this book, you recognize that reflecting on new learning, in both conceptual and embodied ways, is a value I hold for education. Most of the work due in my classes is reflection-based (sample prompts are provided later in the chapter). Reflection encourages connections between what we are learning and our lived experiences, as well as intrinsic motivation for learning. In the "Journal of Applied Learning in Higher Education," professors Sarah L. Ash and Patti H. Clayton (2009) write, "Learning—and understanding learning processes—does not happen maximally through experience alone but rather as a result of thinking about—reflecting on—it" (27).

Reflection gives students the opportunity to create meaning from their learning experiences. James P. Barber, the Senior Associate Dean at William and Mary, as well as Professor of Education uses reflection in his courses. He writes in *The Facilitation of Learning: Five Research-Based Practices to Help College Students Connect Learning Across Disciplines and Lived Experience,*

> I see reflection as an underlying process that enables integration of learning. The act of reflection provides the time and space to process one's experiences, consider how new information fits (or conflicts) with prior knowledge, and undergirds the meaning-making process. (2020, 23).

In addition to these critical thinking components, I hope that students use their reflections to see how they are making progress towards their goals or need to adjust their goals. My prompts[6] are crafted specifically to do this, just as my prompts in this book were created to help you make connections between your current experiences, engagement in this book, and your future goals. Because students engage in reflection weekly in my classes, they get frequent feedback not only on their work, but their process of reflection.

The intrinsic motivation to try, with learning and growing as a person as the rewards, can be throttled by the desire to "make the grade." Psychologist John Condry studied reward and punishment systems in schools in the 1970s and concluded that such systems were "enemies of exploration (1977, 459)." Yet, in dance and theatre classes, exploring is often precisely what we want students to do! However, our reliance on Reward Power, or the grade, leads students to develop extrinsic, rather than intrinsic, motivation for learning. Remember this quote from Alfie Kohn in *Punished by Rewards*:

> If your parent or teacher or manager is sitting in judgment of what you do, and if that judgment will determine whether good things or bad things happen to you, this cannot help but warp your relationship with that person. You will not be working collaboratively in order to learn or grow; you will be trying to get him or her to approve of what you are doing so you can get the goodies. (2018, 57)

Reflection, with its aspects of personal growth and meaning-making, encourages learning and ongoing exploration, rather than assuming learning is something that stops once a grade is assigned. In this way, both the Reward and Coercive Powers are diffused, and personal agency is emphasized.

I try (and often fail) to leave time at the end of class for students to begin their reflective processes. Creating time for reflection in class is a pedagogic practice I am currently working on. My goal with this is to demonstrate how much I value reflection by "giving up" class time to it (I don't see it as giving up anything, as I believe reflection is learning and is where students can translate learning to action). It also gives students a chance to revisit movement experiences as they reflect, or to ask me clarifying questions. Such a time promotes learner safety, and even challenger safety, in the movement studio as students integrate their learning with their lives (however, it also requires vigilant timekeeping, and I tend to be a bit "caught up in the moment" when I teach).

Accommodation as psychological safety

Giving students choice and agency in *how* they display their learning is another opportunity to mitigate the power dynamic created by assessments. Cullen and Oppenheimer found, "Giving students a choice of assessment options might allow for a great sense of autonomy, which as we have seen can powerfully foster motivation (4)." Therefore, students do not have to write their reflective assignments in my classes. My syllabus reads, "These may take the form of written, audio, or video submissions."

This choice allows for different learning and communicating styles and meets the 2024 CAST Universal Design for Learning Guidelines for "Multiple Means of Engagement" and "Multiple Means of Representation." Video and audio support students that may be more confident conversing in English than writing it. Another benefit is that videos encourage embodiment. I can see students' facial expressions and body language. These also humanize students, as I learn more about them as people with a glimpse into their car or room. Barber offers students his classes the reflection options of "thinking, writing, talking, walking, and dreaming" (41).

The rest of this chapter lays out the specific ungrading practices I use in classes, and the care-full purpose of each.

REFLECTION SECTION: "Ungrading"

What is the purpose of grades in the classes I teach? What do students think the purpose of grades is?

_____
_____
_____
_____
_____

What sensations, feelings, thoughts do I notice as I think about ungrading?

_____
_____
_____
_____
_____

What is my current policy regarding late work? What values does this policy impart? How does this policy encourage learning over compliance?

_____
_____
_____
_____
_____

Are there changes I could make to my late work policy that would demonstrate more care for the full lives and humanity of students, or trust in their agency and choices?

_____
_____
_____
_____
_____

Do I currently ask students to engage in reflection in my classes? What are my goals for reflection? Do the methods of reflection encourage autonomy?

Are there places I can add more reflection, or better structure reflection to help students integrate their learning?

Creative input, goal setting, and reflection: Ungrading in movement classes

A goal of movement classes is for students to improve their skills. This may mean pushing themselves physically and/or creatively. You may remember from Chapter 6 this wording in my syllabus:

> This course is structured as a lab in which you are both the scientist and your own (no one else's, including mine!) experiment. In this metaphor, I'm the director of the lab, whose job it is to make sure our experiments are safe and ethical, while still pushing us to new discoveries. I am a co-investigator, with my own experiment of my body and creative practice.

In a laboratory, failure is an expectation; so is safety. My job, as the professor, is to make a space where it is safe to risk, because it is safe to fail. By putting this in writing, reiterating it on the first day of class, and working to embody it daily, I hope to encourage risk-taking and give space for failure, so students are free to work towards their goals without fear of judgment.

In *The Four Stages of Psychological Safety* (2020), Timothy R. Clark emphasizes, "granting learner safety is not a passive act. When we grant it, we make a commitment to create a supportive and encouraging environment. … we commit to share power, credit and resources to enable all to learn: (46). Because the goal is learning, even through failure, I separate one-time execution of a skill (like a jury or audition) from grades.

Instead, I ask students in movement classes to regularly demonstrate their learning by synthesizing it into their activities. In daily "technique experiments,[7]" students choose what new knowledge to embody and are empowered to take creative risks. As the semester progresses, students layer concepts and develop longer phrases. In technique experiments, students create, recall theory, demonstrate embodied learning and skills, and learn from each other, all with the freedom to risk and fail, as they are not assessed. They reflect on their technique experiments, including new insights, challenges, and/or successes in weekly journals. I provide feedback on each journal (since these classes have twenty-four students or less) that may include advice or notes I was unable to give in class, a reframe of the challenge they are facing, or validation of their experience.

Goal setting in movement experiences

If I believe that student learning is the most important activity occurring in a class, and that that activity looks different and happens at a different pace for each student, it would be rather silly of me to attempt to measure all students in the same way. Yet, most traditional assessments do this. Instead, students could be evaluated on their own goals for the class.

To evaluate cumulative learning in the classes I lead, students develop narrative self-assessments, submitted at midterms and finals (these prompts are provided later in the chapter). These assessments begin with setting goals in an Introduction Letter during the first week of class. Students choose five goals from the Movement Experiences Guide (MEG), for the first half of the semester. I created MEG in 2018, initially as a rubric for co-grading with middle and high school dance students, inspired by a colleague, Emi Hilger, who was doing the same with her drama students. It continues to grow and adapt, with influence from students and colleagues. It is now both a goal setting tool and a rubric.

In the article "A Century of Grading Research," Brookhart, et al cite over twenty separate studies from the early 1900s through the early 2000s. They find that while grades can be a predictor of future academic success, "One hundred years of grading research have generally confirmed large variation among teachers in the validity and reliability of grades, both in the meaning of grades and accuracy of reporting" (2016, 833). They offer, "clearer criteria, … and involving students in the development of grading criteria appear to be promising approaches to enhancing grading reliability" (834). The Movement Experiences Guide meets both these suggestions. It shows students the objectives I hold for the class, including technical and life skills, with examples of what that skill looks like at a zero, two, seven, and ten. My syllabus includes the following:

> Guide for Evaluating Movement Experience Goals[8]:
>
> Movement will be a central experience of learning in this class throughout the semester. Please use this to create your goals and self-assess in your letters
>
> We will examine movement experiences for assessment purposes in the following ways:

Category	10 points	7 points	2 points	0 points
Taking Risks, Trying New Things	Willingness to engage in new material to the best of ability. Participates actively and consistently in class and class discussions/videos in the appropriate format. Makes bold personal choices in movement that challenges own preferences/bias/training.	Engages only new material that feels "comfortable" or "interesting". Participates often in class and class discussions/videos in the appropriate format. Often makes choices in movement that challenges own preferences/bias/training.	Rarely engages in new material. Participates occasionally in class and class discussions/videos in the appropriate format. Occasionally makes choices in movement that challenges own preferences/bias/training.	Does not engage new material. Does not participate in class and class discussions/videos in the appropriate format. Does not make choices in movement that challenges own preferences/bias/training.
Critical Thinking applied to Creative Process	Gives attention to instructor, peers, and material, even when that perspective is different than their own. Listens to develop empathy and perspective for difference. Applies new ideas to own creative choices/practice.	Often gives attention to instructor, peers, and material, even when that perspective is different than their own. Often listens to develop empathy and perspective for difference. Often applies new ideas to own creative choices/practice.	Rarely gives attention to instructor, peers, and material, especially when that perspective is different than their own. Rarely listens to develop empathy and perspective for difference. Rarely applies new ideas to own creative choices/practice.	Does not give attention to instructor, peers, and material, especially when that perspective is different than their own. Does not listen to develop empathy and perspective for difference. Does not apply new ideas to own creative choices/practice.

(*Continued*)

Category	10 points	7 points	2 points	0 points
Preparation for Class	Assignments consistently completed. Dressed appropriately for class movement experiences. Is on time which includes being present for the somatic check-in.	Assignments often completed. Often dressed appropriately for class movement experiences. Often on time which includes being present for the somatic check-in.	Assignments rarely completed. Rarely dressed appropriately. Rarely on time often misses somatic check-in.	Does not complete assignments. Does not dress appropriately. Consistently late or consistently misses somatic check-in.
Supporting your Peers and Working in Collaboration	Gives attention to peers, even when their perspective is different from their own. Is aware of the "Space", they are taking up in the room, conversation, or group work. Invites others to conversation when applicable. Offers insightful feedback when appropriate. Takes feedback and ideas from others seriously and looks to integrate all ideas as appropriate in group work.	Often gives attention to peers, even when that perspective is different from their own. Often aware of the "Space", they are taking up in the room, conversation, or group work. Often invites others to conversation when applicable. Often offers insightful feedback when appropriate. Often takes feedback and ideas from others seriously and looks to integrate all ideas as appropriate in group work.	Rarely gives attention to peers, especially when that perspective is different from their own. Is often unaware of the "Space", they are taking up in the room, conversation, or group work. Rarely invites others to conversation when applicable. Occasionally offers feedback. Rarely takes feedback and ideas from others seriously. Occasionally integrates other ideas in group work.	Does not give attention to peers, especially when that perspective is different from their own. Is not aware of the "Space", they are taking up in the room, conversation, or group work. Does not invite others to conversation when applicable. Does not offer feedback. Does not Take feedback and ideas from others seriously. Does not integrate other ideas as appropriate in group work.

(*Continued*)

Category	10 points	7 points	2 points	0 points
Critical Thinking applied to Personal Reflection	Actively and consistently engages in class discussions/threads with awareness of theory, personal meaning-making and preferences, and an awareness of the "space" they are taking up in the conversation. Is consistently aware of how their own positionality affects interpretation.	Often engages in class discussions/threads with awareness of theory, personal meaning-making and preferences, and an awareness of the "space" they are taking up in the conversation. Is sometimes aware of how their own positionality affects interpretation.	Rarely engages in class discussions/threads, or rarely does so with awareness of theory, personal meaning-making and preferences, and an awareness of the "space" they are taking up in the conversation. Is rarely aware of how their own positionality affects interpretation.	Does not engage in class discussions/threads, or does not do so with awareness of theory, personal meaning-making and preferences, and an awareness of the "space" they are taking up in the conversation. Is not aware of how their own positionality affects interpretation.
Staying Present and Intentional	Gives attention and focus consistently throughout the class, including personal somatic check-in, and the material. Creates and consistently assesses personal goals via Letters.	Gives attention and focus often throughout the class, including personal somatic check-in, and the material. Creates and occasionally assesses personal goals via Letters.	Is often distracted throughout the class, including personal somatic check-in, and from the material. Rarely assesses personal goals via Letters.	Does not give attention or focus throughout the class, including personal somatic check-in, or to the material. Does not create or assess personal goals via Letters.

(*Continued*)

Category	10 points	7 points	2 points	0 points
Incorporating Theory, Feedback, and Collaborative Ideas into Creative Work	Consistently incorporates class theories, discussions, and/or collaborative opportunities into personal creative work AND can cite sources. Consistently applies class theories, discussions, and/or collaborative opportunities to personal meaning-making. Works in true collaboration. Consistently uses terminology and vocabulary, as well as embodiment appropriate to the dance genre of class.	Often incorporates class theories, discussions, and/or collaborative opportunities into personal creative work AND can often cite sources. Often applies class theories, discussions, and/or collaborative opportunities to personal meaning-making. Often works in true collaboration. Often uses terminology and vocabulary, as well as embodiment appropriate to the dance genre of class.	Rarely incorporates class theories, discussions, and/or collaborative opportunities into personal creative work AND rarely cites sources. Rarely applies class theories, discussions, and/or collaborative opportunities to personal meaning-making. Occasionally works in true collaboration. Occasionally uses terminology and vocabulary, as well as embodiment appropriate to the dance genre of class.	Does not incorporate class theories, discussions, and/or collaborative opportunities into personal creative work OR does not cite sources. Does not apply class theories, discussions, and/or collaborative opportunities to personal meaning-making. Does not work in true collaboration. Does not use terminology and vocabulary, as well as embodiment appropriate to the dance genre of class.
Centeredness and Balance	Alignment and posture, as well as the ability to play on- and off-center is attended to and consistent.	Alignment and posture, as well as the ability to play on- and off-center is often attended to.	Alignment and posture, as well as the ability to play on- and off-center is rarely attended to and is inconsistent.	Does not attend to alignment, posture, the ability to play on- and off-center.
Coordination and Connectivity	Consistently demonstrates strength, flexibility, and stamina.	Consistently demonstrates 2 of the following: strength, flexibility, and stamina.	Consistently demonstrates 1 of the following: strength, flexibility, and stamina.	Does not demonstrate strength, flexibility, and stamina.

(*Continued*)

Category	10 points	7 points	2 points	0 points
Personal Expressivity	Demonstrates consistent musicality or accurate timing and phrasing. Embodies a variety of movement qualities and dynamics. Makes bold personal choices, appropriate to the genre of the class.	Often demonstrates musicality, with accurate timing and phrasing. Often embodies a variety of movement qualities and dynamics. Often makes bold personal choices, appropriate to the genre of the class.	Rarely demonstrates consistent musicality, with accurate timing and phrasing. Rarely embodies a variety of movement qualities and dynamics. Rarely makes bold personal choices, appropriate to the genre of the class.	Does not demonstrate consistent musicality, with accurate timing and phrasing. Does not embody a variety of movement qualities and dynamics. Does not make bold personal choices, appropriate to the genre of the class.
Embodied Knowing and Meaning-making	Demonstrates thorough comprehension of the content of class, through the embodiment of skills and choices. Can clearly articulate their reasons for choice making and the sensations they experience, as well as the story they desire the audience to receive.	Demonstrates regular comprehension of the content of class, through the embodiment of skills and choices. Can often clearly articulate their reasons for choice making and the sensations they experience, as well as the story they desire the audience to receive.	Rarely demonstrates comprehension of the content of class, through the embodiment of skills and choices. Is rarely able to articulate their reasons for choice making and the sensations they experience, as well as the story they desire the audience to receive.	Does not demonstrate comprehension of the content of class, through either the embodiment of skills or choices. Cannot articulate their reasons for choice making, the sensations they experience, or the story they desire the audience to receive.

(*Continued*)

Category	10 points	7 points	2 points	0 points
Other	If you have another idea that you feel will demonstrate your learning, growing, creating, OR a goal you wish to achieve with your technical movement skills,[9] write it in!			

MEG offers a space for "Other," an opportunity for students to create a goal not listed. With the options to develop their own goal and choose from a variety of goals, students identify what is important to them in learning movement and create their own objectives. Since power dynamics can affect how a person acts, chooses, or speaks in relationship to another, students may not feel free, or in fact be free, to explore their interests or curiosities within classroom content. "Other" is a way I mitigate those power dynamics and encourage students to find what interests them in learning. You could choose to take this a step further and have students entirely design the rubric, or design more than one category.

MEG is a gauge for student learning, as well as an opportunity for students to state what is important to learn. As such, MEG removes the Reward and Coercive Powers of grading, while increasing the sense of learner safety, or that it is acceptable to take risks and fail in this space. Since MEG allows students to focus on their own goals, it also helps alleviate competition mindset, as the student next to them may be working towards totally different goals. Their focus becomes making progress on what is important to them, not impressing me as "better" or "best."

In their self-assessment letters, students must provide a rationale for each score, which they draw directly from their weekly Artist Logs, as well as their midterm and final projects (both the prompts and projects are detailed in the next sections). In nearly ten years of using MEG in some form, I have found most students give themselves an average of eight. As this is a B in a grading scale, this also leaves room for a conversation with me about where I have seen their growth. After a feedback session, in which I validate their learning and risk-taking, I often get to bump their grades up.

I am not the only educator who has this experience in ungrading. Ali Duffy, PhD, a professor of Dance at Texas Tech University conveyed to me:

> Another myth is that there is no rigor in self-assessment and that students will just "phone it in." It is true that students could decide to skate easily through these assignments. As an educator adopting this model, I trust that students will push themselves, and some students may choose not to do that. However, I don't see this happening. Because the students have agency in making what they want to make and the freedom to set goals for themselves, they tend to want to really take some risks and push themselves into doing a lot. In fact, I often find myself gently encouraging students to give themselves a break because their goals for themselves are so big and impressive.

Similarly, Alexia Buono, PhD, who teaches arts integration and dance education in the Department of Education at the University of Vermont has found during ungrading, "Students don't always give themselves A's. Most of them stick to their integrity."

Jessica Zeller, PhD, has sometimes found a different problem. She cautions in *Humanizing Ballet Pedagogies*:

> There is legitimate concern among those in the ungrading and alternative grading communities that students in historically excluded groups who are asked to self-evaluate may do so through the lens of "imposter syndrome," or having internalized the structural prejudices in both the ballet and academic hierarchies. (2024, 153)

To alleviate this concern, transparent conversation about the whys and hows of ungrading, as well as personal conversations with students, can support accurate evaluation.

Emphasizing goal setting, experimentation, and reflection in narrative ungrading unsettles typical learning atmospheres of power, control, and judgment from others. It also encourages personal growth and accountability. At midterms, students may choose new goals or continue with their previous choices. Their ability to adapt because of self-reflection as well as feedback is an integration of their learning and an exercise in personal power and agency.

Reflection and self-assessment in Artist Logs

Weekly journals in the classes I teach are called Artist Logs.[10] I call them this because believe that no matter what class or level students are in, they are already artists able to create. The Logs, like a captain's log on a starship[11] give students a place to chart their progress towards their goals. In fact, if students do their Artist Logs, their midterm and final reflections should be easily cut-and-pasted together or referenced with date stamps and time codes if they have submitted audio or video notes.

Ash and Clayton caution that reflection, "can easily be associated with 'touchy-feely' introspection, too subjective to evaluate in a meaningful way and lacking in the rigor required for substantive academic work" (27). However, in the log, each week's prompt is carefully crafted based on the content of the lessons. They sometimes include a Guiding Question from our syllabus that helps students make explicit connections between their classwork and the goals of the course. Artist Log reflections are not busy work, nor separate from class experiences or goals. Ash and Clayton created "The DEAL Model for Critical Reflection" (41). They describe the process as:

1. Description of experiences in an objective and detailed manner
2. Examination of those experiences in light of specific learning goals or objectives; and
3. Articulation of Learning, including goals for future action that can then be taken forward into the next experience for improved practice and further refinement of learning. (41)

As you design reflective prompts for your classroom experiences, this may be a helpful checklist. While I did not know of this model when I created my prompts, you can see that each prompt below does fulfill these steps. With this type of design, reflective prompts should be easier to write from personal experience, than to generate through a large language model like ChatGPT or similar.

I have not provided all my prompts,[12] but a few examples of how I word these, so students can chart their progress, and see how their work in class supports their growth.

Movement for Actors

- This week was about building awareness of your body.
    - What body parts are easy for you access/use?
    - What body parts do you "ignore?"
    - What class experience(s) illuminated these things for you?
- Course Guiding Questions for the week:
    - What do somatic practice and somatic knowledge offer my creative practice and performance?
    - What are my personal movement preferences at this time?
        - What class experience(s) illuminated these things for you?

Jazz

Read the excerpt provided from *Digging the Africanist Presence in American Performance* by Brenda Dixon Gottschild on the aesthetic of Polyrhythm/PolyCentrism.

- How did this show up in your movement work in class this week?
- What new thoughts on Jazz Dance do you have (from the reading and/or embodying the concept in class)?
- What questions do you have (from the reading and/or embodying the concept in class)?
- What is sticking with you from your reading?

Ballet

This week's theme: *Plier*: to bend and using it to move through space and pose (You may also describe this as yield/connect/deepen).

- How would you describe your sensations in this movement in class?
- What physical movements from class have been easy or exciting?
- What physical movements from class have been challenging, perhaps physically or aesthetically?
- What new knowledge did you gain or how has existing knowledge been reinforced with these experiences?
- Do you have any questions?

Midterm and final projects from movement classes as examples of contributor and challenger safeties

Ungrading and reflective assessments do not mean that students to not have assignments or projects to demonstrate cumulative learning. All my movement courses have midterm and final projects that serve to help students demonstrate their learning, to themselves, their peers, and me.[13] These projects are also designed for students to contribute their own knowledge, preferences, and creativity. In this, the projects build contributor and challenger safeties.

Ballet

My Beginning Ballet midterm and final projects are two of my favorite assignments that I give. In this class, students are learning new vocabulary, in both word and body. These assessments are designed to help students gauge their own retention, and to feel confident in performing it. For the midterms, students, in small groups, create movement to the first forty seconds of Parov Stellar's *Candy Girl*. This song, made famous by TikTok dance challenges, gives students a chance to creatively express ballet vocabulary, as its lyrics are ballet movements in French. With lyrics like *"tendu, plie,"* there is room for students to contribute their own creativity and demonstrate with confidence as they decide which type of those movements to do.

This assignment is an opportunity for students to experience contributor safety. The structure is clearly created by the song and the assignment, but their group collaboration is unique. Each group performs for the class. Despite sharing the same vocabulary from the lyrics, every group has a unique piece. This assignment validates for students not only their learning of ballet, but their own creative contributions.

The final is similar, but now student small groups choose a line dance song. The song must contain lyrics that tell you how to move. Frequent choices are *The Cha-cha Slide* and *Cupid Shuffle*. They must then "translate" the lyrics into ballet terms[14] and execute them properly.

This assignment was created to validate contributor and challenger safeties in the classroom. There is a structure, but students can take creative liberties and explore new options. Not only are they able to do ballet steps, but they have enough knowledge to make choices and create in what is often seen as strict or traditional artform. I love watching these final dances and seeing students confidently perform their ballet knowledge.

In both projects, students work in groups, emphasizing the learning and creating happens in community. I also give class time for these projects. Students only take out-of-class time for these if someone is missing or if they want to. By doing these projects within these containers, I keep them in the contexts of learning, experimenting, and collaborating, rather than separate assessments that must "good" or "perfect."

Movement for Actors

Movement for Actors classes have "monologue workshops" as their midterm and final projects. Simply by calling them a "workshop" rather than an assessment, I emphasize that these are learning opportunities and perfection is not expected.

Students are expected to apply the movement concepts from the first half of the semester to their midterm workshop, and layer on the concepts from the second half at the final. They perform in class and receive "coaching" from me, usually an idea of something else to try.

Students experience contributor safety, as the structure is somewhat set by the class concepts and the piece of text they have chosen, but they are also able to bring their own creative choices to it. Sometimes these creative choices are opportunities to experience challenger safety, as they discover a different interpretation of a character or moment than they assumed or had experienced in an acting class that doesn't emphasize movement. This ability to make bold choices will serve them in the professional theatre world.

Movement for Actors and Bodywork and Conditioning

In Movement for Actors and Bodywork and Conditioning classes I teach, students have a project on creating a movement phrase. For Movement for Actors students, this is framed as a warm-up: how do they prepare themselves for a dance call, rehearsal, or performance? In Bodywork and Conditioning classes students create a ten-minute movement sequence to serve a specific purpose. They may choose to create a warm-up, or a phrase that addresses a specific need they have, such as an injury, or calming and grounding before an exam.

The structure for these is created by Irmgard Bartenieff's "Patterns of Total Body Connectivity,"[15] and students use these as a framework for their movement design. They contribute their own movement choices, deciding what best serves them and their needs. In this, the "assessment" is not for me to know how well they move, but for them to know how well they will be able to meet their own needs when out in the professional performance world and provide feedback on other options or resources.

Assessing technical skills while ungrading

Students need not only creativity and self-awareness in the professional performance world; they need technical movement skills as well. Ungrading does not mean that students' technical skills are not evaluated or addressed; simply that these are not what students' grades are based on.

Instead, juries, auditions, and/or technical assessments for level or program placement or roles are separate activities. In my technique classes that have had level placement, observations took place twice a semester, near the mid- and endpoints by both me and the teacher of the next level class. While these evaluations became part of a conversation with the student, it had no bearing on their grade in my course.

I do not believe it is possible to create learner safety and encourage risk-taking or create contributor or challenger safety and encourage creativity throughout daily class activities if the final grade is based on a single occurrence of movement execution. Such a method enforces perfectionism, fear, people-pleasing, competition mindset, and power dynamics. This is not the classroom culture I want to operate in, so I have found a way to separate creative and learning processes and a final technical product. I recognize that this is not available in everyone's institutional setting, but encourage you to find ways to value learning, and to teach students to appreciate growth and progress, not only a one-time product.

Reflection and self-assessment in midterm and final letters

Learning is not something that can be measured by anyone outside of student themself, and requires a level of self-awareness, group accountability, and cultural context. In ungrading, instead of counting on my measures of that, students are asked to assess themselves, giving themselves a grade and justifying it with a narrative.

The prompts I currently use in classes have been developed from previous semesters' letter prompts, as well as Jessica Zeller's 2020 blog post[16] about her move to ungrading. The midterm and final self-assessment letter prompts look like this:

> You should be able to copy and paste much of this from your Artist Log entries.
>
> - Discuss how you worked towards each goal that you set for yourself this half of the semester. How did your work change throughout?
> - Discuss what working towards each goal taught you about you as a learner? As a dancer? As a creative?
> - What has your work in this half of the semester taught you about your body? Your relationship with the word around you? Relevant issues in the artform? Other concepts, subject areas, or arts?
> - What did your regular pair-and-share and/or group discussion times in class offer your learning, that you would not have had without being in conversation with students with different experiences, backgrounds, and perspectives?
> - Discuss how your knowledge and experience of the dance genre/ movement of class has grown. What questions do you still have?

- Midterm Narrative only: Set 5 more goals for the 2nd half of the semester. These may be the same or different or a combination from your first 5. Use the MEG rubric for guidance.
- Final Narrative only: Roxana Ng's essay[17] (we didn't read this in class, just citing my sources) states that embodied learning is valuable learning, because it contains **resistance, questioning, reclamation, and transformation,** and those integrate our whole selves. How did each of these four aspects of learning show up for you in this course? What are you doing with the knowledge revealed in those experiences?
- With all of this reflection, based on your work, and taking into consideration the context of the semester, give yourself a score out of 50 (each goal equates to 10pts on the rubric, be specific as to what goal gets how much) for your work and your learning in this course.
  - Use the MEG rubric to guide your numerical score. Be sure to account for attendance and lateness as well as these reflections.
  - Remember, if your goal is participation, preparedness, supporting peers, etc., please make sure you are accountable to your attendance.

By answering these questions, students can evaluate their new knowledge with me, so that I can input it as a university-approved grade. Felica Rose Chavez uses a simple prompt in her writing workshops, "What did you learn" (177)?

Alfie Kohn writes in "Speaking my Mind: The Trouble with Rubrics," "when the hows of assessment preoccupy us, they tend to chase the whys back into the shadows (2006, 15)." As an educator, these letters demonstrate *why* I assess—students recognize their progress and name opportunities for more. I am always excited to see these personal assessments in each course, and genuinely enjoy reading, watching, or listening to students claim their learning and their challenges.

Movement student experiences

By embodied work, group work and discussion, and personal reflection, I hope to unsettle the typical learning atmosphere of judgement and encourage personal growth.

> This approach de-centers the focus on the instructor as the fount of all knowledge and pushes students to consider their own prior knowledge, positionalities, and the resulting implications of what they have learned from the course material by considering the ways they may balance and harmonize this new knowledge. (Styres, 34)

Students are encouraged to balance personal reflection and ownership of their learning with an acknowledgement of how the communities they come from and are now in shape that learning. This learning is taking place because they are who they are, I am their teacher, their peers are who they are, and we are all sharing a very particular time and space together—and all of that impacts knowledge creation.

One of my classes may mark the first time a student has been asked to consistently contribute their own embodied knowledge, creativity, or interest to their learning. For those who have experienced trauma, particularly at the hands of a teacher, these moments of ownership support psychological safety and belonging. A student[18] in a ballet class wrote in her final letter, "I feel like this semester I reclaimed ballet for myself as a positive art form and self expression [sic], instead of military as it had been in my life. I feel a little transformed as a dancer and I think it's applied to my life as well."

For some, it allows a return to a time when dance was about expression, rather than perfection, reinforcing personal creativity and power. A student in Jazz wrote:

> Not being traditionally graded in the classroom in a dance setting has revolutionized the way I am in a studio space. I feel more free to learn, move, and take risks. Getting to grade myself makes me think more critically about my own work and how much effort I am putting in.

As they set goals, contribute their own creativity, and self-assess, students use their power and see the impact of their power on their world.

REFLECTION SECTION: Movement class assessments

If I were to create a Movement Experiences Guide for Grading, what categories outside of technical execution to I hope students gain skills in? What do those skills/outcomes look like at various levels?

Skill	0	2	5	7	10

How often do students reflect on their learning in my classes? Is it clear to them that reflection is a part of learning?

How do my assessments demonstrate values of learning, creativity, growth, and progress over perfection or singular execution?

How do my midterm and/or final assessments to encourage contributions or challenges? What are adjustments I can make to my midterm and/or final assessments to encourage contributions or challenges?

What sensations, feelings, thoughts do I notice as I think about changing my grading practices or assessments in these ways?

REFLECTION SECTION: Self-assessment questions

What are questions I can ask to help students evaluate and/or demonstrate their own learning?

___

What do I notice in my body as I consider using these questions with students?

___

Contracts, choice, and self-assessment: Ungrading in lecture/theory classes[19]

Students take General Education or survey courses like Dance or Theatre Appreciation or History for different reasons. Some are genuinely interested in the material, others are looking for an "easy" class, and several are simply put in a class that fits their schedule to meet a graduation requirement. Because of these different reasons, not every student sees an "A" as necessary. Contract grading allows for these different contexts while encouraging choice and accountability in learning. My syllabus for Dance Appreciation, which was a class of 160 students from across the university, stated:

> For this class, we will be using a form of contract grading known as specifications grading aka "specs." This means you will decide your grade, and work to meet the specifications for that grade. The grades are bundles of the work for this class: Weekly Responses, Activity Reflections, Self-Assessment Letters, and a Final Project.

The bundles looked like this:

Letter Grade	Weekly Responses (9 possible)	Activity Reflections[20] (6 possible)	Feedback in Group (13 possible)	Letters (2 possible)	Final Portfolio (1 possible)
A	8	5	11	2	1
B	7	4	9	2	1
C	7	3	8	1	1
D	6	2	6	1	0
F	Anything less than the above				

Each assignment type has specifications that must be met to be "complete" and counted toward the desired quota. The grade bundles do operate as "all or nothing" for each letter grade. To achieve an A, all the totals must be met in the A row.

However, the totals reflect that students have a real life, and outside commitments and priorities, and sometimes unexpected happenings; they promote engagement and effort, not perfection. Students should not be penalized for being human, and the grade bundles to allow for this.

Weekly response specifications

Students choose to submit Weekly Responses in one of five categories. These were developed in conversation with Dr. Danielle Rosvalley, who uses similar methods in her theatre history courses:

- Create four memes.
    - Must include people, dates, topics, etc. we discussed in class.
- Choose an interview subject related to the material and state why you are interested in hearing from them.
    - Develop three to five questions to ask them, and state why you are interested in each answer.
- Complete an Observation Sheet[21] for a video of a dance in the genre studied in class, but not viewed in class.
- Create a three to five video playlist to supplement class viewing of this week's genre.
    - Include about 100 words on what each adds to our knowledge about it.
- Craft a Creative Response (poem, dance, visual art, etc.) to the material.
    - Include a brief statement (200–300 words) about what inspired this.

To be marked as complete, a student's response must fit the above description. Turning the work in on time is also requirement for completion. Another overarching specification reads "I should know you are in this class based on the content you submit." The information included must be specific, and not general.

Offering choices in Weekly Responses is a trauma-informed practice that allows for Working Consent. This type of assignment also supports contributor and challenger safeties. Students have clear structures through which to demonstrate their learning, or they can take the opportunity to decide what it means to them to demonstrate their learning. Some of the Creative Responses I've received over the years have deeply impressed me: full dances created with phrases of movement inspired by studied dance forms, watercolor paintings of each dance genre, and video essays combining text, movement, photos, and music to convey what was meaningful to them in the week's learning. Over 20% of the evaluations I received on this class cited the freedom of assignments as the best thing about this class.

With a class of this size, I cannot provide feedback every assignment, every week. Therefore, part of my contract with them is that they will get feedback from me twice during the semester. However, students receive weekly feedback from each other, as a requirement of each grade bundle.[22] A student wrote in their final letter,

> The activities and discussions done with my group and class taught me how other people's perspectives differed from mine ……… I learned what my peers thought which broadened my understanding of the dance. … doing activities like this isn't just about dance, but it helps you think about situations differently.

Because the measures of learning include interaction with others, and sharing learning experiences, their peers depend on them to aid their learning. Diana Taylor describes this as, "What we know, in part, depends on our being there, interacting with others, unsettled from our assumptions and certainties, forging at times the conditions for mutual recognition, trust, and solidarity" (2020, 9). By completing this part of the grading contract, students gain insight into the material and our learning community and develop skills for working with others.

Weekly Responses, and the accompanying feedback to a peer, make up 80% of final projects (see below), as well as contribute to the bundles. These are not "busy work;" students have tangible proof that ongoing investment in their own learning and our class community impacts their final outcomes. Because of this, students are also encouraged to "meet spec" on all assignments, not just the ones I give feedback on; they know I will see much of their work in their final project, and an incomplete final would result in a C or less.

Midterm and final assessments in theory/lecture classes as examples of contributor and challenger safeties

In these classes, students do a midterm self-assessment letter from a prompt like the one provided for Movement Classes. This is also a time for them to count their completed assignments and see if they are on track for the letter grade they desire. At this point, I provide personal feedback to each student on their work and progress.

For their final projects, students turn in a portfolio of their work over the class. As mentioned above, Weekly Responses form the basis of these projects. My syllabus for these courses reads,

> The goal of the Final Project is to synthesize your learning from the course. You will have to do some additional writing and/or creating. But, if you have kept up with your Weekly Responses, Activity Reflections,

and Letters, you should be able to do a lot of cutting/pasting or linking things together!

In every final project, it should be obvious that you were in this class. The vocabulary used, people/places/genres referenced, etc.

The following examples are the Final Projects[23] for a recent section of Dance Appreciation. As you can see, these tie back to the types of Weekly Response students could submit.

Final Type	Description	Instructions	Specs
Observation Sheets from Weekly Reflection	Compare and contrast 1 from each module (Dance as Record-Keeping, Dance as Performance, Dance as Community). If you are missing one, create one now.	• Compare and contrast each dance's use of the categories. • Use proper vocabulary that we have covered in this class. • Synthesize your findings with meaning-making and interpretation, as well as your own preferences and experiences.	• Every category on the Observation Sheet must be mentioned, but not all 3 dances need to be addressed in every section. • Reference which Weekly Responses you revisited for this project. • Essay should be 1–2 pages. Video essay should be 1–2 minutes. • Turn in the Observation Sheets with your essay or video essay. • Include a bibliography-links must be cited. • Turned in on time.

(*Continued*)

Final Type	Description	Instructions	Specs

Dance Appreciation Video Playlist	Use your video suggestions from your Weekly Responses to create. If you did not suggest the required amount during the semester, you can bring them forward now.	• Suggest at least 3 for each module. (9 total, or more!)
		• Turn in a doc with the link to the play list and an essay or video essay that addresses:
		  a. What module or unit you would create to introduce these. You cannot use my titles.
		  b. Why would these be required viewing? What would you hope students would learn from viewing each?
		  c. What order your modules would go in, and why.
		  d. What order you would show the videos in, and why.
			• 9 or more videos.
			• Answers all of the above, in your own words, not AI generated.
			• Reference which Weekly Response you revisited for this final project.
			• Essay should be 1–2 pages. Video essay should be 1–2 minutes.
			• Include a bibliography-links must be cited.
			• Turned in on time.

(*Continued*)

Final Type	Description	Instructions	Specs

Interview	Choose one of the subjects you suggested in a Weekly Response for an interview.	• Actually interview them (or do research to ascertain their answers) with the questions you proposed.
		  a. If you are going to record them, audio or video, you must ask for their consent. Even if you are not going to share it with me.
		    i. If you are going to share the audio or video file with me, please share with them that you are, and that it will be a digital file in our LMS. With AI concerns, some folks may wish to opt out of that.
		    ii. If you need help finding someone with a certain job or connecting with folks, please reach out to me. While I likely can't get you an interview with Misty Copeland, I can get you an interview with a professional dancer.
		• Include in your essay/video essay:
		  a. An introduction to them and their relation to dance.
		  b. Why you wanted to interview them.
		  c. Their answers to your questions.
		  d. Your own meaning-making- Use our Statements of Meaning format we've gone over previously in class.
			• Answer everything above.
			• Reference which Weekly Response this is inspired by.
			• This should be obviously your own work, not AI generated (especially if you are doing research and not a live interview).
			• Essay should be 1-2 pages. Video essay should be 1-2 minutes.
			• Include a bibliography- links must be cited.
			• Turned in on time.

(Continued)

Final Type	Description	Instructions	Specs

Digital Creative Showcase	Compile your Creative Responses into video, gallery, PDF, or something else.	• At least five creations from previous work.
		• Add one (or more if you did not have five from the responses) new creation I have not seen/heard/experienced before.
		• Accompany the Showcase with a 1-page document or 1-minute video detailing:
		   a. Why you are showcasing these creative works. What meaning do they hold for you?
		   b. Why are these pieces in the order they are in? What story does the
		   c. Showcase tell, as a whole.
			• Six or more original creative works
			• Reference which Weekly Responses you are using.
			• 1-page document answering the above. Video description should be 1–2 minutes.
			• Include a bibliography-links must be cited.
			• Turned in on time.

Since these projects are built off previous and highly structured, this is a time for students to experience contributor safety. They have the skills and the knowledge, and can demonstrate the outcomes of learning in personal, creative ways!

I have received some amazing final projects with these instructions, including video interviews of dancers at other schools and students' former studio teachers, wonderful videos for playlists that broadened my horizons of dance and what I could show students, and solo choreography inspired by the studied dance forms. When given the opportunity to claim their knowledge in personally meaningful ways, many students rise to, or even go beyond, the challenge.

One class was ready for challenger safety even beyond the Creative Showcase option and asked me about designing their own finals that didn't fit these categories. I agreed, but students had to submit their own spec sheet at a specified date that detailed what would be included, so that I could ensure the work was comparable to that of their peers and that it connected to the work of the class. This has now become a regular part of Final Project offerings.

Dance studies student experiences

The midterm and final self-assessment letters in this class include a count of assignments for their bundles and a reflection. A student in Dance Appreciation wrote in their final letter:

> I did achieve the grade that I wanted! An A! I did every assignment and came to nearly every class. I am very happy and proud of myself to have stuck with the grade I wanted and ensured that I received it. I also just wanted to thank you for such a great semester and let you know how much I feel this grade has helped me grow.

Her commitment to herself and her class resulted in not only a "good grade," but personal transformation.

My favorite student comment though, was:

> Truthfully, I signed up for this class as a bullsh*t credit. I did not think I would get much out of this and was just taking this to ensure I was a full-time student. However, the amount of information I learned, the sheer number of things that I enjoyed, and my overall enjoyment with this entire class was simply incredible.

To take a class that can feel "just a requirement," or where a student is one of so many that they could feel lost or ignored, and know that they not only learned, but enjoyed learning, is care-full teaching.

REFLECTION SECTION: Theory/lecture classes assessments

What are adjustments I can make to my assessments to encourage contributions or challenges?

_____

_____

_____

_____

_____

What sensations, feelings, thoughts do I notice as I think about changing my grading practices or assessments in these ways?

_____

_____

_____

_____

_____

Common misconceptions around ungrading

Ungrading is not a new concept. But it is not widely used in academic programs. Traditional academic power dynamics do provide a level of security, to both the teacher and the students, because it is familiar. I wrote in the *Dance Teacher* article:

> Transparent conversations around the "why" and "how" of ungrading will likely be necessary with students, colleagues, and administration. Grading has become an entrenched part of teaching, and the reasons why and how we do it are often left unexamined.

In my desire to do assessment and grading differently, in ways that are trauma-informed, consent-forward, and psychologically safe, I have found ways that work for me, and many of the students I work with. I also continually seek ways to grade with more care.

For many movement instructors, touch remains the sole point of discussion and change when it comes to being consent-forward and trauma-informed in class. I have surprised quite few colleagues with the stance that traditional grading does not honor consent, and that is why I seek to do it differently. Their objections and concerns about ungrading tend to be one of the following explored below.

Ungrading lacks rigor

As with the syllabus, this is only true if one conceives of "rigor" as "one size fits all," or that there is only one way to be successful. In my conversation with Dr. Alexia Buono, she said that many students and professors confuse conformity with rigor. "While ungrading does not require conformity, to do it well, rigor is required of both the teacher and the students."

I have found rigor to be required in communication and application of ungrading for all parties. I must write excellent prompts that help students assess and progress. I must spend time in feedback. Ungrading requires that I spend the time and effort to create Learner Safety for students. Then, students must engage with integrity and hold themselves accountable to their own goals.

Care-full pedagogy recognizes that all students have different needs, experiences, and goals. Ungrading helps us support all these truths. Ungrading also recognizes that there are many ways to be successful as an artist and a student, and it may be different than the way the teacher conceived of. Ungrading demands the best of us for it to work.

Students won't have the technical skills they need

Students are still working on their skills in class. But in ungrading, they are measuring their progress towards their own goals for those skills, rather than an idea of "good," or "perfect," or "better than" someone else. Ungrading alleviates competition mindset as well as Expert Power and allows students to learn and contribute without fear.

Not doing traditional assessments or grades does not mean that students are not learning. As Dr. Jessica Zeller said in our conversation, "Grades and the learning are not the same." Also, if you can assess technical skills in a feedback-only, nongraded situation like mentioned above, this point is alleviated.

Students won't have the skills they need for the "Real World"

For students entering the professional performance their worlds will be different. Some will belong to incredibly collaborative companies that work in consent-forward, trauma-informed ways. Some will join traditional arts organizations that run with typical hierarchical power structures. Some will create their own work. We have no idea where these students will end up, so we should be giving them skills to succeed everywhere: proactive and professional communication, the ability to set goals and self-assess, collaboration, awareness of power dynamics and their effects, and self-advocacy. Ungrading methods do this.

Also, as I've mentioned before, in the arts we are in the business of creating new worlds. We know that the "Real World" is often not consent-forward, trauma-informed, or psychologically safe. But that doesn't mean it should or needs to be this way. Why should we teach students to settle for a world that denies their autonomy and humanity? Let's teach them to see the world as it is, and to create the world they want to live and work in.

If I don't grade, I won't be fulfilling my job responsibilities

In conversation, Dr. Jessica Zeller brought this up as a concern she hears from colleagues. She then followed it with, "What if grading isn't actually my job?"

Grading isn't our job; teaching is. For many instructors turning in grades is listed on our job duties. But how we get to those grades, and what value they hold in our classrooms are open to individual processes. Ungrading promotes individual learning—and we can still turn in grades at the end. As we've seen in this chapter and other places in this book, the power dynamics and traumatic potential of grades can keep students from learning. When we ungrade, we fulfill our job duties but enable teaching and learning.

Ungrading takes too much time

I heard this one recently in a webinar I led for NDEO on ungrading in dance. The truth is, it does take more time for me to read, listen to, or view Artist Logs, Weekly Responses, and Self-assessment Letters than if I gave a multiple-choice test, or used a single jury or technical assessment as the basis for final grades. But I would miss so much of the humanity and personal creativity students bring if I did that. I wrote in *Dance Teacher*:

> For me, ungrading has been both rewarding and fulfilling. I have found that the work I receive from ungraded students is much more compelling, because they are invested in it. Personal assessments I receive from students are inspiring and interesting. ... they provide important insights into their humanity and learning process.

We are also at time right now when AI tools have caused many teachers to reexamine what they are truly trying to assess, how they do that. This may be a great time to experiment in these more personal ways of assessment and feedback.

Conclusion

Susan Blum writes in her introduction to *Ungrading*, "in going gradeless, most...act on the conviction that our principal task is educating all students, not ranking them" (2020, 5). A care-full pedagogy works to create an atmosphere of collaboration and trust. Students trust that their peers are there to learn and support each other's learning, that their teacher will use their power to create a space and practice of safety and equity, and that their own interests and needs are worthwhile.

Cullen and Oppenheimer remind us, "there is a dearth of research validating interventions to promote autonomy in higher education" (2024, 6). While this chapter did not quantify research, it provided theoretical underpinnings, practical examples, the experiences of other educators, and student outcomes to provide rationales and templates for movement educators to promote student power and autonomy, even in assessment. Creating care-full assessments can mitigate the power dynamics of grades, and honor the complexities of students, including the possibility of trauma, particularly the traumas caused by evaluation, judgment, and/or lack of choice.

For the *Dance Teacher* article about ungrading, I interviewed several colleagues from around the country. I asked them specifically about the connection of ungrading and consent-forward and trauma-informed pedagogies. Autonomy and agency came up in many answers. Dr. Ali Duffy told me, "I believe ungrading absolutely connects to consent-forward pedagogy because it offers students space to enter the content from wherever they feel empowered and comfortable." Heather Castillo, MFA, an Associate Professor of Dance Studies at CSU Channel Islands, felt ungrading was both consent-forward and trauma-informed because, "It helps dismantle the idea of hierarchy and can tackle imposter syndrome."

Drs. Jessica Zeller, Andrea Markus, and Alexia Buono instead position ungrading in a liberatory or abolitionist pedagogy. As Buono described it for *Dance Teacher*:

> A liberatory educational model depends on the how. It reworks education to remind us we are all human, learning is not linear, it never ends. It invites space for our students and us as professors to be the humans that we are, rather than strive for perfection. It is a way to not just say we are refusing grading, but we are rebuilding a liberatory system with our students—in collaboration with students.

I quoted Zeller in the article, stating, "equity has improved because it gets me out the way—interrupts any bias I hold." Markus told me that ungrading helps her ask "How do we teach so that every body learns?"

The article, and even my chapter thus far, could not hold all the wisdom and insights these colleagues shared. So, I have included some more of their applicable words on why they ungrade here to close this chapter.

Alexia Buono, PhD, Professor of Early Childhood Education at the University of Vermont:

> What is the purpose of education? What are strategies that actually get us towards this? This is humanizing modes of assessment.

Heather Castillo, MFA, Associate Professor of Dance Studies at CSU Channel Islands:

> Having discussions around the practices of grading, giving students agency in grading, and rethinking why we grade is important to developing critically thinking students who take agency and responsibility for their learning process and education.

Ali Duffy, PhD, Professor of Dance at Texas Tech University,

> I find that students can become hyper focused on points, numbers, and letters when grades represent the primary way for them to illustrate learning and growth. This has the effect of distracting the students away from what I want them to be curious about—their choreography! I see traditional grading as more of an authoritarian, top-down approach, whereas I believe an empowered, shared, co-created learning experience in a classroom to be most effective … When educators take the pressure off of the mighty grade, possibilities open for greater depth, diverse expression, and risk taking in choreography.

Andrea Markus, EdD, Adjunct Professor of Dance at NYU and Marymount Manhattan College:

> Those of us whose teaching practices are centered around care, love, and joy will sometimes meet students who will only respond to authoritarian practices. Some students are complicit in abusive education practices by accident, because they only respond to "old-school," or authoritarian ways of being in the dance classroom.

Gina T'ai, MFA, Associate Professor of Performing and Applied Arts at Beloit College:

> I want all of our learning outcomes to be on growth and not skills. Everything is in service of the individual's growth, and we grow within community.

Jessica Zeller, PhD, MFA, Professor of Ballet at Texas Christian University:

> I don't think it's possible to have a student-centered class if the professor is the sole assessor.

There is no single approach or timeline to demonstrating care in assessments, nor to ungrading. I have, over several years, found methods that I feel promote care for the whole student—their choices, experiences, and growth. I hope this chapter inspires you to create assessments with care, as well as assessments that promote care.

Chapter reminders

- Grades are examples of Reward and Coercive Powers.
- Grades, and the rewards they represent through recognition, validation, and/or pleasing authority, support the power imbalance of teacher over student.

- "Ungrading" is not one tool or method, but rather is a way of assessing that center autonomy and growth over compliance or a single demonstration of mastery.
- Ungrading practices fit a care-full pedagogy:
  - They ease the demands of power dynamics, as meeting my expectations is not the standard for success.
  - They are opportunities for Working Consent, as students have tangible agency over their grade.
  - They are trauma-informed, as they limit opportunities for harm that occur in systems built on power, competition, and hierarchies.
- Grades are given and sought for different reasons. Knowing the purpose of grades in your class is key to care-full pedagogy.
- Reflection, with its aspects of personal growth and meaning making, encourages learning and ongoing exploration, rather than assuming learning is something that stops once a grade is assigned.
- Ungrading is a relationship of trust between teacher and students.

Notes

1. Much of this chapter was originally published as the in-practice article "Assessments of Care" in the 2025 special issue of the *Journal of Dance Education*. In this book, I reordered pieces and have been able to go more in depth in examples and explanations. However, you may experience a bit of deja vu in some places if you read that article, as it serves as the source material for this chapter.
2. Since this chapter is focused on practice, while I cite sources, please know that there are many more resources and scholarship on grading and alternative methods of grading available. I have offered some of my favorites in the "Resources" section.
3. The article is linked in the "Resources" section. For this article I interviewed colleagues from around the country, who used different methods of ungrading in different types of courses. Some of their quotes were used in the article, and some have stayed in my notes, and now live in this book. Each professor has given consent for their words to be used in this context, even if they didn't appear in the original piece.
4. I have included the accompanying slides for this discussion in the "Resource" section.
5. However, there is a way to earn more tokens! Here is where I put assignments that used to be "extra credit" that now earn a token: see a show and write a review, write a letter to your art form as if it were a person, or attend an outside movement class and discuss it through the lens of what we are learning in our class.
6. Prompts crafted this way also help address the AI issue, as raised in Chapter 6.
7. Detailed in Chapter 7.
8. Included in this chapter is the MEG to with its most categories and descriptions. I do not, in every class, use all these examples or all of this wording.

9. For ballet, I have specific technical offerings I suggest to students for inclusion.
10. I am certain a brilliant colleague came up with this term before me, however, I do not remember who. If this was you, I'm sorry, and please tell me.
11. Have you noticed I might really like *Star Trek*?
12. A simplified version of Artist Logs, meant for studio use, exist for sale at Momentum Stage. You can use the link in the "Resources" section to find these if you would like actual logs for your students. However, I encourage you to consider crafting your own, as you know your classes and students far better than I.
13. I will give examples of the types of feedback students may experience in these settings in the next chapter.
14. This assignment was inspired by dance professor colleague Nicole Y. McClam. See the "Resource" section for full citation.
15. As found in Hackney, Peggy. *Making Connections*. See the "Resource" section with citations for full citation.
16. Linked in the "Resources" section. She includes a new set of evaluation questions, for both midterm and final self-reflections in her book, *Humanizing Ballet Pedagogies*.
17. I always reference this essay, even in classes that do not read it, as part of my own ethical pedagogic practice. It is linked in the "Resources" section.
18. Students quoted in this chapter and the previous have given permission for the words to be used anonymously.
19. While not necessarily "movement pedagogy," I have included my methods of ungrading for theory/lecture courses here because:
    - You are likely to teach one of these types of classes in your career, even in movement fields.
    - You may find inspiration from these methods for your movement classes.
    - I also use the "bundles" described here for the Artist Log "grade" in technique classes.
20. I do not go into detail on the Activity Reflections in the chapter. However, there is a paragraph in the "Resource" section dedicated to this if you are curious!
21. Like the Artist Log prompts requiring reflection on class experiences, this point exposes AI use, because the generators do not know the specifics of our classroom activities or students' embodied experience.
22. There is much more giving and receiving feedback, from both teachers and students, in the next chapter.
23. There is more information on each project in a presentation I use to accompany Final Project Instructions, that I give usually about four weeks before Final Projects are due. You can see this presentation in the "Resources" section.

10
Practices in assessment: Feedback

Theories of feedback in higher ed movement classes

Giving feedback, or notes, like touch in movement or dance classes, is often taken for granted because it is such an ingrained part of class. However, leaving the giving of feedback unexamined means its potential to rely on power dynamics, deny consent, or even cause trauma remains unaddressed. Or, as Alfie Kohn reminds us in *Punished by Rewards*, "it takes skill and care and attention to encourage people in such a way that they remain interested in what they are doing and don't feel controlled" (2018, 112).

The power dynamics of Expert and Legitimate Powers can influence students during times of feedback, whether it be from instructors or peers. When I as the instructor give feedback in movement classes, I must be aware of the powers I hold, and the things that influence me: my cultural context, training and experiences, and preferences.

Effective, care-full, and creativity-building feedback requires:

- That I know my own biases.
- That I put the artist's purpose(s) above my own experience.
- That I value the creative process, not just the product (no fixing or promoting my way of creating or doing).

Because power dynamics and pressure can also exist from peer-to-peer, my responsibility as an instructor who gives feedback is to help students account for these things as well.

Since feedback can sometimes be given in ways that promote the speaker's point of view over the artist's choices and creative autonomy, feedback can feel invalidating, dismissive, or even activate a trauma response, like fight or flight. However, when done well, feedback is an opportunity for learning and to demonstrate care.

Liz Lerman and John Borstel's (2003) *Critical Response Process*, Larry Lavender's (1996) *Talking about Dance*, and studies in Nonviolent Communication have been formative to my own thoughts and instructions regarding feedback. My methods have also been influenced by Mary Parker Follett's ([1933] 1973) "law of the situation" and Felicia Rose Chavez's (2021) *The Anti-Racist Writing Workshop*, as you will see later in the chapter.

Liz Lerman's *Critical Response Process*, is a feedback method designed for groups and consists of four steps:

1. Statements of Meaning: Responders state what was meaningful, evocative, interesting, exciting, striking in the work they have just witnessed.
2. Artist as Questioner: The artist asks questions about the work. After each question, the responders answer.
3. Neutral Questions: Responders ask neutral questions about the work. The artist responds.
4. Opinion Time: Responders state opinions, subject to permission from the artist. The usual form is "I have an opinion about _____, would you like to hear it?" The artist has the option to say no. (2020, 1)

Larry Lavender uses ORDER to create a feedback formula, specifically for dance and choreography classes:

- **O**bservation
- **R**eflection
- **D**iscussion
- **E**valuation
- **R**ecommendations for revisions (2006)

Nonviolent communication (NVC) was codified by Marshall Rosenberg[1] to deal with conflict in ways that keep us connected to ourselves and to the person we are speaking to. While giving feedback is not a conflict, it can sometimes feel like that to the person receiving it, especially if the feedback does not fit with their worldview, artistic point of view, or is not given to enable learning or action.

Rosenberg writes, "The first component of NVC entails the separation of observation from evaluation (2003, 26). I have found this principle to be incredibly useful in giving feedback, as it allows me, and the student artist I am giving feedback to, to remember that my interpretation and evaluation are *based* on what I observed, but they are *not* what I observed. Therefore, my meaning-making and experience are mine alone, and say more about me, than they do about the artist. My observation is what speaks about the artist and the art.

NVC also asks us to remember that everyone is simply trying to get their needs met. When working with students, we need to be curious about *which* need they are trying to meet. *Are they creating something to share a specific message? Are they working towards a particular goal? Are they trying to impress the teacher or their classmates or get a "good" grade? Are they trying to challenge themselves or to feel good about themselves?* Understanding which need students are trying to meet through their work in class can lead to effective and useful feedback for them, and a deeper understanding of the learners in our spaces for us.

Another principle of NVC is to create and maintain connection. Communicating in ways that foster connection with others is also a crucial part of teaching with care.

I have found worthwhile objectives and methods in each of these processes, and, through combining them with my knowledge or power dynamics, consent, and trauma, I have created a Care-full Feedback Method.

Curating care-full feedback

In both movement and lecture courses, feedback from others is a component of learning. However, feedback in many performance-related courses is traditionally not consent-forward nor trauma-informed. Nor is it often delivered in a space that values psychological safety. I wrote for *Dance Geist*:

> Often when we give feedback, we *think* we are centering the artwork. But, what we are usually doing is trying to convey the ways we (as teacher, critic, or audience) would "fix" the work to fit what we want it to be—which may have nothing whatsoever to do with the artist's vision of it.
>
> Another common use of feedback is to show how informed or correct the viewer is. By passing judgment on another's work as less than, we can show off our high standards. When we praise something that fits our personal construction of art, we validate our own point of view. Unfortunately, neither of these is of any assistance to the artist, which should be the point of feedback.

Because feedback, from me and from peers, is a required part of the courses I teach, I approach it with great deliberateness, taking time to teach how to both give and receive feedback in care-full ways. We start similarly to how I introduced ungrading, by asking "What is the purpose of feedback?" Often, the answer from students is something like "so I know what to fix." Offering a correction or solution is one reason to provide feedback. But as noted above, other reasons may include "fixing" it for someone else (which does not foster consent or creativity) or the critique-giver proving how "right" they are (which relies on Expert Power dynamics). Feedback like this tells us much more about the person giving the critique, than the artist or the artwork.

Other reasons to offer feedback may be:

- To provide encouragement.
- To deepen or check understanding.
- To share how I, the viewer, experienced the work.
- To build community as multiple parties engage in the creative process.
- To cultivate creativity and help the artists fulfill their vision of the artwork.

Through our discussion, students realize that not everyone wants the same type of feedback or wants to give or receive feedback for the same reasons. When it comes to sharing work, sharing points of views, and cultivating community and creativity are all useful forms of feedback. Feedback that offers "fixes" or corrections *can* be useful, but only if that type of comment is desired (See Lerman's *CRP* Step Four) or fits with their personal experiences.

If we have not done this already in class when we get to our feedback lesson, I include here the Story People exercises and Selective Attention Tests found in Chapter 5. These experiences serve as practice for students to remove their own preferences and assumptions that exist when viewing others, including the artwork of others.

REFLECTION SECTION: The purpose of feedback

What is the purpose of feedback in my classes?

What makes "good" feedback?

What do students think makes "good" feedback?

Are there assumptions I am making from power dynamics, or my own positionality or values that students may not, and do not have to share? How do I account for this in feedback sessions? How do I help students do this for each other?

The care-full feedback process

With all these inspirations and reflections, my feedback model for myself, and that I teach in classes and workshops, so that the feedback given is full of care, follows four steps:

1. Witness and Reflect.
2. Describe.
3. Recognize the Art in the Process.
4. Answer the Artists' Questions.

Witness and reflect

Bearing witness requires a level of detachment. A witness in a court must be able to relay the facts as they know them, without their own judgment, so that others may draw their own conclusions. So too, in movement class. When we witness each other's movements, we attempt to see them for what they are, not what we may want them to be. In doing so, we must also remove our own values from the description. Reflection gives us time for that.

In this step the person giving feedback asks themselves, "What am I seeing?" and reflects on what they witnessed. Lavender describes reflection as an activity that "helps students become conscious of the nature of their perceptual experience before hearing the responses of others" (69). This is an internal step for the person giving feedback.

Describe

After observing and reflecting, we are ready to share our findings. However, before we do so, we ask, "How can I share what I see in ways that do not center my aesthetic values or position?"

Grounding feedback in observation is one of the steps of communicating nonviolently, as is recognizing the difference between observation and evaluation. Rosenberg offers that, "observations are to be made specific to time and context" (32). He offers the example, "'Hank Smith has not scored a goal in twenty games,' rather than 'Hank Smith is a poor soccer player'" (32). In movement class this description may be, "I noticed that you did not include *specific skill we are working on in class*," "I saw this *skill or element in* this moment," or "you have missed three class so far this semester." None of these have judgment or criticism, they are observable facts.

Like Lerman's "Neutral Questions," describing in this way attempts to account for personal preferences and to use unloaded, nonjudgmental language to communicate what they are viewing. This is like the "clinical" or observational writing students did in Observation Exercises. This is not always easy for me, as my teacher brain often wants to offer my point of view, in the name of education. But my point of view is only that, mine, and likely will not help the student achieve their goals.

The phrases "It was good" or "I liked it" are expressly forbidden in feedback sessions in classes I facilitate. When trying to be positive, we forget that "telling someone her work is good is every bit as much a value judgment as saying it is bad (Kohn 2018, 102). In addition, sentences like these tell us about the values of the person giving the feedback, and not about the art! Instead, describing what we see in unloaded terms helps set us up to recognize the art and answer the artists' questions aware of our biases and assumptions.

This is not necessarily a step the viewer shares with the artists, although it may be. But these observational statements become the basis for step three.

Recognize the art in the process

When we witness the creative and expressive movement of others, even in process, we witness art. It does not have to be completed "piece" or performance. It may not be our preferred type or style; we may not even "get it." But those things don't make it less art. It was a creative attempt to make something new that would share, communicate, or express the inner thoughts of the creator to the viewer.

Like Lerman's "Statements of Meaning," the feedback given to the artist in this step states what the viewers were made to think about, wonder, feel, image, remember, want to know more about, etc. because of the piece. Or viewers might share how the piece impacted their artistic perspective. Building on the last step of Describe, this step sounds like: "I saw ____, and it made me feel/think/wonder," or "you use of x skill reminded me of...," or "when you ____, I felt ____."

Many students, and teachers for that matter, have not done a deep examination of their aesthetic values. Being able to do so, and honestly assess the power dynamics that are a part of these aesthetics, is a necessary part of being able to give care-full feedback.

To help with this, I have started giving dance students an Artist Log prompt created by Crystal U. Davis in her book *Dance and Belonging*:

> Describe what beautiful dancing looks like to you. How do you determine what is beautiful? How did you come to know the markers what signify beauty? More specifically, how did you come to know what dances are of artistic quality and what dances are not? How did you come to know the markers that signified that a dance is of quality? Where did you receive guidance, modeling, experience, in articulating the words and defining features of a high-quality dance work? Were there people who had a different opinion than you at that time? If so, how did you come to know that the people who shared with you the elements of a quality dance work were experts to be trusted? How did you discern that this expert should be the authority on what determines quality instead of a different person who may have a different option? (2022, 65)

Students complete this journal prompt after the feedback lesson and before they enter into feedback sessions in class.

Answer the artist's questions

Now that the artist knows what art the audience is witnessing, they can assess how this aligns with the art they aimed to create. Like Lerman's "Artist as Questioner," this is a time for artists to ask the audience something specific about the piece. These questions may come from the feedback they heard or may have been formulated ahead of time. In my classes, I usually require students to come to midterm or final presentations with two questions for the audience, but with the option to drop those if they hear something in the feedback of the moment they would rather address. In answering the artist's questions, the feedback giver should first ask themselves, "How can my observations, descriptions, and/or meaning-making support the art the artist is trying to make?"

Feedback to movement experiences or movement sharing in class

In creative work

Care-full feedback has three defining features:

- It gets the student closer to their goals or helps them see how to move towards their goals.
- It is actionable.
- It does not compare artistic works.

In her writing workshops, Felicia Rose Chavez asks students what kind of feedback they are looking for. She writes:

> Were they toying with new ideas and techniques and wanted encouragement? Were they expelling a messy draft in hopes of discovering what pops? Were the finalizing a draft for publication and wanted line edits? Just because all of my students completed an identical assignment didn't mean that their relationship to the work with identical. (156)

While I have never tried this in a movement class, I suspect it could be equally applicable. *Do they need encouragement as they try new things? Do they need a statement of meaning from an audience, or to discover it for themselves? Do they need technical and precise feedback to prepare them for a jury, audition, or performance?* This could be tailored to fit the goals the students set in their self-assessment letters. Differing learning needs and goals create different feedback needs.

Coupled with ungrading, feedback from me is free to meet the student's needs in their creative expression. As Jessica Zeller reminds in *Humanizing Ballet Pedagogies*, "If I don't have to levy a grade, my perspective serves as a resource rather than the standard" (2024, 150). My feedback becomes about moving students toward their goals, not my preferences.

Care-full feedback does not have to be full of praise. Remember, Reward Power exists and can quickly become coercive as those with less power become more motivated to please the person in power. Alfie Kohn wrote in *Punished by Rewards*:

> With every comment we make–and specifically, every compliment we give–we need to ask whether we are helping that individual to feel a sense of control over his life. Are we encouraging him to make his own judgments about what constitutes a good performance? (106)

Instead, care-full feedback gives the student information they need to make choices, or to be able to put their own choices and judgements into action.

Giving actionable feedback means that the student knows what to do next. This is not a directive, as in, "you should change levels on count eight" or "you should ____." Unless it is a technical or safety issue, feedback that begins with "you should" is about the giver's opinion, not about the art becoming what the artist wants it to be, or even about the student's learning goals.

Actionable feedback instead helps students realize what their next step(s) could be. Edmonson describes feedback in a psychological safe space to be "concerned with future impact" (2019, 179). Our feedback should be as well—how will this feedback shape what comes after, and create a future in which the artist is autonomous and confident in their work? In this way, feedback is a gift, an idea supported by NVC.

Finally, care-full feedback also avoids comparing students and/or their work to one another. While this may seem obvious, subtle comments like "ask so-and-so how they did that," or even offering more or less feedback to one student than to another can feed competition mindset. Kohn writes:

> Avoid praise that sets up competition.... [It] encourage[s] a view of others as rivals rather than as potential collaborators. What's more, [it] leads people to see their own worth in terms of whether they have beaten everyone else—a recipe for perpetual insecurity. (109)

When we praise, we usually want to bolster students' confidence and creativity, but the wrong kind of praise results in the opposite.

In technical corrections

Another change to my own teaching methods has been depersonalizing corrections and instructional feedback. Based on Mary Parker Follett's "law of the situation" ([1933] 1973) this way of speaking to students removes some of the power dynamics inherent in the student-teacher relationship, by putting the focus on the shared goal of the work to be done. In moving my language to depersonalization, it is my goal to alleviate feelings of personal shortcomings on behalf of students, as well as their desire to please me as the teacher.

In ballet class, for example, this could look like stating: "The aesthetic of ballet requires us to point our toes," rather than "Student, you need to point your toes!" With this change, I've reminded them of the physical action to take, and the "why" for doing it—to do the work we are here to do, ballet. We are both listening to the aesthetic of ballet for what we should do; in the words of Mary Parker Follett, "both should agree to take their orders from the situation (58)." I do not offer a correction because I find the student personally disappointing, or because it gives me my desire. Rather the correction serves the work we both agreed to—in this example, create ballet. Likewise, students do not have to make the change because I said so, but rather because they are there to do the work.

Here we are reminded of a key part of Follett's "law of the situation," "Our job is not how to get people to obey orders, but how to devise methods by which we can best *discover* the order integral to a particular situation" (59). I appreciate this idea applied to pedagogy; our job as teachers is not to order students, but rather to create space and experiences for them to engage in the work, so that they learn what is needed to do the work.

Feedback to reflective or self-assessing assignments

In learning, questions are almost always more valuable than answers. Questions help us see what we still don't know, and where we can deepen our understanding. When students demonstrate a phrase or turn in their Weekly Responses or Self-assessment Letters, I make much of my feedback questions, rather than comments. I go to step three of Lerman's CRP, "Neutral Questions," and try to create questions that will help students discover more of what they want their art to be, or more of what they want to learn. These questions might be, "Why do you think that is," "what do you think your next step is," or "can you tell me more about ___?"

In *Dancers Talking Dance*, Larry Lavender writes, "Indeed, when a teacher's critical voice dominates in the classroom, students are usually exposed to judgments derived from undiscussed and possibly arbitrary criteria" (51). Making feedback a question instead of a statement also keeps me from exerting Expert Power over the student. Giving feedback is not a time for me to impose my values or preferences, but rather to give students an opportunity to reestablish themselves in the learning.

Questions also remind me, and students, that there are multiple solutions to creative problems. Particularly in classes where students can make their own choices and may have a different movement background or aesthetic than I, their answers to the questions can provide me with important context about their creative process, so I do not make assumptions based on my own experiences or unexamined biases. Lavender cautions:

> Therefore, to press upon students prevailing critical standards actually teaches them nothing about how to discover the ways art influences our perceptions or about the fundamental nature of critical discourse.... Moreover, lists of criteria tend to silence students who might propose (either in discussion or through their creative works) different artistic values. (34)

Using students' stated goals from MEG as stated in their letters is often how I start my questioning process.

Feedback from the class

Giving and receiving feedback to movement experiences/experiments in my classes are another opportunity to practice Working Consent. When students share, I ask them if they would like feedback from the class and me.

Not every student is in the frame of mind or body on any given day to accept more information about their work. But, whether from true desire or due to the power dynamics of teacher/student, they nearly always say "yes."

Similarly, students may offer feedback to movement experiences, but it is not required. This also honors the time it takes to enter the feedback process. Not every student will be able to move through their steps and have something to offer in the time provided. Not every student will be able to do this for every piece. Instead, I ask them to make sure they have offered feedback at least once in class.

When I offer feedback, I go last, making sure students have the opportunity to share, before the power dynamic of Expert Power enters the conversation. By waiting, I can also use my time to address or redirect some of the other comments that were made.

In movement experiments

In daily classes, the feedback process may only be the first two steps, *Witness and Reflect*, and *Describe*. By engaging in these steps regularly, students become more attuned to their own movement preferences and habits in seeing and describing movement. This practice makes the sharing process more efficient and equitable.

Sometimes students or small groups will "pair-and-share" after movement experiments. Those sessions are usually guided to include the *Recognize the Art in the Process* step, as students are asked to share how they saw their partner or other group fulfill the experiment with their choices, especially if the choice made was something different than how they chose to complete the experiment.

The following are examples of feedback experiences for midterm and final projects (described in Chapter 9).

Ballet

For both the midterm and final projects,[2] observing students, and I as the instructor, are asked to *Recognize the Art in the Process*. These statements should include naming ballet vocabulary and validating choices. For example, "I was surprised by your choice to make the plié in second, but thought it made a useful transition," or "I never would have thought to use the pas de chat to change formations and found that exciting."

The presenting dancers are asked to come with two questions, so the feedback can also *Answer the Artists' Questions*. Past examples are: "The next section of the *Candy Girl* song says____ and we didn't know how to fulfill that, so we stopped it here. What are your ideas for that lyric," and "What ballet vocabulary and lyric match most surprised you?" Because these projects often inspire a lot of conversation around ballet vocabulary as a creative tool, if time permits, the audience may ask a neutral question like, "How did you come up with____," or "Why did you want to use ___ for ___ lyric?"

Movement for Actors

In Movement for Actors classes, students enter a monologue workshop for both midterms and finals.[3] They are asked to accept feedback on their performance from me and their peers.

By spending the full semester rehearsing one piece, students explore a lot of choices and get feedback on those choices. I give class time for rehearsals the two weeks leading up to a workshop and students often use that time both to work alone, and then to invite me or a few peers to view it and offer feedback in unofficial sessions.

During the monologue workshops, observing students are asked to *Recognize the Art in the Process*. These should include the movement vocabulary and concepts we are working on in each half of the semester. For the final performance, these could also include changes and/or growth since the midterm presentation.

The performer then asks audience two questions on their performance. In past classes some of these have been, "I want the character to appear ____, so I _____. Did that connect for you," and "Last time you said you felt/saw _____. Did that continue for you?" We use this time to *Answer the Artist's Questions*.

My role for feedback in the monologue workshop is different than my role in dance classes. Since these are called workshops, we all recognize that the work is not complete, and is still progress. So, during monologue workshops I go last, and ask for new choices. When we get to the first time I speak, I remind students that these are offers and choices. I say something like:

> When I suggest of a different choice, it is only that, a different choice. You might not want to try it, and you don't have to. You might try it and discover you hate it, and it makes you feel disconnected from the character or the moment. You might try it and discover you want to play with

it more, because while that wasn't "it" for you, it gave you a new idea of what might be. You might try it and love it! You might try it and think it's fine, but you still like your way best. All of that is part of the learning and exploring in creating characters and movement.

Then I ask, "Would you be interested in trying a different option at *x point?*" The student may say "yes" or "no." Again, due to the power dynamics of teacher/student and director/actor, they nearly always say "yes."

My offers frequently center the questions the actor has asked the audience, or what I know the students' goals to be (there may be times I make offers based on the context of the play and what I know has happened right before or is about to happen right after, but these are rarer). These sound like, "You said you wanted your character to appear____. Another way to do that might be to ____. Would you be interested in trying that?" Again, I offer an opportunity to consent to the feedback.

Besides giving the performing student more options for their character, feedback like this reinforces to everyone in the room that there are many choices available, and they aren't right or wrong. After students perform with the new option, I ask "How did that feel," or "What did you notice?" Students have a tendency, because of the power dynamics to answer, "How did that feel?" with "Better." If that happens, I say something like "Why? What about how the character communicated was "better?" I also try to remind them that it is quite fine for it to not feel better! I might have made a terrible suggestion for their body, character, or impulses. The work and learning are in the trying, not in telling me I'm right.

On "written" work

Some classes have feedback information included in the syllabus. The following is from the Dance Appreciation course used as an example in the previous chapter. Feedback was a requirement on written assignments and counted towards their grade bundles. The guidance for feedback was:

> Your attendance and participation in your group is crucial. See the section above on our Class Community. Because the Weekly Responses[4] feed directly into your Final Projects, the feedback should let your peers know if they are on the right track with their thoughts, or missing some pieces. Feedback does not have to be intense and should not be policing. You can:
>
> - Validate someone's creative choice or personal interpretation.
> - Ask a neutral question around their interpretation or offering.

- o "Neutral question" comes from Liz Lerman's *Critical Response Process* and has no judgements or assumptions in the words.
- o So, instead of "Did you mean for that interpretation to be so dark?" we ask, "Can you tell me what led you to that interpretation?"
- o Questions that start with "Can you tell me more about _____?", "How/why did you choose _____?" are often neutral.
- o "I'm curious about ...." can often be a neutral statement
- Comment on how it supported your own learning:
  - o "I didn't think of ____ that way!"
  - o "I had forgotten ____. Thanks for reminding me"
- Reminder of the specs, without shaming.
  - o "Hey, you're missing _____!"

The goal is open opportunities for the creator to dive more deeply into an aspect of their work.

Specs for Feedback

- Every assignment that you turn in has a matching feedback response. In this class, we recognize that we support everyone's learning, not just our own.
- Does one of the above dot points.
- Turned in on time.

Student feedback on feedback

When students provide feedback to each other, the opportunities to learn are doubled. The receiver hears a new perspective other than the usual mine and theirs, and the giver learns to assess their biases, speak with meaning-making and connection in mind, and/or put the goals of others above their own. This is why I do feedback work in every class. And students have found it worthwhile! The following was from a student in a lecture course:

> I think one thing that surprised me the most was how my peer's reflections and responses to my weekly assignments and activity discussions helped me. I feel like we started to give better feedback toward the middle of the semester and it helped us become better and more detailed towards our assignments.

REFLECTION SECTION: The feedback process

Complete the journal prompt provided by Crystal U. Davis on page 260 for yourself. What new insights did you have about perspective and/or feedback methods?

_____
_____
_____
_____

Do I have a specific formula or method I use for giving feedback, or having students give feedback, in classes? How does this account for differences in power and privilege? How does it support the work of the artist? How does it encourage connection and/or creativity versus simply sharing or having an opinion?

_____
_____
_____
_____

Are giving and receiving feedback consent-based activities in class? Are there changes I could make in instructions or structure to foster autonomy?

_____
_____
_____
_____

How often does feedback given in my classes (by me or others) ask a question versus offer an opinion?

Conclusion

Much like ungrading, there is no one way to do feedback care-fully. I have found ways that work well in the classes I lead. I hope the tools and resources offered in this chapter will assist you in thinking critically and creatively around how feedback is given and received in your classes, so that students experience psychological safety in the very vulnerable processes of sharing and viewing artistic works.

The student receiving the feedback should still feel inclusion safety and that they and their artwork belong. The students offering feedback should feel contributor safety, and that they are able to apply their learning in meaningful ways for both themselves and others. They may even feel challenger safety as they speak with a voice of expertise, and may offer something no one else has. All students should experience learner safety as they risk sharing their art and opinions with each other, so they are met with thoughtful consideration that helps them continue to learn.

Chapter reminders

- Leaving the giving of feedback unexamined means its potential to rely on power dynamics, deny consent, or even cause trauma remains unaddressed.
- Effective, care-full, and creativity-building feedback requires:
    o That I know my own biases.
    o That I put the artist's purpose above my own experience.
    o That I value the creative process, not just the product (no teaching, fixing, or promoting my way of creating or doing).
- Feedback can serve a variety of purposes. Be clear on what purpose feedback serves in your class.
- The Care-full Feedback Process follows four steps:
    o Witness and Reflect.
    o Describe.
    o Recognize the Art in the Process.
    o Answer the Artists' Questions.
- Care-full feedback:
    o Gets the student closer to their goals or helps them see how to move towards their goals.
    o Does not compare artistic works.
    o Is actionable.

- Depersonalized corrections are about doing what the work of the class needs, not about pleasing the teacher.
- Student-to-student feedback doubles the learning opportunities.

Notes

1. Rosenberg is a white man, and as such, his system has some privileges built in. If you are interested in learning more about nonviolent communication, I'd also recommend Meenadchi, who offers virtual courses on both nonviolent communication and feedback from the point of view of a woman of color. Her website is linked in the "Resources" section.
2. See descriptions in Chapter 9, p. 228–229
3. See descriptions in Chapter 9, p. 229–230
4. See descriptions in Chapter 9, p. 238

11
Conclusion

We need care.

I am writing this conclusion on November 6, 2024, and I have never felt so deeply the need to demonstrate care as an educator. To help students know that they are powerful. That they are deserving of bodily autonomy. That their creativity and individual experiences are valuable. That community and inclusion are the best launching pads for risk-taking. That distrust and fear do not help us learn or create.

With a pedagogy of care, we demonstrate that the purpose of education is not only to learn facts and theories, but to learn more about ourselves and the people around us. Care-full educators believe learning cannot be measured by an outside eye or instrument but can only be demonstrated by daily application and personal growth.

As artists, we are constantly creating new worlds and making them real to those around us. We do this as educators, too. Our classrooms are the testing grounds of the world we want to live in. Demonstrating care, from the syllabus to the final exam, and every moment in between is one way I bring the world I want to live and work in into existence. As you engage in care-full pedagogic practices, you are creating a world I want to live and work in, too.

We, as educators creating and offering care, are often bridging the space between the hierarchical and kyriarchical traditions of both academia and performance spaces, and the truly collaborative, equitable, and creative spaces we desire. We must teach and train students to live in the world "as it is," while giving them the tools and psychological safety to create what "could be." A pedagogy of care is a practice of demonstrating what could be: equitable creative teams, a society that values embodied knowledge from a multiplicity of experiences and backgrounds, transparent communication, a desire to avoid harming others, and joy in learning.

DOI: 10.4324/9781003596301-14

Conclusion

As you demonstrate care in your classes, you may face resistance—from your boss, your colleagues, even the students and yourself! When you do, I hope you come back to this book—to the theories of the past 100 years that support your changes, your personal reflections of how you envision movement education can be, and the examples of how care can make for better teaching and learning. I hope you give yourself grace when you make mistakes, as they are inevitable when we are making something new. I hope you give yourself time to make changes and do not crush your own hope with urgency. I hope you are well resourced with care for yourself, both from yourself and others. I hope you hope.

Jessica Zeller, PhD writes in *Humanizing Ballet Pedagogies:*

> In acknowledgement that there in no one "correct way to approach student driven pedagogies—no "best practices" that will apply to all ballet teaching contexts—I discuss them in the plural to broaden possible points of entry and make space for the development of methodologies that can function inside the many environments in which ballet is taught and learned. These pedagogies are ultimately for the individual teachers to devise—the act of pedagogical thinking …. (2024, 43).

Her words apply to all dance and theatrical movement classes. You have your own pedagogical thinking and will devise the tools that fit your content and classes. I hope this book has been useful in providing tools "done for you," and in helping you think about ways you can create your own to foster more access, equity, consent, and care in your classroom.

I, too, am continuing to grow and learn. At various places throughout this book, I have been transparent about what I am still working on and/or what isn't working quite the way I'd hoped. Personally, another next step is to co-create syllabi and/or course outlines with students, rather than show up with them already completed. This feels exciting to consider from the standpoint of equalizing power and giving opportunities for consent!

Teaching is a journey that requires learning and change. As the world shifts, so must our methods of instruction and our demonstrations of care. In the words of Mary Parker Follett, "Life is an art. Life … is an endless interplay" (1924, 141). This book is at its end. But as educators, may we never be done learning, teaching, and caring.

In that spirit, there is a final "Reflection" Section on the next page, about your goals and strategies for creating a care-full pedagogy of movement in your classes. These are for you to design your next steps. I wish you much joy and success on the journey, because the world needs more care.

REFLECTION SECTION

What does a Care-full Creativity look like to me?

What do I hope for, for myself? The students I work with? The institution I work in?

How can a care-full pedagogy bring these hopes to fruition?

What is something from this book that I am carrying with me?

Conclusion 275

What is something from this book that I am letting go of, because it doesn't fit my values, my institution, my reality, etc.?

_____
_____
_____
_____

What is a change I can and will make right now to make my pedagogy more care-full?

_____
_____
_____
_____

What is a change I can and will make over the next year to make my pedagogy more care-full?

_____
_____
_____
_____

What is a change I am interested in making to make my pedagogy more care-full, but will require me to speak to colleagues, get permission from a chair, etc., before I am able to implement? What step can I take now get that process started?

_____
_____
_____
_____

How do I feel when I envision these as a new reality? What sensations do I notice?

_____

_____

_____

_____

_____

What has this book made me curious about, that I would like to learn more about, to make my pedagogy more care-full?

_____

_____

_____

_____

_____

Part 3
Resource Section

Sources and Resources

This section includes references for in-text citations and supplemental materials to support each chapter.

The first section is academic citations of works cited or referred to in the text[1]. Those sources that occur in many chapters (i.e., Follett, Freire, etc.) are included only in the chapter where they first occur.

The second section of "Resources" is all the tools and templates I have created and refer to in the text. These are available as downloads or links. Where a link is not included with the reference, please see the Routledge Resource Centre at https://resourcecentre.routledge.com/books/9781032979502. These downloads are meant for your use in your classroom(s). Slide decks are meant for you to copy and create a version that is relevant to your class and needs. If you wish to recommend the downloadable resources to another, please refer them to this book, or send them to: https://www.momentumstage.org/arts-education?category=teaching+resource.

The final section of supplemental materials is meant to support your own exploration of topics that interest you. Many are links to resources or scholars I appreciate but could not work into the text.

Note

1. I have purposefully used theories from the social science, business, and education, as well as the arts, as I know that you are likely dealing with administrators from outside the arts that will need "proof" that care-full methods are not just arts teachers being "soft" or "touchy-feely."

References

Accessible Syllabus resources: https://www.accessiblesyllabus.com/.

Ahenkorah, Elise. 2023. "Safe and Brave Spaces Don't Work (and What You Can Do Instead)." Medium, October 18, 2023. https://medium.com/@elise.k.ahen/safe-and-brave-spaces-dont-work-and-what-you-can-do-instead-f265aa339aff.

All student correspondences included in this text were from the Fall of 2023 and/or the Spring of 2024. Permission was granted to use these comments anonymously.

Ash, S.L., and P.H. Clayton. 2009. "Generating, Deepening, and Documenting Learning: The Power of Critical Reflection in Applied Learning." *Journal of Applied Learning in Higher Education*, 1(1): 25–48.

Bannon, Fiona. 2012. Rep. *Relational Ethics: Dance, Touch, and Learning*. London, England: HEA.

Barber, James P. 2020. *Facilitating the Integration of Learning: Five Research-Based Practices to Help College Students Connect Learning Across Disciplines and Lived Experience*. New York, NY: Taylor and Francis Group.

Beard, Mary. 2018. *Women and Power: A Manifesto*. London, England: Profile Books.

Bedera, Nicole, PhD. "Resources." https://www.nicolebedera.com/copy-of-news-1.

Birdwell, M.L.N., and Keaton Bayley. March 2022. "When the Syllabus Is Ableist: Understanding How Class Policies Fail Disabled Students." In *Teaching English to Young Children* 49(3): 220–237.

Blum, Susan, ed. 2020. *Ungrading: Why Rating Students Undermines Learning (and What to Do Instead)*. Morgantown: West Virginia University Press.

Brookhart, Susan M., Thomas R. Guskey, Alex J. Bowers, James H. McMillan, Jeffrey K. Smith, Lisa F. Smith, Michael T. Stevens, and Megan E. Welsh. 2016. "A Century of Grading Research." *Review of Educational Research* 86(4): 803–48. https://doi.org/10.3102/0034654316672069.

Buono, Alexia, PhD. 2024. Personal correspondence. June.

Castillo, Heather, MFA. 2024. Personal correspondence. June.

Center for Nonviolent Communication. *Feelings and Needs Inventory*. https://www.cnvc.org/store/feelings-and-needs-inventory.

Chavez, Felicia Rose. 2021. *The Anti-Racist Writing Workshop: How to Decolonize the Creative Classroom*. Chicago, IL: Haymarket Books.

Clark, Timothy R. 2020. *4 Stages of Psychological Safety: Defining the Path to Inclusion and Innovation*. Oakland, CA: Berret-Koehler Publishers, Inc.

Condry, John. 1977. "Enemies of Exploration: Self-initiated versus Other-Initiated Learning." *Journal of Personality and Social Psychology* 35: 459–477. https://doi.org/10.1037/0022-3514.35.7.459.

Cullen, Simon, and Daniel Oppenheimer. 2024. "Choosing to Learn: The Importance of Student Autonomy in Higher Education." 17 July. In *Science Advances*. https://www.science.org/doi/10.1126/sciadv.ado6759

Davis, Crystal U. 2022. *Dance and Belonging: Implicit Bias and Inclusion in Dance Education*. Jefferson, NC: McFarland and Company.

Deikman, M.D., Arthur J. 1990. *The Wrong Way Home: Uncovering the Patterns of Cult Behavior in American Society*. Boston, MA: Beacon Press.

Denial, Catherine J. 2024. *A Pedagogy of Kindness*. Norman, OK: The University of Oklahoma Press.

Duffy, Ali, PhD. 2024. Personal correspondence. June.

Dweck, Carolyn, PhD. 2007. *Mindset: The New Psychology of Success*. New York, NY: Ballantine Books.

Edmonson, Amy C. 2019. *The Fearless Organization: Creating Psychological Safety in the Workplace for Learning, Innovation, and Growth*. Hoboken, NJ: Wiley.

Follett, Mary Parker. 1924. *Creative Experience*. New York, NY: Longmans, Green, and Co.

Follett, Mary Parker. [1933] 1973. *Dynamic Administration*. London: Pitman.

Follett, Mary Parker, Pauline Graham, and Mary Parker Follett. [1925] 1995. "The Giving of Orders." In *Prophet of Management: A Celebration of Writings from the 1920s*. Boston, MA: Harvard Business School Press.

Freire, Paulo. [1973] 2006. *Pedagogy of the Oppressed*. 30th edition. New York, NY: Continuum.

French, John R.P., and Bertram Raven. 1959. "The Bases of Social Power." Massachusetts Institute of Technology. Accessed February 17, 2021. https://web.

mit.edu/curhan/www/docs/Articles/15341_Readings/Power/French_&_Raven_Studies_Social_Power_ch9_pp150-167.pdf

Gablik, Suzi. 1992. *Has Modernism Failed?* London, England: Thames & Hudson.

Goldsman, Akiva. 2021. "Context is for Kings." Episode. *Star Trek: Discovery.*

Gottschild, Brenda Dixon. 1996. *Digging the Africanist Presence in American Performance: Dance and Other Contexts.* Westport, CT: Praeger Publishers.

Gray, Judith Anne. 1989. *Dance Instruction: Science Applied to the Art of Movement.* Champaign, IL: Human Kinetics Books.

Guarino, Lindsay, and Wendy Oliver. 2015. *Jazz Dance: A History of the Roots and Branches.* Gainesville, FL: University Press of Florida.

Hackney, Peggy. 2002. *Making Connections: Total Body Integration Through Bartenieff Fundamentals.* New York, NY: Routledge.

Hamilton, Patrick. 1938. *Gas Light.* New York, NY: Samuel French, Inc. (This play is sometimes known as *Angel Street.*)

Hemphill, Prentis. 2021. "A Reminder." *Instagram.* Meta. https://www.instagram.com/p/CNSzFO1A21C/.

Hemphill, Prentis. 2025. "Boundaries are evidence of our interconnection, not a denial." *Instagram.* Meta. https://www.instagram.com/p/CLpZ9FqAMWN/?igsh=MWRvNTQ2NnFqcTFpeQ%3D%3D.

Hilger, Emmi. 2020. "Engagement Rubric." Chicago: Beacon Academy.

Hill, Devin. 2024. *Creating Change Conversation: Disability and Neurodiversity in the Arts.* Panel Discussion hosted by Momentum Stage. July.

Jackson, Naomi. 2022. *Dance and Ethics: Moving Towards a More Humane Dance Culture.* Chicago, IL: Intellect.

Jowitt, Deborah. 1989. *Time and the Dancing Image.* Berkeley: University of California Press.

Keltner, Dacher. 2017. *The Power Paradox: How we Gain and Lose Influence.* New York, NY: Penguin Books.

Kohn, Alfie. 1992. *No Contest: The Case Against Competition.* Boston, MA: Houghton Mifflin.

Kohn, Alfie. [1993] 1998. "Choices for Children." In *What to Look for in a Classroom and Other Essays.* San Francisco, CA: Jossey-Bass Publishers.

Kohn, Alfie. [1994] 1998. "Grading: The Issue is not How, but Why." In *What to Look for in a Classroom and Other Essays.* San Francisco, CA: Jossey-Bass Publishers.

Kohn, Alfie. 2006. "Speaking My Mind: The Trouble with Rubrics." *The English Journal* 95(4): 12–15. https://doi.org/10.2307/30047080.

Kohn, Alfie. 2018. *Punished by Rewards: The Trouble with Gold Stars, Incentive Plans, A's, Praise, and Other Bribes.* 25 Anniversary Edition ed. Boston: Houghton Mifflin.

Lakes, Robin. 2005. "The Messages behind the Methods: The Authoritarian Pedagogical Legacy in Western Concert Dance Technique Training and Rehearsals." *Arts Education Policy Review* 106(5): 3–18.

Lavender, Larry, PhD. 1996. *Dancers Talking Dance: Critical Evaluation in the Choreography Class.* Champaign, IL: Human Kinetics

Lerman, Liz. 2020. *Critical Response Process in Brief.* https://lizlerman.com/critical response-process/

Lerman, Liz, and John Borstel. 2003. *Liz Lerman's Critical Response Process: A Method for Getting Useful Feedback on Anything you Make, from Dance to Dessert.* Takoma Park, MD: The Dance Exchange, Inc.

Markus, Andrea, EdD. 2024. Personal correspondence. June.

McClam, Nicole Y. 2022. "Translating Ballet to Change Perceptions and Engage Community College Students." *Dance Education in Practice* 8(4): 7–11. https://doi.org/10.1080/23734833.2022.2099685.

McLaren, Brian. 2020. "Learning How to See with Brian McLaren: 5: What You Focus on Determines What You Miss." *Apple Podcasts.* Center for Action and Contemplation. November 1. https://podcasts.apple.com/us/podcast/5-what-you-focuson-determines-what-you-miss/id1532685433?i=1000496893026.

Merriam-Webster.com Dictionary, s.v. "psychology," accessed November 7, 2024, https://www.merriam-webster.com/dictionary/psychology.

Miller, Valerie and JASS Associates. https://www.powercube.net/wp-content/uploads/2009/12/Power_Matrix_intro.pdf.

Morgan, Chels. 2025. *Accountability, Apology, and Healing.* For Intimacy Professionals Education Collective. https://www.ipecintimacy.com/.

Ng, Roxana. 2018. "Decolonizing Teaching and Learning Through Embodied Learning: Toward an Integrated Approach." In *Sharing Breath: Embodied Learning and Decolonization*, edited by Sheila Batacharya and Yuk-Lin Renita Wong. Edmonton: Athabasca University Press.

Noddings, Nel. [1984] 2003. *Caring: A Feminine Approach to Ethics and Moral Education.* Berkley, CA: University of California Press.

Perry, Nicole. 2024. "A Look at Teaching—and not Grading—Dance in Higher Education." *Dance Teacher*. 30 September. https://dance-teacher.com/not-grading higher-ed/#gsc.tab=0.

Perry, Nicole. 2025. "An Assessment of Care." *Journal of Dance Education*, June, 1–6. doi:10.1080/15290824.2024.2447017.

Roddenberry, Gene. 1988. "Home Soil." Episode. *Star Trek: The Next Generation*.

Rosenberg, Marshall B. 2003. *Nonviolent Communication: A Language of Life*. Encitias, CA: PuddleDancer Press.

Rosvalley, Danielle, PhD. 2023. Personal correspondence. August.

Schenck, Molly W. nd. Dancing the Autonomic Color Wheel. https://www.mollywschenck.com/product-page/dance-the-autonomic-color-wheel-replay.

Schenck, Molly W. 2021. *Introduction to Trauma Informed Creative Practices*. Grey Box Collective.

Schenck, Molly W. 2023. *Trauma-Informed Teaching Practices for Dance Educators*. Human Kinetics. https://us.humankinetics.com/products/trauma-informed teaching-practices-for-dance-educators-online-course.

Schussler Fiorenza, Elizabeth. 2001. *Wisdom Ways: Introducing Feminist Biblical Interpretation*. Maryknoll, New York: Orbis Books.

Smith, Clyde. 1998. "On Authoritarianism in the Dance Classroom." In *Dance, Power, and Difference: Critical Feminist Perspectives on Dance Education*, edited by Sherry B. Shapiro. 123–146. Champaign, IL: Human Kinetics.

Stanislavski, Constantin. 2008. *An Actor's Work: A Student's Diary*. Translated by Jean Benedetti.

Stommel, Jesse. 2020. "How to Ungrade." In *Ungrading: Why Rating Students Undermines Learning (and What to Do Instead)*, edited by Susan Blum. Morgantown: West Virginia University Press.

Stuart Fisher, Amanda. 2020. "Introduction: Caring performance, performing care." In *Performing Care*. Manchester, England: Manchester University Press. https://doi.org/10.7765/9781526146816.00007.

Styres, Sandra. 2019. "Literacies of Land: Decolonizing Narratives, Storying, and Literature." Essay. In *Indigenous and Decolonizing Studies in Education: Mapping the Long View*, edited by Linda Tuhiwai Smith, Eve Tuck, K. Wayne Yang, and Sandra Styres, 24–27. New York, NY: Routledge, Taylor & Francis Group.

Substance Abuse and Mental Health Services Administration (SAMHSA), ed. 2014. "SAMHSA's Concept of Trauma and Guidance for a Trauma-Informed Approach." *SAMHSA's Trauma and Justice Strategic Initiative* 1, no. 1, July 27.

https://www.nctsn.org/sites/default/files/resources/resource-guide/samhsa_trauma.pdf.

Swedo E.A., Aslam M.V., Dahlberg L.L., et al. 2023. "Prevalence of Adverse Childhood Experiences Among U.S. Adults—Behavioral Risk Factor Surveillance System, 2011–2020." In *Morbidity and Mortality Weekly Report* 72: 707–715. http://dx.doi.org/10.15585/mmwr.mm7226a2.

T'ai, Gina, MFA. 2024. Personal correspondence. June.

Taylor, Diana. 2020. *¡Presente!: The Politics of Presence.* Durham, NC: Duke University Press.

The Dance Data Project. January 2025. *Season Overview 2023–24.* https://www.dancedataproject.com/ddp-research/season-overview-2023-2024/.

The Dance Data Project. March 2025. *2025 Performing Arts Centers' Programming and Leadership Report.* https://ddp-wordpress.storage.googleapis.com/wp-content/uploads/2025/03/07154126/2025-Performing-Arts-Center-Leadership-and-Programming-Report.pdf.

The Dance Education Equity Association: https://wwwdanceequityassociation.com

Thompson, James. 2015. "Towards an Aesthetics of Care." *Research in Drama Education* 20(4): 430–441. https://doi.org/10.1080/13569783.2015.1068109.

Thompson, John. 2023. *Care Aesthetics: for artful care and careful art.* New York, NY: Routledge.

Tonn, Joan C. 2003. *Mary P. Follett: Creating Democracy, Transforming Management.* New Haven, CT: Yale University Press.

Tuck, Eve, and K. Wayne Yang. 2012. "Decolonization Is Not a Metaphor." *Decolonization: Indigeneity, Education & Society* 1(1): 1–40.

Venet, Alex Shevrin. 2021. *Equity-Centered Trauma-Informed Education.* New York, NY: W.W. Norton and Company.

Whittier, Cadence. 2017. *Creative Ballet Teaching: Technique and Artistry for the 21st Century Ballet Dancer.* New York, NY: Routledge.

Wilson, Shawn. 2008. *Research Is Ceremony: Indigenous Research Methods.* Halifax, NS: Fernwood.

Womack, Anne-Marie. February 2017. "Teaching is Accommodation: Universally Designing Composition Classrooms and Syllabi." In *College Composition and Communication* 68(3): 494–525.

You can find the image and a video explainer for FRIES here: https://www.plannedparenthood.org/learn/relationships/sexual-consent.

Zeller, Jessica. 2020. "Pedagogy for End Times: Ungrading and the Importance of Arson." August 16. https://www.jessicazeller.net/blog/pedagogy-for-end-times.

Zeller, Jessica. 2024. *Humanizing Ballet Pedagogies: Philosophies, Perspectives, and Praxis for Teaching Ballet*. London, England: Routledge.

Zeller, Jessica, PhD. 2024. Personal correspondence. June.

Resources to support material in the text

Tools and templates referenced from Momentum Stage and Nicole Perry

Chapter 5

Momentum Stage's Land Acknowledgement can be found in the middle of this page. https://www.momentumstage.org/.

Honor Triad Template

Boundary Worksheets.

Boundary Zone or Comfort Zone graphics (both with text and blank).

Boundary Conversation Handout.

Story People Images (for reference only. Please see the link in the next section to purchase.).

Chapter 6

Dress code link: https://www.discountdance.com/search/mylist:603490.

Slides for my AI lesson.

Totentanz project from Momentum Stage: dancers.ai

Resolution Pathway (both with text and blank).

Chapter 7

Somatic Check-in Examples and Instructions for 5-4-3-2-1.

Context Check-in Script.

Check-in Questions List.

Yes/No Card Template.

Body Metaphors, Idioms, and Imagistic Language.

Chapter 8

Momentum Stage for the Ethics of Touch course, now a part of the Care-full Creativity Accreditation program for dance studios, conventions, and academic departments: https://www.momentumstage.org/carefull-creativity-accreditation.

Chapter 9

Grading Discussion Presentation.

Artist Log purchase link: https://www.momentumstage.org/artist-log-journals.

More information about Activity Reflections:

> I believe we cannot teach an appreciation of movement, or even ethically learn a movement style's history, without embodiment. So, even in these large "lecture" courses, I include at least bi-weekly movement experiences during class. Even though this can be a risk in large classes, and with students whose experience in or motivation for learning movement may be low, I truly believe embodied learning is crucial to understanding. I was gratified that in my evaluations, over 20% of students cited movement in class as a highlight.
>
> These activities are followed by a reflection, in which students choose a guiding question from the syllabus (See Chapter Six) and answer how that activity provided more information for them about that aspect of our studies. Students are not always clear on how material fits course objectives, so by routinely returning students to the goals of the class, they are able to make connections between content, embodiment, and learning outcomes. Again, there is no "busy work," but rather activities explicitly designed to support the overall curriculum and translate into their grade.
>
> Specifications for a complete activity reflection included a word count and deadline. Students were reminded that their reflections did need to include specific information about the activity, so that it could not be generated by an AI. If a student was absent, they were unable to do the activity, therefore, their email to me about their absence had to include a plan to make up this work, to complete their bundle.

Final Project Presentation full instructions (Also provides info on token use at the end of the semester.).

Chapter 10

The Care-full Feedback Process and Conversation Starters.

Resources to support material in the text

Other links and offerings

Introduction

Intimacy Professional Organizations and Links:

I trained with Intimacy Directors International and was certified through Intimacy Directors and Coordinators. I now teach this work and hold certification through the Intimacy Professionals Education Collective https://www.ipecintimacy.com.

Chapter 1

The Dance Education Equity Association. https://www.danceequityassociation.com/

Chapter 3

The Centre for Healing has two free courses to learn about trauma and trauma-informed practices. They have several paid courses as well. https://www.thecentreforhealing.com/free-courses

Dr. Peter Levine talking about trauma in the body: https://youtu.be/ByalBx85iC8.

Fox, Ruby Rose. 2024. *Superplay: Your Instrument is You (The Fox Method)*. www.muscle-music.com. This book offers a look at the nervous system, from the lens of performance. She also offers tools for grounding.

Porges, Stephen. 2011. *The Pocket Guide to Polyvagal Theory*. New York, NY: W.W. Norton. https://wwnorton.com/books/9780393707878.

Other trauma researchers you may want to look up:

- Deb Dana
- Dr. Daniel Siegel (Window of Tolerance)

Chapter 5

Land Acknowledgements

To learn more about Joseph Cloud and/or book a Land Acknowledgement workshop visit: https://www.josephcloud.me/workshop.

Website for finding your tribal lands: https://native-land.ca/.

Boundary conversations

Intimacy Direction in Dance: https://www.intimacydirectionindance.com/.

Prentis Hemphill has a fantastic podcast called *Finding Our Way*, that incorporates somatics and justice work. Learn more or listen here: https://www.findingourwaypodcast.com/.

Hemphill, Prentis. 2025. "Boundaries are evidence of our interconnection, not a denial." Instagram. Meta. https://www.instagram.com/p/CLpZ9FqAMWN/?igsh=MWRvNTQ2NnFqcTFpeQ%3D%3D.

Observational practices

Selective Attention Tests I use:

1. Monkey Business: The Monkey Business Illusion. https://www.youtube.com/watch?v=IGQmdoK_ZfY
2. The Door: The "Door" Study. https://www.youtube.com/watch?v=FWSxSQsspiQ

Story People images for purchase: https://www.dreamstime.com/.

Chapter 6

Universal Design resources: https://udlguidelines.cast.org/.

Totentanz: dancers.ai.

Actors' Equity Workplace Safety Resources for Harassment, Bullying, Abuse or other Unsafe Work Environments:

- Submit a report online or call 833-550-0030.
- See their YouTube series about Reporting and Safety. https://youtu.be/hLgM8BW3Pw8?si=dRVHWpCQQF-D_Azv
- You do not have to be a member to use this, there simply must be at least 1 Equity contract on the show.

AGMA

- Unsafe working conditions reporting. https://www.musicalartists.org/faq-help/help-page/unsafe-working-conditions/
- Sexual harassment reporting. https://www.musicalartists.org/faq-help/help-page/sexual-harassment-policy-information-portal/

SAG-AFTRA reporting and resources website. https://servicesagaftra.custhelp.com/app/sh/home/session

JDoe: https://www.jdoe.io/.

Theatre Advocacy Project also provides reporting options at https://www.theatreadvocacyproject.org/anonymous-report

Chapter 7

This article is one of my favorite things to give undergrads to read in ballet and/or the ballet section of dance history:

Fisken, Marlo. 2020. "A Letter to the Pole Community: It's Time We Talk about Toe-Point Supremacy." *Flow Movement by Marlo Fisken*. August 19. https://flowmovement.net/poleflowblog/2020/06/alettertothepolecommunity.

Guarino, Lindsay, Carlos R.A. Jones, and Wendy Oliver. 2024. *Rooted Jazz Dance: Africanist Aesthetics and Equity in the Twenty-first Century*. Gainesville, FL: University Press of Florida.

Chapter 8

National Dance Education Organization's Online Professional Development Institute for the *Ethics of Touch* course: https://www.ndeo.org/Learn/Online-Courses.

Bannon, Fiona. 2018. *Considering Ethics in Dance, Theatre and Performance*. London: Palgrave MacMillan.

Website for Hannah Fischer. "Research." http://www.fischerdance.org/research.

Integrated Movement Studies: https://www.imsmovement.com/.

Chapter 9

Buck, David. "Alternative Grading Resources." Handout. https://docs.google.com/document/d/1PzQ05JAyFquUNJSigV7xKcNOUMCDb8E1LUfg2xl75c8/edit?tab=t.0#heading=h.eofoscb4mw0z. Buck also runs a website with to ungrading resources: https://ungrading.weebly.com/.

Feldman, Joe. 2019. *Grading for Equity: What It Is, Why It Mattes, and How It Can Transform Schools and Classrooms*. Thousand Oaks, CA: Corwin.

Rosvally, Danielle has an account on TikTok @YassifiedShakespeare, where she talks about her ungrading practices, and other fun theatre things.

Stommel, Jesse. 2023. *Undoing the Grade: Why we Grade and How to Stop*. Denver, CO: Hybrid Pedagogy. Stommel also has a great website and blog: https://www.jessestommel.com/.

Chapter 10

Lerman, Liz, John Borstel, and Christóbal Martinez. 2022. "The Critical Response Process: Aesthetics of Time." Essay. In *Critique Is Creative: The Critical Response Process in Theory and Action*, 207–19. Middletown, CT: Wesleyan University Press.

Meenadchi. https://www.meenadchi.com/pages/websitehome

NVC Academy: https://www.nvcacademy.com for more Nonviolent Communication learning.

Index

accommodation 46, 49–50, 66, 77, 107, 124
Adverse Childhood Experience 143
Ahenkorah, Elise 78
Artificial Intelligence (AI) use 140–41, 146
Artist Logs 226–27; examples 227–28
Ash, S.L., and P.H. Clayton 213, 227
assessment: and autonomy 214–15, 248–49; examples of 228–30; multiple forms of 66, 214; power and 208–10; traditional 211; *see also* Movement Experiences Guide; self-assessment; ungrading
attendance 147–51, 165, 211–12, 232, 266

Ballet: Artist Log example 227; assessments for 46, 228–29; boundaries in 110, 118; class exercises 170–72, 179; dress code 140; feedback in 159, 262, 264–65; touch in 202
Bannon, Fiona 189
Barber, James P. 214–15
Baseline Boundaries 110–11, 193, 195–97; *see also* boundaries
Beard, Mary 42
Bedera, Nicole PhD 155
Birdwell, M.L.N., and Keaton Bayley 148
Blum, Susan 248
boundaries 51, 72, 78, 120–21, 129, 142, 163–64, 166, 185; conversations for 117–21, 166–67; to instructional touch 187, 190, 193–95; knowledge of 111–14; and needs 32–33, 51, 110, 120, 134; props for 166–67; *see also* Baseline Boundaries
Boundary Zone 114, 116
brave space 78–79

Brookhart, Susan M., Thomas R. Guskey, Alex J. Bowers, James H. McMillan, Jeffrey K. Smith, Lisa F. Smith, Michael T. Stevens, and Megan E. Welsh 219
Buono, Alexia, PhD 212, 226, 246, 249

care: and community 97, 129, 134; culture of 1, 3, 150; definition of 2–4, 93, 163; in feedback 254–55, 258; in grading 212–13, 246, 250–51; relationships of 17, 32, 93; in teaching 6, 8–12, 17, 32, 34, 38, 272–73; trauma-informed 71–74, 83, 209
Castillo, Heather MFA 249
Chain of Communication *see* conflict resolution
Chavez, Felicia Rose: and choice 185; and dialogue 66; and feedback 254, 261; and grades 210–11, 232; and liberation 5; and students 76, 126, 182
challenger safety: definition of 87–89, 92, 94; in feedback 270; in grading 214, 230–31, 243; in teaching 180–81, 185; *see also* psychological safety
check-ins: for boundaries 166–68, 195; and consent 65, 163–64; for context 165–66; for learner safety 176–77, 184–85; somatic 106, 125, 164–65
check-outs 176, 178, 184
choice: as autonomy 18, 86–87, 132, 170, 178, 182; and boundaries 166–67; as challenger safety 181; as collaboration 43, 125; and competition mindset 33, 39; as contributor safety 178–79, 229–30; definition of 180; and learner safety

164–65, 174, 176–78; as a trauma-informed practice 72–74, 77
Clark, Timothy R.: and human beings 121, 185–86; levels of psychological safety 82, 86, 87–88, 94, 174, 218
Class Contracts 98–100, 105, 129, 159
coactive control 42–43; *see also* collaboration; power-with
Coercive Power 93, 98, 102; definition of 20–23, 25; in grading 208, 214, 225, 250
collaboration: and consent 65; as power-with 43–44, 52; and psychological safety 78, 82, 93; as a trauma-informed practice 72–73, 76–77; see *also* coactive control; power-with
Community Agreements *see* Class Contracts
competition mindset: in class 72, 117, 129; definition of 30–33, 39; in feedback 262; in grading 225, 231, 247
Condry, John 214
Confidence Zone 114–16, 120
conflict resolution 143–44
consent: and boundaries 114, 166–67, 193; and conflict resolution 144; definition of 63–69; with electronic devices 100, 142–43; and feedback 256, 266; and instructional touch 188, 193–94; and power 13; and psychological safety 93, 159; see *also* consent-forward; Working Consent
consent-based *see* consent; consent-forward
consent-forward: definition of 2, 13; feedback 255; grading 209–10, 246–47, 249; instructional touch 193–94, 196–97, 200, 206; language 169; staged intimacy 5, 8; syllabus 142, 153, 159; teaching 63–69, 163; and trauma-informed practices 77; *see also* consent; Working Consent
contract grading 237–43; *see also* ungrading
contributor safety: definition of 86–87, 92, 94; in feedback 270; in grading 229–31, 243; in the syllabus 141; in teaching 99, 101, 178–80; *see also* psychological safety
Critical Response Process 254, 267
Cullen, Simon, and Daniel Oppenheimer 209, 214, 248

Dance Appreciation 237, 240–41, 244, 266
Dance Data Project, The 52

Dance Education Equity Association 46, 116
Dance Geist 30, 70, 73, 206, 255
Davis, Crystal U. 260
decolonization 170, 172
Deikman, M.D., Arthur J. 20–23, 30–33, 66, 187
Denial, Catherine J. 66–67
dialogue: and boundaries 116, 167; as disruptive to power 65–67; and trauma 71–72, 77; and Working Consent 65–67, 76
differing modes of engagement 174–75
Dixon Gottschild, Brenda 171, 179, 228
Dress Code 140
Duffy, Ali, PhD 226, 249–50
Dweck, Carolyn, PhD 114

Edmonson, Amy C.: and fear 72, 93; and feedback 261; and psychological safety 79–80, 82–86
electronic devices 100, 134, 142–43
empowerment 57–58, 73
ensemble 97, 101, 109, 123, 129
Ethics of Touch Statement 193–96
Eurocentric 4–5, 64, 171–72, 211
European *see* Eurocentric; European-derived
European-derived 3, 7, 43
Expert Power: and challenger safety 88; and contributor safety 135; definition of 19, 22, 24; and feedback 256, 263–64; and grading 247; and Invisible Power 53; and learner safety 135; in the syllabus 147, 150, 154

Freire, Paulo: banking model of education 4, 65–66; and dehumanization 44, 73, 209; and dialogue 66
French, John R.P., and Bertram Raven: "The Bases of Social Power" 18, 208; types of power 19, 23, 27, 41–42, 61, 83

Gablik, Suzi 126
gaslighting 52–53, 56
goal setting 213, 218–19, 226
Goldsman, Akiva 126
grades *see* ungrading
Gray, Judith Anne 4–5
"Growth Mindset" 114
Guarino, Lindsay, and Wendy Oliver 171
Guiding Questions 135–36, 152, 227, 287

Hamilton, Patrick 52
Hemphill, Prentis 113
hierarchical *see* hierarchy
hierarchies *see* hierarchy
hierarchy: in academia 38, 43, 73, 80, 99, 226; and competition mindset 30, 32; in cults 22; in dance 70; and fear 72, 79–80; and grading 208–9, 211, 251; and kyriarchy 8, 18, 30, 38, 58, 272; and power 17; structures of 19, 34, 44, 47, 133, 247
Hilger, Emmi 219
Hill, Devin 53

inclusion safety: definition of 83–84, 92, 94; in feedback 270; in language 169; in the syllabus 135, 150; in teaching 97–98, 101, 129, 165, 171; *see also* psychological safety
Informational Power 21–22, 25
Intimacy Direction in Dance 110, 119
Intimacy Professionals Education Collective 6, 119
Invisible Power 51–54

Jackson, Naomi 38
Jazz: Artist Log example 228; class exercises 179–80; language in class 171–72

Keltner, Dacher 71
Kohn, Alfie: and competition 31–32; and feedback 253, 259, 261–62; and grades 85, 232; and relationships 21, 214; and rewards 20, 102; and students 79, 85, 93
kyriarchy 18, 30, 32, 51, 58, 73

Lakes, Robin 6, 38, 54
Land Acknowledgements 97–98, 124
late: policy 149–50; work 212
Lavender, Larry, PhD 254, 258, 263
"the law of the situation": definition of 45–46, 49; in feedback 254, 262; in the syllabus 159; in teaching 97–98, 101, 112–13, 118; *see also* Parker Follett, Mary
learner safety: definition of 83–87, 92, 94; in feedback 270; in grading 212, 214, 218, 225, 231, 246; in the syllabus 131, 136, 147; in teaching 99, 106, 126, 163, 165, 169–70, 172, 176–78, 184–85; *see also* psychological safety
Legitimate Power: definition of 20, 24; and feedback 253; and Invisible Power 53
Lerman, Liz 254, 256, 259–60, 263, 267
Letters: Introduction 124–25, 219; self-assessment 222, 225, 231–33, 237, 239–40, 244, 248, 261, 263
low-touch teaching 199–205
Lozoff, Sarah 110, 119

Markus, Andrea, EdD 249–50
McLaren, Brian 125
Miller, Valerie 43, 51
Modern: class exercise 180–81; class exercise with differing modes of engagement 175; language in class 170
Momentum Stage 98, 114
Movement Experiences Guide (MEG) 219–25, 232, 263
Movement for Actors: assessments for 229–30; class exercise with differing modes of engagement 175; class exercises 177, 180–81, 201; Dress Code 140; example of Class Contract and needs for learning integration 106–7; language in 170–71

needs: as boundaries 32–33, 110–13, 115, 117, 134, 142, 166–67, 195; inventory of 105; for learning 105–9, 124, 129, 135, 261
Noddings, Nel 3, 10–11, 46, 66, 83
no-touch teaching 199–205
nonviolent communication: Center for 105; techniques 110, 254–55

Observational Practices 125–27, 129, 259

Parker Follett, Mary: and community 58, 61; and power 41–44, 47, 57, 66; and "the law of the situation" 45, 174, 254, 262, 273; *see also* "the law of the situation"; power-over; power-with
participation: grades 102, 110, 149–50, 152, 211, 232, 266; Zones of 174–75

Index

power dynamics: and consent 64–65; definition of 17–21, 42; in grading 209–10, 225, 246–49, 251; mitigating 38, 44, 77–78, 93, 117, 193–95, 202; recognizing 23, 25–31, 33–37, 187–88; relationships of 23; in the syllabus 132–33; and trauma 72–73

power-over 42–43, 58, 61, 66, 80, 93

Power To: definition of 57, 59–60, 62; and psychological safety 82, 88; in teaching 170, 178

power-with 42–43, 47, 51, 61–62; *see also* coactive control; collaboration; Parker Follett, Mary

Power Within: definition of 51–53, 57, 59, 61–62; and psychological safety 82–83, 85, 88; in teaching 165, 167, 170; and trauma-informed practices 76

psychological safety: definition of 79–80; levels of 82–94; *see also* challenger safety; contributor safety; inclusion safety; learner safety

Referent Power: and competition mindset 32–33; definition of 22–23, 26; and psychological safety 83

reflection: in feedback 254, 258; and grading 211–15, 217–18, 222, 226–27, 231–32, 235, 251; and psychological safety 85

Reward Power: definition of 19–23, 25; and competition mindset 30–32; and feedback 261; and grading 208–10, 214, 225, 250; and instructional touch 187; mitigating 98, 102, 225; and psychological safety 85, 93

Rosenberg, Marshall B. 254, 258

Rosvalley, Danielle, PhD 212, 238

safe space 78–79

Schenck, Molly W. 164, 178

Schussler Fiorenza, Elizabeth 18

self-assessment 225–26, 231, 239, 240, 248, 261, 263; *see also* assessment; ungrading

Shevrin Venet, Alex: and care 150; and power 57; and students 154, 187; and trauma-informed 70–71, 74, 76

Smith, Clyde 23, 53

somatic awareness 163–64, 185

Stommel, Jesse 208–9

Stuart Fisher, Amanda 2, 93

Styres, Sandra 172, 232

Substance Abuse and Mental Health Services Administration (SAMHSA) 71–74, 209

Swedo E.A., Aslam M.V., Dahlberg L.L., et al. 143

syllabus: accessible 131–32; policies 131–62

T'ai, Gina, MFA 250

Taylor, Diana 239

Thompson, James 2, 163

Tonn, Joan C. 41–42, 58, 61

touch: and boundaries 111, 113–14, 117, 119–21, 166–67; and consent 46, 65–66, 73; instructional 187–207; and power 32

trauma 70–74, 76–77, 143, 164; and feedback 253, 255; and grades 208–9, 233, 248–49; and power 33; and touch 187, 194, 196, 199, 202; *see also* trauma-informed

trauma-informed 70–74, 76–77; grading 209–10, 213, 238, 246–47, 249, 251; and psychologically safe 83, 93; syllabus 142, 149, 159; teaching 163, 169, 193, 206; *see also* trauma

Tuck, Eve, and K. Wayne Yang 172

ungrading: misconceptions about 246–48; and power 208–9; practices for movement classes 218–36; practices for theory courses 237–45; practices overall 209–12, 248–51; and psychological safety 212–15; *see also* assessment; self-assessment

visual syllabus *see* syllabus: accessible

Wilson, Shawn 44

Womack, Anne-Marie 132, 159–60, 162

Working Consent 65–69, 110, 133, 143, 174, 187, 209; *see also* consent; consent-forward

Zeller, Jessica, PhD: and bodies 147; and identity 62; and teaching 273; and ungrading 226, 231, 247, 249–50, 261

For Product Safety Concerns and Information please contact our EU representative GPSR@taylorandfrancis.com
Taylor & Francis Verlag GmbH, Kaufingerstraße 24, 80331 München, Germany

www.ingramcontent.com/pod-product-compliance
Lightning Source LLC
Chambersburg PA
CBHW071806300426
44116CB00009B/1218